£63·75

Tax efficient foreign exchange management

JOHN F. CHOWN

Tax efficient foreign exchange management

QUORUM BOOKS
New York · Westport, Connecticut

Published in the United States and Canada by
Quorum Books, Westport, Connecticut

English language edition, except the United States and Canada,
published by Woodhead-Faulkner (Publishers) Ltd.

First published 1990

Library of Congress Cataloging-in-Publication Data

Tax efficient foreign exchange management / edited by John Chown.
   p. cm.
   Includes bibliographical references.
   ISBN 0-89930-541-5 (lib. bdg. : alk. paper)
   1. Foreign exchange. I. Chown, John F., 1929- .
HG 3851.T37   1989
332.4'5- -dc20   89-10884
                                                CIP

Library of Congress Catalog Card Number: 89-10884

ISBN: 0-89930-541-5

Typeset by Pentacor Ltd, High Wycombe, Buckinghamshire
Printed in Great Britain by BPCC Wheatons Ltd, Exeter

Contents

Preface

It is a commonplace that business and investment these days know no frontiers. Major companies in Europe and the United States have, of course, a long tradition of setting up subsidiaries and branches overseas, while from the last century the City of London was providing not only short-term finance for the world's trade but longer-term capital for African mines, Far Eastern plantations and South American railways. Even then, British private investors regularly diversified their portfolios, holding a significant proportion of foreign shares either directly or through investment trusts. Other countries such as France, Germany and the United States have much more recently followed suit, while Japanese finance is now a major force in the world.

The Euro markets and their Asian equivalents which developed after the Second World War added to the mobility of funds and ensure that there is no longer any necessary relationship between the currency borrowed, the nationality of the borrower, the nationality of the lender and the location of the market in which the transaction is arranged. A Japanese company might raise money for an Australian acquisition by issuing a Swiss franc convertible bond with the help of an American investment bank based in London.

It is also commonplace that currency markets have been decidedly choppy and that foreign exchange risk is a major preoccupation of the financial and indeed the general management of companies and of investors. New markets have grown up, swaps, futures, options and their derivatives, which make it easier for borrowers and investors to fine tune and manage their risk. The complexities of these markets are now, in general, well understood.

When I began my career I was fascinated by currency markets and worked for a time with a firm of international economic consultants. My then chief, Maxwell Stamp, and I tried to persuade companies that they needed specialist and continuous advice on their international financial exposures. They did not, in those days, perceive this as a serious problem (although it was soon to hit them) but many of them said that they were having difficulty in getting constructive advice on international tax problems involving more than one country. J F Chown & Company Limited was therefore born to fill this market need.

Given this background, it is perhaps inevitable that we should specialise in the tax treatment of foreign exchange. We saved our first corporate victim from the 'foreign currency borrowing' trap as far back as 1972. Since then the problem has multiplied. United States legislation is fiendishly complicated, and frequently changing, while the United Kingdom is still only discussing changing the law to deal with a tax trap that has cost companies billions over the past decade or so. Although market instruments and the understanding of them has developed rapidly, the tax treatment remains a mystery, only taken seriously by a few of us scattered around the world. To these, most of whose names appear in the bibliography, I am grateful for the many brain-storming sessions which, coupled with twenty years' experience, have gone into the making of this book, and am particularly grateful to my old friend and new colleague, Jill Pagan, who has applied a down-to-earth barrister's analysis with the more extreme flights of my economist's imagination.

This is not a detailed reference book for tax practitioners, although I hope they will find some meat within its pages. It is more directed to the general financial practitioner, the finance director, the treasurer, and the banker and to show why, and how, it is absolutely essential to incorporate tax thinking into any aspect of international financial strategy which involves currency risk. I particularly hope that it will appeal to the next generation of finance directors, those now going through Business School. I have taught some of the tricks to some of their recent predecessors whose questioning minds have taught me more than I have taught them.

Part One

Managing foreign exchange taxation

1

The problem stated

Foreign exchange markets have been decidedly choppy, at least since 1971. Everyone trading internationally, or even just travelling, knows that. The problems of foreign exchange risk are familiar enough; the related tax problems, only too often, are not.

The tables at the end of Chapter 3 give some key figures for the period. Year after year, changes in exchange rates typically exceed interest rate differentials and sometimes exceed interest rates themselves. Over the period discussed the average absolute annual movement in the value (plus or minus) of each of the major currencies against the US dollar was over 11 per cent.

Planning for international taxation, and for foreign exchange and interest risk, are inextricably linked. Any attempt to do one without the other or, almost as bad, to delegate the two problems separately to two different departments, or to two different outside advisers who do not communicate with each other, is a sure road to disaster.

There are problems, traps, and for the well-advised, opportunities which can only be solved, avoided or exploited by looking systematically at the related factors of international tax, exchange risk, interest, and inflation. A significant improvement in after-tax profits can be obtained by an integrated professional approach to tax-efficient treasury management: what one American client, when it was explained to him, characterised as a 'holistic' approach.

The tax treatment of currency risk is too important to be left either to tax experts – or to currency specialists. In the early days it seemed that all we had to do was to get the tax and currency people to talk to each other. In practice, this proved to work no better than getting domestic tax specialists from the United States, Japan and West Germany round a table and expecting them to come up with useful international advice. These subjects can be tackled only if they become a central part of financial and general management.

The most serious problem is 'tax fragmentation'. The tax treatment of foreign exchange gains and losses is, under UK and US law in particular, neither rational, logical nor coherent. In one of the Australian cases discussed, the tax authorities actually sought (unsuccessfully but they went all the way through the courts) to tax a company on its foreign exchange gain in one year, while disallowing the exactly corresponding loss in another. The US Hoover case shows how a US company can (or could in 1967) get both its foreign exchange and its tax planning hopelessly wrong. Expecting devaluation of the pound, it hedged the assets of its UK subsidiary, lost money by getting its timing wrong, and failed to get a deduction for its losses.

Tax fragmentation arises from the different tax treatment of different transactions having similar economic consequences, and takes four main forms. The most virulent is peculiar to the United Kingdom, and arises from the non-symmetrical treatments of capital gains on assets and liabilities. A UK company borrows $12 million when the pound is $2.40, and buys a US asset. A few years later, the pound being $1.20, the asset is sold for the same $12 million, and the loan is repaid.

Commercially, there is neither gain nor loss. However, the UK Inland Revenue will assess on the basis that the *asset* was acquired for £5 million and disposed of for £10 million, a chargeable capital gain of £5 million. No relief is available for the exactly corresponding loss on the *liability*. There is a tax charge of £1.5 million even where there is no economic gain.

The Marine Midland case, and the subsequent Revenue Statement of Practice let some victims (mainly UK subsidiaries of foreign banks) off the hook, but for most the trap is still there. It has been addressed by a Working Group, the report of which is appended to Chapter 10, but amending legislation is still awaited. (As we go to press a Consultative Document has been issued by the Inland Revenue, and there is some prospect of action in 1990.)

In the United States, proposals first drafted in early 1980 re-emerged in 1985 in *Treasury 2* and were substantially enacted in the Tax Reform Act of 1986. This is a genuine attempt at a rational approach, but even after many subsequent technical amendments there remain many loose ends. There was no sign there of tax advice becoming a declining industry and, indeed, as Chapter 13 shows, American companies need genuine international advice more than ever before.

American parent companies are now having to reappraise international tax strategy to take account of the general implications of the far-reaching Tax Reform Act of 1986. Tax rates were reduced, accompanied by a significant broadening of the tax base. Rates are now lower than in many other countries. It is no longer sufficient to assume that foreign taxes do not matter because they are creditable against US tax. Old-style tax planning relied on careful juggling with the tax credit rules. Many US-based multinationals will now have a surplus of foreign tax credits; tax planning tactics may have to be reversed to minimise foreign, rather than domestic, taxes. 'European'-style international tax skills will become more relevant to US corporations; are we about to see a 'brain drain' of tax talent across the Atlantic?

One warning for American readers. Before reading a book by an American author on international tax or 'international' anything, check the footnotes, and see whether the author takes a genuinely international approach or whether he has only read what other Americans have written.

Over the years there have been some pretty serious disasters, which in the early 1970s sometimes threatened the very existence of the enterprise (Dunlop and J. Lyons are the classic UK examples). In 1976 we were told by a thoroughly unreliable source (a ministerial reply in the House of Commons) that UK companies had lost no less than £5,000 million in a non-tax deductible form! They had borrowed dollars or other foreign currencies, encouraged by the Bank of England and by the 'Lever amendments'. These had relaxed the restrictive circumstances under which the interest on foreign borrowings was deductible. When sterling fell out of bed, the cost of interest and repayment rocketed in sterling terms, turning an apparently cheap loan into a very expensive one. Many companies then found, to their shock and surprise, that they could not even get tax relief for these losses!

This 'foreign borrowing' trap of the 1970s was not buried particularly deeply in the obscurities of tax law, but it was well documented. The problem was that it never occurred to the bankers concerned with raising the money to look at the tax aspects and, outside the small circle of *international* tax specialists, the typical tax partner in a firm of lawyers or accountants knew nothing about currencies. It never occurred to him to advise on the possible consequences of currency fluctuation. British companies raised thousands of millions on international markets without seeking any advice from international tax specialists. In spite of the huge losses suffered by companies, no professional advisers appear to have been sued for negligence, although there are cases of in-house advisers being sacked. The trap is still there; a change in the law is long overdue.

Just at the time when companies were becoming more sophisticated about *exchange* rates they faced another problem – unpredictable *interest* rates. Companies that had been complaining that the interest

rates had failed to keep pace with inflation, with disastrous consequences to the funding of their pension funds, found the problem had
reversed itself. Interest rates shot up, in real as well as nominal terms,
and seriously prejudiced their financing plans. Too many had borrowed
at 'floating rates' – loans showing misleadingly in the accounts as
'medium' term.

In the late 1980s there has been a dramatic improvement in company
profitability. Many companies who thought they needed to manage the
currency mix of their *debt* now find themselves with the new challenge
of administering spare cash; this, too, is a good subject for strategic
planning.

There are other problems of tax fragmentation. The second and most
obvious arises from the relationship between interest and foreign
exchange risk. These are closely related through the forward market. If
dollar interest rates are 12 per cent, while yen rates are 6 per cent, the
market is expecting, and the forward market is offering, a 6 per cent
appreciation in the yen over the year. (The market may well be
mistaken, a complication which in practice is not as serious as it sounds
since it can be handled by appropriate hedging techniques; see Chapter 3.)
This seems simple enough – until we remember that in the English-
speaking countries at least, interest and capital gains are not treated in
the same way. (Although the rates of tax on trading income and capital
gains are now the same in some countries the rules remain different and
this point is still significant.)

Major companies have subsidiaries or other taxable presences in
many countries. They have tax problems and opportunities in all of
these, and can often choose where to borrow money or take currency
exposure. A close study of the relevant laws of many countries often
reveals some unexpected opportunities.

The third variant really only concerns the timing of tax liabilities and
when gains or losses are recognised. This can work in the taxpayer's
favour although the more aggressive 'straddle' technique is generally no
longer available. The fourth variant arises from anomalies in the
calculation of double tax relief. These variants are complex and a study
of them can be rewarding. They are discussed in Chapter 11 (United
Kingdom) and Chapter 13 (United States).

As well as the difference between anticipated and unanticipated
exchange risk, there is another uncertainty – on the tax treatment itself.
Instead of merely putting a tax dimension on to currency risk
management, we have to apply a 'risk management' approach to
international tax planning itself. Wherever there is uncertainty as to the
outcome of a transaction there is always a danger that the tax treatment

will not be *symmetrical*. The taxman's share of the upside potential may be greater than his share of the downside risk, which is a serious distortion of the odds. The good tax planner is aware of these dangers and will try to ensure that the Inland Revenue's share of the downside is at least as large as its share of the upside. In currency risk management we can live with a 50 per cent or even a 60 per cent tax charge – provided that we have equivalent deduction for losses. But, if the Inland Revenue stands to take a higher (even slightly higher) proportion of the gains we will be cleaned out just as surely as the gambler is cleaned out by the zero on the roulette wheel.

Chapters 2–8 give a general account of foreign exchange and interest rate risk, and the main problems and opportunities arising from the tax treatment of interest paid and received, and of foreign exchange gains and losses. We then go on to explain the principles on which key decisions on where and how to borrow, to invest and to hedge are taken.

Even in a relatively short time there have been major changes in relevant tax law, particularly in the United States, Australia and New Zealand. In the United Kingdom, where the subject remains a mess, and Canada, where on the whole it is not, there have been few changes affecting the taxation of foreign exchange gains and losses. In both these countries there have been other major changes affecting financing. Corporate finance in Canada will never be the same again following changes in the preferred share rules and the Bronfman case.

Chown (1986) included a chapter on 'Some modern financing techniques' covering financial futures, options, swaps, caps, collars and their variants. This subject has increased in importance and now pervades the whole book. Some difficulties, such as the old UK Case VI 'heads I win, tails you lose' trap have gone, and tax law has at some points, caught up with market reality. Some 'straddle'-type *opportunities,* in the United States and elsewhere, have gone. Problems remain: the UK 'swaps trap' is still claiming eminent victims, while conflicts on whether a US hedging transaction is within Section 988, Section 1256, or both, will keep tax lawyers happy and well fed for many years to come. Other techniques, such as cross-border leasing and captive insurance companies have become relatively less important – at least for a time.

The second half of this book deals with individual countries. The treatment is not intended to be comprehensive or definitive: law and practice changes too rapidly, and the subject is too complex to make that possible. No book, not even a weekly updated loose-leaf service, can be a substitute for an appropriate team of professional advisers. Rather, these chapters are intended to give to finance and corporate strategy management, more generalist international tax practitioners, and investment bankers a clear feel for the constraints, and an idea of the traps and opportunities. Keen readers will look beyond the countries in which they are immediately interested; there may be the odd nugget buried in an unexpected place.

The law in these country chapters is, subject to the usual proviso, correct at end 1988. Developments in early 1989 are noted, but not consistently. Given the aim of providing the more generalist financial executive with an overview, it would have been unnecessarily pedantic to use a consistent cut-off date.

2

The foreign exchange consequences of trading transactions

The simplest form of foreign exchange exposure, 'transactions exposure', arises from straightforward trading transactions. Whether the exporter invoices in his own or in his customer's currency, this will be 'foreign currency' for one, and occasionally for both, parties. Generally, this raises no problems of definition or of tax; the seller will bring his actual home currency receipts, and the buyer his actual costs, into trading accounts for tax purposes.

The problems and opportunities of tax fragmentation arise on capital account transactions and longer-term exposures, but before examining these it is well worth while starting with a thorough analysis of the 'simple' case. Even those familiar with the finer points will find it worth while to return to first principles occasionally.

Trading transactions

Assume a US company is owed £1,000 (invoiced in sterling) by a British customer and payment is expected in three months time. The spot rate of exchange is $1.60 and the US company may therefore regard itself as being owed $1,600. If the rate of exchange falls to $1.50 it will receive only $1,500. This could be an important loss of expected profit even for a high-margin manufacturing company; for a low-margin export merchant, who might have bought the goods for $1,550, such losses could, in total, be disastrous. There is, of course the possibility of receiving $1,700, but the company does not regard itself as being in the business of speculating in foreign exchange.

What steps can we take to deal with this exposure? The simplest is to hedge in the forward currency market. The selling company could sell £1,000 sterling for US dollars three months forward at the ruling market price which might be $1.58. This is the most elementary form of hedging and normally raises no tax problems. The loss or profit of the hedging transaction will be a straightforward trading loss or gain and the US company will be taxed on the basis of the number of dollars it eventually receives. Even this, very simple, example reveals some significant points.

First, the company will receive, not $1,600 but $1,580 – the 'cost' of $20 being sometimes regarded as insurance against a possibly greater loss. The 'insurance' analogy is in fact misleading. What the seller should do, but often does not, is to base quotations on the *forward* price ruling at the date of payment expected – not on the spot price at the date of quoting. If the US company wanted to be sure of receiving $1,600 it should have quoted a sterling price of £1,013 (i.e. $1,600 at $1.58). Currency risk needs to be appraised before pricing decisions are taken. The alternative of invoicing in one's own currency, merely shifts the problem to the customer. A surprising number of UK companies continued to invoice in sterling in the 1970s when sterling was weak. This had a double disadvantage. If the customer expects sterling to fall, he would delay payment for as long as possible in the hope of getting a better rate, thus adding to the seller's financing costs. If sterling actually fell, the sterling proceeds would be worth less in dollars, Deutschmarks or whatever than it would otherwise have been.

The *second* problem is one of timing. Unless the transaction is settled by a bill of exchange maturing on a specified date, the hedge will not be a 'perfect' one. Trade debts are often settled on open account, and although the US supplier will know roughly when to expect payment he will not know exactly. In practice, payment may be received at a different date and converted at a different rate from the rate of maturity of the forward contract.

The *third* problem arises even before the order is placed. Alfred Kenyon (1981) discussed the 'life cycle' of currency exposure from conception to death and discussed the antenatal period between 'conception: when we commit ourselves to a mismatch' and 'birth: when the commitment becomes a commercial or contractual reality: it has ceased to be unilateral'. He also refers to this in a later chapter as 'the worst problem, the tender period'. The difficulty here is when the would-be seller has to quote a firm price in a foreign currency and the exchange rate may well move before the customer has to make up his mind. There is a unilateral risk which cannot be covered by hedging; options can help, but may, in this context be expensive. It is sometimes possible to shift it to a credit insurer such as the Exim Bank or the Export Credit Guarantee Department. Such agencies are well aware of the problem and have made helpful arrangements.

There is a similar problem for parties to law-suits where the settlement is to be in a currency other than that which he wants (as plaintiff) or may have to pay (as defendant). Option markets may also be appropriate in those cases.

Fourth, it is not realistic to assume that the reference currency (usually the currency of the parent company's own country) is itself stable. A perfect currency hedge may mislead the company into accepting the distortions produced by the home country's inflation. The implications of this are discussed in Chapter 3.

Matching assets and liabilities

Exchange risks of a trading nature can also be hedged by altering the currency mix of assets and/or liabilities. For instance, the US exporter in the first example could borrow £1,000 from his bankers, convert them into spot dollars and deposit the resulting $1,600 with the bank. When payment is received the transactions would be reversed. The 'cost of hedging' would then be the interest differential and, because of interest arbitrage, the cost of the alternatives would (on a large scale) tend to be about the same. For instance if sterling interest rates were 12 per cent, dollar interest rates were 8 per cent and the spot exchange rate was $1.60, the transactions over three months would be:

	Borrow £	*Deposit* $
Borrow	1,000	
Convert at $1.60		
Deposit		1,600
Interest paid 3 months at 12%	30	
Interest received 3 months at 8%		32
	£1,030	$1,632

After three months, the hedger therefore receives $1,632 and has to repay £1,030, both sums including interest at the appropriate rate. The closing transactions exactly match out if the dollars can be converted into sterling at $1.585. This therefore is going to be, give or take a tiny fraction, the three months' forward rate at the start of the transaction.

This interest arbitrage relationship is fundamental; it will re-emerge, in a more complex and subtle guise as the 'implicit forward exchange rate'.

Groups of companies

If even a simple hedge reveals some intriguing features, we can learn even more by turning to the more amusing aspects of the subject. First of all, what happens when an international group of companies has foreign currency exposures with tax consequences in more than one country?

Step 1. must be to compute exposure in local currency in each country. This exercise must be thorough and accurate. A liability to pay Portuguese escudos next month is not the same as a liability to pay in September next year and needs to be recorded separately.

Step 2. is to calculate *group* exposure in after-tax terms, treating each subsidiary in exactly the same way as if it were an independent company, taking account of tax factors in its country of residence but (at this stage) ignoring tax factors at parent company level.

Step 3. is to centralise the information. The parent, or a fellow subsidiary, may have matching risks and it may be advisable to net out the exposure on a group basis before taking any steps to hedge.

An exposure in one direction in a subsidiary may be matched by a risk in the opposite direction (or a hedging transaction may be deliberately set up) in a subsidiary in another country.

Armed with this information we can look at our overall strategy. It is easy enough to set out a schedule balancing these out in pre-tax terms – again provided we have scheduled liabilities by maturity as well as by currency.

Tax does now come into the analysis, and it is essential to continue the calculation in post-tax terms. To take an obvious example – if there is a $10,000 exposure in a country with a 50 per cent tax rate, a 10 per cent movement in the exchange rate will produce a gross loss (or profit) of $1,000, but this will be reduced by tax to $500. If the hedge is carried out through a tax haven affiliate, it may only be necessary to hedge half the amount – $500.

Each country will compute gains and losses with reference to its own currency. An obvious, but again sometimes overlooked, problem arises on intercompany debt. If a US company is owed money by a UK 100 per cent affiliate, the exposure (ignoring tax) balances out at group level regardless of whether the debt is denominated in sterling, dollars, or even a third currency. If the debt is in dollars, fluctuations in the dollar/

sterling rate will have tax consequences in the United Kingdom, but not in the United States; *vice versa* for a sterling debt.

There is one serious potential trap here. A client may assure us that the debt is denominated in a particular currency. It is then always worth asking for photocopies of the ledger entries relating to the loan in both companies. Usually, there is no problem but in a significant minority of cases, each company books the transaction in its own home currency. This may not matter, but any ambiguity is a serious hostage to fortune. The tax authorities can look at the transaction in whichever way suits *them* best.

Branches

Yet another complication arises where the same profit or gain is liable to tax in more than one country. Under the laws of many countries the income and gains of an unincorporated foreign branch of a domestic company are subject to domestic tax. The same income will be taxable in the host country, but in principle this tax will be available as a credit against home country tax. However, as each country will calculate gains and losses in its own currency, this can produce anomalous results. Although branches as such are relatively rare (except for banks) in international operations, the point is becoming increasingly important with the spread of 'controlled foreign corporation' legislation. This may in certain circumstances result in undistributed profits in a foreign subsidiary being taxed transparently, i.e. 'as if' it were a branch.

3

The economics of exchange risk

Chapter 2 discussed the simplest form of foreign exchange exposure, and showed that there were some subtle angles even there. Longer-term exposures, particularly those associated with multicurrency financing and cross-border acquisitions, are more complex.

As a practical matter, we can only advise on the tax aspects of a transaction if we really understand the nature of the transaction itself. It is remarkable how often an apparently intractable tax problem, particularly one involving modern financial instruments or (say) a cross-border leveraged buy-out, falls beautifully, and profitably, into place when we analyse it into its component parts.

Some key relationships

This chapter discusses the underlying economic relationships. Foreign exchange exposure is easy to recognise but difficult to define. It cannot usefully be expressed just as a single figure, and it is certainly not a figure which can be derived from traditional year-end accounts. A full analysis needs to take account of the majority of assets and liabilities; guilders receivable next month cannot simply be netted against guilders payable next year. *Uncertain* receipts and liabilities need to be incorporated in the model. Exchange rate risk is merely one aspect of a general problem which includes price risks and interest risks.

Fluctuations in *exchange* rates are associated with two other rates – the *inflation* rate and the *interest* rate. The relationship between these three sets of figures is of central importance in analysing real-life problems. There are three relationships between three sets of figures. Changes in exchange rates are associated with changes in relative price levels in the countries concerned. Exchange rate changes and, more specifically, expected exchange rate changes are associated with the difference in interest rates in two currencies. Domestic interest rates bear a relationship to domestic inflation rates; the 'real interest rate' is the difference between the two figures. These three relationships, sometimes referred to in the textbooks as 'purchasing power parity theory', 'Fisher open' and 'Fisher', respectively, have two things in common. First, they are highly imprecise. Second, they are very important.

The paradox is easily resolved. As this chapter will show, although these relationships have some validity in the long run, the short-run deviations can be dramatically important, sometimes more important than changes in the raw data. One part of a particular exchange rate movement may be in harmony with these economic 'laws', while there is another part which is not. Currency fluctuations which follow, and those which depart from, some aspect of equilibrium need handling, for treasury management and tax planning purposes, in quite different ways.

The tables at the end of the chapter are designed to illustrate these points. Tables 3.1 and 3.2 give, for six major countries, the year-end exchange rate, and the year-end retail price level. Table 3.3 shows the year-on-year percentage changes against the US dollar. In several cases, they exceed 20 per cent, and for all the currencies over an eighteen-year period the absolute mean (i.e. ignoring the direction of change) was over 11 per cent.

(Tables 3.13 and 3.14 summarise more detailed data. They show the average annual movement, in absolute terms, for each month in the period compared with the corresponding previous month. Against the US dollar the 1980s have been even more volatile than the 1970s, but the cross-rates tell a different story.)

Types of exposure

A fascinating short paper by Stonehill, Ravn and Dullum (1982), based on experiences in managing Novo, the Denmark-based multinational, identifies and discusses four levels of currency exposure:

1. Transaction exposure – 'outstanding accounts receivable, accounts payable, and unexecuted forward contracts'.
2. Impact on 'medium term cash flows assuming *equilibrium* between foreign exchange rates, national inflation rates and national interest rates'.
3. Impact on 'the same medium term cash flows but this time assuming *disequilibrium* between foreign exchange rates, national inflation rates and national interest rates'.

4. 'Impact on long run cash flows . . . . At this strategic level a firm must take into account the reaction of existing and potential competitors.'

The authors define foreign exchange economic exposure as 'the possibility that the net present value of a firm's expected net cash flows will change due to an unexpected change in foreign exchange rates'. They distinguish between the effective changes 'assuming equilibrium' (level 2), 'assuming disequilibrium' (level 3), and between foreign exchange rates, national inflation rates and national interest rates. There are relationships between exchange rate movements on the one hand, and interest rate differentials ('the Fisher effect') and inflation differentials ('purchasing power parity'). It may be important to distinguish between an exchange rate movement where one of the classical relationships actually holds, and one where it does not. The appropriate corporate strategy and the tax consequences could be very different indeed.

Exchange rates and inflation

If, over a period, internal prices in one country double while prices in another remain stable, one might *expect* the par value of the first country's currency to halve in relation to the second. There would then be no change in the comparative export competitiveness of the two countries. A traveller from the second country to the first would then find that, although local prices had doubled, he could obtain twice as many units of currency for his own currency. Prices in terms of his own money would therefore be unchanged. Over a long period exchange rates do tend to follow the 'purchasing power parity' but *deviations* from purchasing power parity are a significant and often overlooked problem (or opportunity) for the corporate treasurer.

The purchasing power parity index

We have found this a particularly useful statistic in analysing the movement of currencies. The 'purchasing power parity index' (PPPI) shows the extent to which a country's exchange rate has risen or fallen in a way which is *not* explained by movements in relative prices.

For example, at the end of 1980 the value of the pound was $2.39. If we look at Table 3.2 during the next four years consumer prices rose by 26.1 per cent in the United States, and by 33.6 per cent in the United

Kingdom. If 'purchasing power' had held, the pound would have fallen to $2.26.

		In the *United States*	*In the* *United Kingdom*
1980	Cost of 100 units of goods in dollars	$239	£100
1985	Cost of same goods	$301.38 (plus 26.1%)	£133.60 (plus 33.6%)
	(£133.60 at 2.26 = $301.38)		

In fact the pound, actually fell to $1.16. A customer who found his UK and US suppliers equally good value at the end of 1980, could at the end of 1984 find what he wants in the United States for $301 – but needs only to pay £134 at $1.16 – or $155 – for UK goods. The ratio between 207 and 312 (66 as an index number) is the PPPI and is a measure of relative change in competitiveness. British goods were (relatively) costing half the price of US goods as compared with four years earlier. This figure can be read directly from Table 3.4.

During the next four years, to end 1988, US prices rose by 13.7 per cent, while UK prices rose 18.6 per cent. During this period the pound, instead of falling, recovered shortly to $1.81. The purchasing power parity index rose to 83.7, recovering much of its fall and relinquishing most of the gain in competitiveness.

The PPPI is calculated as

$$PPPI = \frac{\text{Domestic price index}}{\text{US price index}} \times \text{Exchange rate (as \$ per unit)}$$

Table 3.4 gives this statistic for five countries against the United States. The UK example is actually not particularly extreme. At the end of 1980 the Swiss and Japanese currencies were nearly *twice* the level that PPPI, based on figures at the end of 1970, would have suggested; most of this over-valuation had run off by the end of 1984 – the high point of dollar strength, but then the figures again went into reverse. The yen is now over two-and-a-half times the 1970 level; the Swiss franc kept its end up until 1987, and then fell from grace.

The PPPI figures are of some limited value in making an economic appraisal of the strength or weakness of a currency. The fact that some forecasters have placed undue emphasis on it does not mean it should be ignored. A high PPPI suggests that a country is 'uncompetitive'; if a currency is at the top of its range, it may be in for a fall, or vice versa. This is of little use as a forecasting tool; the tables show that the PPPI figure can easily deviate by 40 per cent or 50 per cent either side of an average figure. The PPPI can in any case be corrected by changes in price levels, and needs to be examined alongside inflation forecasts. The figure is in fact of more use to business strategists in its own right, as a guide to competitiveness.

From either point of view, Table 3.4 has three weaknesses. First, it uses the United States as a reference, and we cannot immediately tell whether a fall in the PPPI for a country is a result of that country becoming more, or the United States becoming less, competitive. It is better for some purposes to use 'trade weighted' figures for the calculation. Trade weighted exchange rate indices are given in Table 3.5 and some PPPI figures derived from them are given in Table 3.6.

Second, when is a country 'competitive'? It proved convenient to take the end of 1980 as the reference, but there is no suggestion that this coincided with some perfect equilibrium.

Third, Table 3.4 is based on retail price indices – a general measure of inflation. This a good guide for the holidaymaker who wants to know whether the South of France will be relatively cheaper or more expensive than last year. For our purposes, it is not ideal as it includes goods and services which are not internationally traded. Whatever index is used, we cannot be sure that the price of particular goods will follow that particular index. The price levels facing a particular business deviate substantially from the index, giving yet another area of risk. An obvious alternative, the wholesale price index, is also flawed; deviations from purchasing power parity tend to be smaller because the index is made up of a large proportion of internationally traded goods whose prices are themselves heavily influenced by changes in the exchange rate. The economist's art is to use different figures to illuminate the same facts in different ways. This may sound inconsistent, but is in fact helpful.

Using this approach, we may well conclude that there *is* a good explanation for a deviation in PPPI, and that it may persist. For instance, oil prices have had a dominating effect on the UK economy. High oil prices strengthen sterling, but also reduce industrial competitiveness – and vice versa – and the effect is reflected as a structural change in the PPPI relationship. Similarly, Japan's exports are based on industries in which real production costs have been falling – an upward trend in PPPI was to be expected, and is indeed observed.

The presentation used in this chapter is deliberately intended to highlight the deviations in PPPI and not to explain them. The point is to show that foreign exchange risk is *not* a proxy for inflation risk, or even for differential inflation risk, and that there are quite separate risks associated with PPPI. The following two examples will illustrate.

Some years ago a British company entered into a contract to produce capital goods at a fixed price in US dollars. The work was in fact to be done by a Swedish subsidiary. Three countries were involved. What was their exchange risk? Should they sell forward dollars, buy forward kronor, or what? A little clear thinking soon revealed that the main risk the company was taking was a rise in Swedish wage rates as expressed in US dollars. It does not matter whether this is brought about by a rise in kronor wage rates, with an unchanged exchange rate, by unchanged domestic wage rates accompanied by a strengthening of the kronor, or by a combination of the two.

It was not really an exchange risk problem at all; most of the danger was from inflation. One way of hedging some of the risk would have been to index the contract to US wage rates. This would in practice have been more appropriate than currency hedging. It would have been totally effective if and only if any difference in wage rates in the two countries was reflected in the exchange rate. The main commercial risk was of a change in the purchasing power parity index.

Some apparent long-term currency risks (e.g. assets in foreign countries) are more in the nature of 'trading' or 'differential inflation' rates than pure long-term currency risks. If a company owns one office block in Rio, and another in Philadelphia, these have real values which should not be affected directly by the weakness of the cruzado or the strength of the dollar. If a British shipyard contracts to sell a ship for yen, part of its risk is the future level of wages of British shipyard workers – as converted into yen. It is vitally important to use common sense to analyse the real risk, and not simply to apply inflexible rules of thumb.

Profitability and exchange risk

The central theme of this book is that the disciplines of treasury management and tax planning are intimately related. Even today, after a decade or so of companies being educated in the hard school of experience, this integrated approach, although more widespread than before, is still the exception rather than the rule. Some aspects go beyond treasury management and into corporate strategy and general management. They are difficult to analyse systematically, but cannot be ignored.

Exchange rate movements affect national profitability, and therefore affect the profits of different parts of a group of companies. This is a more subtle aspect of the PPPI analysis. Suppose a US parent company has an operating subsidiary in West Germany. From the treasurer's point of view this has current assets (net receivables and cash balances) on which there is a 'translation' risk. There are also 'real' assets (fixed assets and inventories) which need treating in a different way. So far so good. The group seems vulnerable to a fall, and will profit from a rise, in the dollar value of the Deutschmark.

But what if the West German subsidiary is a major supplier of products to third markets? In such circumstances a strong Deutschmark which really and fairly exactly reflects lower German inflation rates will not affect the trading position. If, as happened in the late 1970s, the Deutschmark rises even more than relative price levels justify, what is the result? Sure enough the group makes a profit, even allowing for tax on its translation exposure, but it may find its German factory becoming uncompetitive in terms of costs. Its profits would be squeezed and the value of the going concern reduced by a strong Deutschmark. If this strength of the Deutschmark had been anticipated, the correct strategy might have been to move production away from West Germany. An *unanticipated* rise might result in a loss on trade account exceeding the gain on purely financial account. The true 'exchange risk' of the group may be the opposite of what was originally supposed. The PPPI concept is important here. An increase in PPPI is a decline in competitiveness, and is a risk quite distinct from a change in exchange rates as such.

It is therefore essential with exchange exposure to look at each country (or at least currency area) separately, both as a production centre and as a market, and at least make some attempt to estimate the effect on cash flows and product margins of various possible exchange rate scenarios. The fact that it is difficult to obtain an exact measure of exposure on this basis is no excuse for not making at least a qualitative attempt.

Exchange rates and interest rates

This is the second of the major relationships. If over a period of, say, a year, one currency is *expected* to depreciate by 5 per cent in terms of another, we might also *expect*, subject to the limitations of exchange controls and market imperfections, that interest rates in the weaker currency would be five points higher than interest rates in the stronger currency. This particular relationship is based on *expected* and not on *historical* rates.

Expectations are not always fulfilled. Table 3.7 shows average annual yields on three-month Treasury bills or the equivalent in the six countries. These show wide discrepancies both over time and between countries, while Table 3.8 shows the power of compound interest: £100 becomes £577 over eighteen years but 100 Swiss francs becomes only Sw Fr 155.2. In the event, the francs were the better investment. Table 3.9 translates the figures in Table 3.8 into US dollars, while Table 3.10 shows the year-on-year change in dollar terms.

The US-based investor in yen would have made returns of over 30 per cent per annum in three consecutive years; the US company *borrowing* yen would have *paid* these amounts. In one year, though, yen returns were negative.

The superior growth of the Swiss franc, Deutschmark and yen occurred in the first part of the period. In 1979 and 1980 the foreign-based investor in sterling did brilliantly. In 1982, the investor in Swiss francs suffered low nominal interest rates and a *loss* on currency. Looked at the other way, a US company borrowing Swiss francs in 1982 (or, for instance, pounds or yen in 1975) enjoyed a negative cost of funds.

The relationship between exchange rate changes and interest rate differentials is obviously of central importance to the corporate treasurer. The interest arbitrage relationship, explained in Chapter 2, is the key to this analysis. Assume the treasurer needs to raise Sw Fr 10 million for a period of twelve months. The two most obvious possibilities open to him are to borrow Swiss francs for twelve months at an interest cost of 4 per cent, or to borrow dollars at 10 per cent, convert into Swiss francs at the ruling rate of exchange, assumed to be Sw Fr 1.60 = $1. When the Swiss francs are received they will be converted into dollars at the *then* ruling rate and the proceeds used to repay the loan.

If the treasurer expects the value of the dollar to fall over the twelve-month period, what should he do? The answer is of course that it depends how far the dollar is likely to fall. The break-even exchange rate is in fact Sw Fr 1.5125. If the dollar fell below that, it would be a 'cheaper' borrowing in spite of the higher coupon. If it fell by less (and ignoring tax, of which more – indeed much more, in the rest of this book) the Swiss franc borrowing would be the better bargain.

Another strategy is available: borrow dollars, buy Swiss francs spot and sell Swiss francs forward at whatever rate the market is quoting. The 'interest arbitrage' relationship explained in Chapter 2 is a key concept. Given the six-point interest differential in favour of the dollar, the Swiss franc must be priced in the forward market at 1.60 × (1.04)/(1.10) or Sw Fr 1.5125 since, otherwise, arbitrageurs would be *guaranteed* a positive return. In terms of foreign exchange exposure, this is equivalent to borrowing, not dollars but Swiss francs. Forward exchange rates reflect (and to some extent cause) the exchange rate differentials. Subject to market frictions, which these days are relatively minor, a 2 percentage point interest rate differential on three months' money between two currencies will result in the three months' forward rate being a 0.5 per cent discount on the spot rate.

As the tables show, the forward exchange rate does not necessarily, or even usually, predict the likely future spot rate. *Interest* rates are normally determined by domestic monetary policy and the forward rate would merely be a reflection of this differential. Sometimes the forward rate thus derived will differ from what the rate is expected actually to be.

(If the consensus of opinion on currency markets believes that the Sw Fr 1.51 figure understates the likely weakness of the dollar and that the spot rate in three months' time is more likely to be Sw Fr 1.55, what will happen? Speculators will buy forward dollars against Swiss francs in the hope of a profit. As they are entering into forward *contracts*, no money changes hands at this stage, but their activities might bid up the forward price to Sw Fr 1.52. Banks would now be able to borrow Swiss francs at 4 per cent buy spot US dollars at Sw Fr 1.60 and sell forward at 1.62. They would only need to earn 9.5 per cent on the dollars to break even, while the market is offering 10 per cent and would therefore make about 50 basic points arbitrage profit on the round trip.

The normal arithmetical relations would be restored in one of the three following ways:

1. Funds might be withdrawn *from* the Swiss banking system, leading to an *upward* pressure on Swiss interest rates.
2. Funds might flow *into* the US banking system, leading to a *downward* pressure on US interest rates.
3. Spot funds could flow from Switzerland to the United States putting *upward* pressure on the *spot* value of the US dollar.

Speculative movements can affect internal interest rates, and governments may use internal interest rates as a means of influencing exchange rates. The example is simple but important. It is intended to show clearly the relationship between interest differentials and exchange fluctuations.

Hedged arbitrage is undertaken for tiny margins by the banking system and ensures that the ordinary trader will get about the same rates for the same risk. There is generally little to choose in pre-tax terms. Unhedged arbitrage is another matter altogether. Table 5.10 shows the effective dollar cost of borrowing (or return from investing in) the various currencies in each year. They range from 43.7 per cent (when dollars cost 7.7 per cent) to *minus* 15.2 per cent.

Inflation and interest rates

Interest rates might also be expected to bear some relationship to inflation rates: a third relationship. A country experiencing high rates of *inflation* will also have the high rates of *interest*. If an investor invests $10,000 at 10 per cent interest he will get back $11,000 principal and interest at the end of the year. If prices have meanwhile risen by 10 per cent, his *real* return will be nil. If the investor is to obtain a real return, the rate of interest offered must be higher by some margin than the rate of inflation, even if he does not pay tax. (A taxpaying investor will have a much harder battle.)

Table 3.8 shows the effect of investing continuously in three-month Treasury bills or the nearest equivalent in each currency. The 'roll-up' figures show 'the power of compound interest' as enthused over by life assurance salesmen. The more sceptical of us will compare them with price figures (Table 3.2). Table 3.11 shows the fate of the domestic investor in each country correcting the 'interest' return for the consumer price index, while Table 3.12 shows the annual real returns.

There was a period in the late 1970s when investors actually suffered (and borrowers enjoyed) negative return (even before tax) in all the countries but most particularly in the United Kingdom and Japan where, briefly, real rates hit 'double digit negative'. Real returns (and, significantly for our purpose, real costs of borrowing) turned positive in 1980. This is a very important economic phenomenon with implications for savers, corporate and government borrowers, pension funds and the general economy.

Real interest rates corrected for expected or past inflation can, for many purposes (not all), be more important than nominal interest rates. Just as exchange rate changes need breaking down into 'nominal' and 'PPPI' elements, we need to do the same with interest rates.

Table 3.1 YEAR-END EXCHANGE RATES AGAINST US DOLLAR

Year	United Kingdom	West Germany	France	Switzerland	Japan
1970	2.39	3.65	5.52	4.32	357.7
1971	2.55	3.27	5.22	3.92	314.8
1972	2.35	3.20	5.12	3.77	302.0
1973	2.32	2.70	4.71	3.24	280.0
1974	2.35	2.41	4.44	2.54	301.0
1975	2.02	2.62	4.49	2.62	305.2
1976	1.70	2.36	4.97	2.45	292.8
1977	1.91	2.11	4.71	2.00	240.0
1978	2.03	1.83	4.18	1.62	194.6
1979	2.22	1.73	4.02	1.58	239.7
1980	2.39	1.96	4.52	1.76	203.0
1981	1.91	2.25	5.75	1.80	219.9
1982	1.61	2.38	6.73	1.99	235.0
1983	1.45	2.72	8.35	2.18	232.2
1984	1.16	3.15	9.59	2.59	251.1
1985	1.44	2.44	7.50	2.06	200.3
1986	1.46	1.97	6.48	1.65	162.0
1987	1.86	1.60	5.40	1.29	123.5
1988	1.81	1.77	6.06	1.50	125.0

Table 3.2 CONSUMER PRICE INDEX (1980 = 100)

Year	United States	United Kingdom	West Germany	France	Switzerland	Japan
1970	47.1	27.1	61.0	39.9	61.6	42.3
1971	49.1	30.3	64.1	42.1	65.6	45.0
1972	50.8	32.5	67.7	44.7	70.0	47.2
1973	53.9	35.5	72.4	47.9	76.1	52.7
1974	59.8	41.1	77.4	54.5	83.5	65.0
1975	65.3	51.1	82.0	60.9	89.2	72.6
1976	69.1	59.6	85.6	66.8	90.7	79.4
1977	73.6	69.0	88.7	73.0	91.8	85.9
1978	79.2	74.7	91.1	79.7	92.8	89.5
1979	88.1	84.8	94.9	88.2	96.1	92.8
1980	100.0	100.0	100.0	100.0	100.0	100.0
1981	110.4	111.9	106.3	113.4	106.5	104.9
1982	117.1	121.5	111.9	126.8	112.5	107.8
1983	120.9	127.2	115.6	139.0	115.9	109.9
1984	126.1	133.6	118.4	149.3	119.3	112.3
1985	130.5	140.8	121.0	157.9	123.4	114.6
1986	133.1	145.7	120.7	161.9	124.3	115.3
1987	137.9	151.7	121.0	167.3	126.1	115.4
1988	143.4	158.5	122.5	171.8	128.5	116.2

Table 3.3 YEAR-ON-YEAR PERCENTAGE CHANGES AGAINST US DOLLAR (%)

Year	United Kingdom	West Germany	France	Switzerland	Japan
1970					
1971	6.7	−10.4	−5.4	−9.3	−12.0
1972	−7.8	−2.1	−1.9	−3.8	−4.1
1973	−1.3	−15.6	−8.0	−14.1	−7.3
1974	1.3	−10.7	−5.7	−21.6	7.5
1975	−14.0	8.7	1.1	3.1	1.4
1976	−15.8	−9.9	10.7	−6.5	−4.1
1977	12.4	−10.6	−5.2	−18.4	−18.0
1978	6.3	−13.3	−11.3	−19.0	−18.9
1979	9.4	−5.5	−3.8	−2.5	23.2
1980	7.7	13.3	12.4	11.4	−15.3
1981	−20.1	14.8	27.2	2.3	8.3
1982	−15.7	5.8	17.0	10.6	6.9
1983	−9.9	14.3	24.1	9.5	−1.2
1984	−20.0	15.8	14.9	18.8	8.1
1985	24.1	−22.5	−21.8	−20.5	−20.2
1986	1.4	−19.3	−13.6	−19.9	−19.1
1987	27.4	−18.8	−16.7	−21.8	−23.8
1988	−2.7	10.6	12.2	16.3	1.2
Mean	−0.6	−3.1	1.5	−4.7	−4.9
Absolute mean	11.3	12.3	11.8	12.7	11.1
Standard deviation	13.7	13.0	13.8	13.7	12.6

Table 3.4 PURCHASING POWER PARITY INDEX (CONSUMER PRICES)

Year	United Kingdom	West Germany	France	Switzerland	Japan
1970	58.8	69.5	69.4	53.3	51.0
1971	65.8	78.3	74.2	60.0	59.1
1972	62.9	81.6	77.7	64.3	62.5
1973	63.9	97.5	85.3	76.7	70.9
1974	67.6	105.3	92.8	96.8	73.3
1975	66.1	93.9	93.9	91.8	73.9
1976	61.4	102.9	87.9	94.3	79.7
1977	74.9	111.9	95.2	109.8	98.7
1978	80.1	123.2	108.8	127.3	117.9
1979	89.4	122.0	112.6	121.5	89.2
1980	100.0	100.0	100.0	100.0	100.0
1981	81.0	83.9	80.7	94.3	87.7
1982	69.9	78.7	72.7	85.0	79.5
1983	63.8	68.9	62.2	77.4	79.5
1984	51.4	58.4	55.8	64.3	72.0
1985	65.0	74.5	72.9	80.8	89.0
1986	66.9	90.2	84.8	99.6	108.6
1987	85.6	107.5	101.5	124.8	137.6
1988	83.7	94.6	89.4	105.1	131.6

Table 3.5 ANNUAL AVERAGE TRADE WEIGHTED INDEX (MERM)

Year	United States	United Kingdom	West Germany	France	Switzerland	Japan
1970	128.6	133.2	61.2	99.1	48.6	70.2
1971	125.4	133.6	63.3	97.3	50.2	71.7
1972	116.4	129.2	65.4	100.5	51.0	80.1
1973	106.8	116.6	72.9	105.2	57.0	86.2
1974	109.5	112.8	76.7	98.1	61.8	80.7
1975	106.7	104.1	77.7	106.0	69.4	79.1
1976	112.2	89.2	81.4	101.4	75.3	82.4
1977	111.7	84.6	87.8	96.8	77.4	91.1
1978	102.1	84.9	93.3	96.8	96.2	112.1
1979	99.9	90.9	99.0	99.0	100.2	104.0
1980	100.0	100.0	100.0	100.0	100.0	100.0
1981	112.7	98.9	92.7	89.4	96.6	113.1
1982	125.9	94.2	96.5	81.3	102.7	106.6
1983	133.2	86.7	98.8	74.2	104.8	117.4
1984	143.7	81.9	96.1	69.7	100.3	124.1
1985	150.2	81.5	95.9	70.4	99.2	127.1
1986	122.5	75.9	106.4	74.7	111.5	161.0
1987	108.0	75.6	114.5	76.5	120.5	174.2
1988	102.0	79.6	113.6	74.8	118.8	192.9

Table 3.6 PURCHASING POWER PARITY INDEX – TRADE WEIGHTED

Year	United States	United Kingdom	West Germany	France	Switzerland	Japan
1970	138.9	84.6	85.6	90.7	68.7	68.1
1971	134.1	88.2	88.4	89.2	71.7	70.3
1972	123.2	87.5	92.2	93.6	74.4	78.8
1973	111.3	80.1	102.1	97.5	83.9	87.9
1974	111.9	79.2	101.5	91.4	88.2	89.7
1975	107.2	81.8	98.0	99.3	95.2	88.3
1976	110.1	75.5	99.0	96.2	97.0	92.9
1977	107.7	76.5	102.1	92.6	93.1	102.6
1978	98.7	77.4	103.8	94.2	109.0	122.5
1979	98.6	86.3	105.2	97.8	107.8	108.1
1980	100.0	100.0	100.0	100.0	100.0	100.0
1981	113.0	100.5	89.5	92.1	93.4	107.8
1982	124.5	96.7	91.2	87.1	97.6	97.1
1983	129.5	88.6	91.8	82.9	97.6	103.7
1984	139.0	83.9	87.3	79.8	91.8	106.9
1985	144.1	84.4	85.3	81.7	90.0	107.1
1986	117.1	79.4	92.3	86.9	99.6	133.4
1987	104.0	80.1	96.7	89.4	106.1	140.4
1988	99.0	85.4	94.1	87.0	103.3	151.7

Table 3.7 AVERAGE YIELDS ON THREE-MONTH TREASURY BILLS

Year	United States	United Kingdom	West Germany	France	Switzerland	Japan
1970	6.4	7.0	9.4	8.9	6.8	8.3
1971	4.3	5.6	7.2	6.3	1.2	6.4
1972	4.1	5.5	5.6	5.5	2.7	4.7
1973	7.0	9.3	12.1	9.1	3.6	7.2
1974	7.9	11.4	9.9	13.0	6.0	12.5
1975	5.8	10.2	5.0	7.8	2.8	10.7
1976	5.0	11.1	4.3	8.7	1.5	7.0
1977	5.3	7.7	4.4	9.2	2.5	5.7
1978	7.2	8.5	3.7	8.2	0.7	4.4
1979	10.0	13.0	6.7	9.5	1.0	5.9
1980	11.6	15.1	9.5	12.2	2.3	10.9
1981	14.1	13.0	10.6	15.2	2.9	7.4
1982	10.7	11.5	8.0	14.7	1.3	6.9
1983	8.6	9.6	5.6	12.6	1.8	6.4
1984	9.6	9.3	5.7	11.9	3.3	6.1
1985	7.5	11.6	5.0	10.1	3.8	6.5
1986	6.0	10.4	3.9	7.8	3.2	4.8
1987	5.8	9.3	3.3	8.2	2.5	3.5
1988	6.7	9.8	3.8	7.8	2.2	3.6

Table 3.8 NOMINAL ROLLUP (LOCAL CURRENCY)

Year	United States	United Kingdom	West Germany	France	Switzerland	Japan
1970	100.0	100.0	100.0	100.0	100.0	100.0
1971	104.4	105.7	107.4	106.5	101.2	106.6
1972	108.9	111.8	115.3	113.3	102.3	113.6
1973	113.5	118.0	121.9	119.7	105.1	119.0
1974	121.6	129.4	137.4	130.9	109.0	127.8
1975	131.5	144.8	151.5	148.8	115.6	144.6
1976	139.3	160.1	159.2	160.8	118.8	160.6
1977	146.4	178.7	166.2	175.2	120.7	172.1
1978	154.3	192.8	173.6	191.9	123.7	182.1
1979	165.7	209.8	180.1	208.1	124.5	190.2
1980	182.9	238.4	192.5	228.6	125.7	201.7
1981	205.1	276.5	211.4	257.8	128.6	224.5
1982	235.6	314.2	234.7	299.3	132.4	241.6
1983	261.8	351.9	254.1	345.8	134.2	258.7
1984	285.1	386.9	268.7	391.6	136.7	275.7
1985	313.4	424.2	284.2	440.2	141.3	292.9
1986	337.6	475.4	298.6	486.3	146.7	312.3
1987	358.2	526.6	310.3	525.3	151.4	327.5
1988	379.5	577.0	320.6	569.8	155.2	339.1

Table 3.9 NOMINAL ROLLUP IN US DOLLARS

Year	United States	United Kingdom	West Germany	France	Switzerland	Japan
1970	100.0	100.0	100.0	100.0	100.0	100.0
1971	104.4	114.4	122.5	115.5	117.8	123.3
1972	108.7	111.4	134.4	125.3	123.9	137.0
1973	116.5	116.2	168.4	143.9	148.1	154.9
1974	126.0	129.0	212.6	167.0	195.9	154.7
1975	133.5	124.1	215.6	187.7	201.5	172.6
1976	140.3	115.5	251.6	183.2	221.5	199.9
1977	147.9	144.8	293.7	210.7	275.5	261.3
1978	158.8	166.1	353.8	260.0	348.6	340.9
1979	175.3	197.5	388.3	293.2	359.8	289.1
1980	196.5	241.7	366.3	286.4	326.2	361.9
1981	225.7	224.0	350.5	253.9	326.3	372.0
1982	250.9	214.6	367.7	251.8	303.9	374.6
1983	273.1	216.5	348.4	234.5	281.1	406.0
1984	300.3	190.4	318.1	231.2	241.0	400.0
1985	323.4	259.1	434.5	332.4	313.2	532.7
1986	343.2	294.4	565.3	424.9	405.9	702.3
1987	363.6	415.5	723.2	550.8	535.9	966.1
1988	388.5	443.1	675.5	532.4	472.5	988.5

Table 3.10 TOTAL US DOLLAR RATE OF RETURN

Year	United States	United Kingdom	West Germany	France	Switzerland	Japan
1971	4.4	14.4	22.5	15.5	17.8	23.3
1972	4.2	−2.6	9.7	8.5	5.2	11.1
1973	7.2	4.3	25.3	14.8	19.5	13.0
1974	8.1	11.0	26.2	16.1	32.3	−0.1
1975	5.9	−3.8	1.4	12.4	2.9	11.6
1976	5.1	−6.9	16.7	−2.4	9.9	15.8
1977	5.4	25.4	16.7	15.0	24.4	30.7
1978	7.4	14.7	20.5	23.4	26.5	30.5
1979	10.4	19.0	9.7	12.8	3.2	−15.2
1980	12.1	22.4	−5.7	−2.3	−9.3	25.2
1981	14.9	−7.3	−4.3	−11.4	0.0	2.8
1982	11.1	−4.2	4.9	−0.8	−6.9	0.7
1983	8.9	0.9	−5.3	−6.9	−7.5	8.4
1984	9.9	−12.2	−8.7	−1.4	−14.3	−1.5
1985	7.7	36.1	36.6	43.7	30.0	33.2
1986	6.1	13.6	30.1	27.9	29.6	31.8
1987	6.0	41.1	27.9	29.6	32.0	37.6
1988	6.8	6.6	−6.6	−3.3	−11.8	2.3

Table 3.11 REAL ROLLUP (USING CONSUMER PRICE INDEX)

Year	United States	United Kingdom	West Germany	France	Switzerland	Japan
1970	100.0	100.0	100.0	100.0	100.0	100.0
1971	100.1	96.3	102.3	100.9	94.7	100.2
1972	100.8	94.7	102.4	100.4	90.9	100.1
1973	101.9	95.1	108.3	102.6	86.3	95.8
1974	99.1	91.4	111.9	102.5	83.2	86.0
1975	95.8	78.9	111.0	98.7	79.8	85.5
1976	95.1	74.9	110.9	98.0	79.7	83.6
1977	94.1	69.0	111.9	98.2	80.7	81.6
1978	93.9	69.4	113.1	97.5	80.4	81.8
1979	93.1	69.5	116.1	96.7	78.3	83.8
1980	91.8	68.1	121.3	96.1	77.0	86.8
1981	95.9	69.3	127.0	98.7	74.2	89.1
1982	100.7	71.7	130.8	102.4	71.0	93.0
1983	106.4	75.4	134.0	106.1	70.2	97.2
1984	112.4	78.9	138.5	111.4	70.5	101.2
1985	117.1	84.1	142.5	116.7	70.8	105.8
1986	122.0	90.3	148.4	123.1	72.5	110.3
1987	124.8	95.3	153.0	129.4	73.3	114.2
1988	128.4	100.6	157.0	136.3	73.6	117.5

Table 3.12 REAL RATE OF RETURN (LOCAL CURRENCY) (%)

Year	United States	United Kingdom	West Germany	France	Switzerland	Japan
1970						
1971	0.1	−3.7	2.3	0.9	−5.3	0.2
1972	0.7	−1.6	0.1	−0.6	−4.0	−0.1
1973	1.1	0.4	5.7	2.3	−5.0	−4.3
1974	−2.8	−3.9	3.4	−0.1	−3.6	−10.2
1975	−3.3	−13.7	−0.8	−3.7	−4.0	−0.6
1976	−0.7	−5.1	0.0	−0.7	−0.2	−2.2
1977	−1.1	−7.8	0.9	0.2	1.3	−2.4
1978	−0.2	0.5	1.0	−0.7	−0.4	0.2
1979	−0.9	0.1	2.7	−0.8	−2.6	2.3
1980	−1.4	−1.9	4.5	−0.6	−1.7	3.6
1981	4.5	1.7	4.7	2.7	−3.5	2.7
1982	5.1	3.4	3.0	3.7	−4.3	4.3
1983	5.7	5.3	2.5	3.6	−1.2	4.6
1984	5.6	4.6	3.4	5.0	0.4	4.1
1985	4.2	6.6	2.9	4.7	0.4	4.6
1986	4.1	7.4	4.2	5.5	2.5	4.3
1987	2.4	5.5	3.1	5.1	1.1	3.5
1988	2.9	5.6	2.6	5.4	0.4	3.0

Table 3.13 AVERAGE ABSOLUTE RATES OF CHANGE–EXCHANGE RATES AGAINST US DOLLAR

Decade	Australia	Canada	France	West Germany	Japan	Netherlands	Switzerland	United Kingdom
1960s	0.28	1.37	0.86	1.22	0.45	0.87	0.26	1.84
1970s	6.71	3.63	8.04	10.02	9.64	8.09	11.18	7.15
1980s	9.42	3.81	14.71	13.38	12.88	13.68	13.04	12.22
All	5.56	2.97	7.92	8.30	7.76	7.63	8.33	7.10

Table 3.14 ABSOLUTE RATES OF CHANGE – CROSS RATES

Decade	Japan West Germany	United Kingdom West Germany	Switzerland West Germany	France Netherlands	Australia United Kingdom
1960s	1.49	2.82	1.22	1.56	1.92
1970s	7.43	8.99	6.38	6.20	8.55
1980s	10.14	8.82	3.30	4.17	11.69
All	6.36	6.96	3.72	4.05	7.46

4

Covering longer-term exposures

Short-term trading exposures, and their corresponding hedges, are normally 'tax-neutral', at least in a single country. Normally, also, there are formal *forward* markets for transactions between the major currencies for periods of about one year. The most distant contract in currency *futures* against the US dollar is also about a year. Where such a market does exist, the interest arbitrage relationship can be seen clearly and analysed accordingly.

Until a few years ago it was difficult to hedge longer-term exposures. It was even difficult to persuade client companies that these exposures could at least be analysed rationally. We developed the concept, explained in the following chapter, of the 'implicit forward exchange rate'. At that time this was particularly valuable in handling the type of 'tax fragmentation' problem on long-term capital assets and liabilities. Nowaday longer-term instruments, including swaps, are available to cover longer-term risks. In the event, our tool has proved even more valuable, ensuring that our corporate clients can make an accurate calculation of the real costs and benefits of financial products offered to them.

Where a company places an order for a major capital item, such as a construction project or a ship, the contract may provide for payments over several years. One party, and possibly both, will then have a long-term currency exposure. Long-term exposures arise, even more commonly, from financing operations. A US parent may issue twenty-year bonds via a Dutch subsidiary, and make the funds so borrowed available from the expansion of its Australian subsidiary. There is a whole bundle of exchange risks, and techniques for hedging them, which must be analysed rationally.

Chapter 2 set the scene with a description of the simpler forms of short-term currency hedging. Tax was not, typically, a major problem. Longer-term exposures need non-sophisticated analysis and do raise major tax questions. 'Tax fragmentation', indeed, is the major theme underlying this book.

Tax fragmentation

There are two closely related tax matters of concern to the company treasurer or strategic planner. One is the best way to set up a deduction for interest paid, or to optimise the tax treatment of interest received, and this is discussed in Chapter 6. The other is the tax treatment of foreign exchange gains and losses. Here the main, but not the only, problem or opportunity arises from tax fragmentation.

The tax treatment of gains, losses and costs arising from foreign exchange transactions of any complexity is, in most countries, neither simple nor rational. Corporate taxpayers have to accept the risks of currency movements; they might feel entitled to expect that the tax treatment of the resulting gains and losses is symmetrical and predictable. Unfortunately, it is not. In many countries, particularly the United Kingdom, relevant law is still a complete muddle, resulting in expensive tax traps and, for the well-advised, some profitable opportunities. The United States, in pursuit of the rational solution, has produced a complex jungle of imperfectly digested new legislation still awaiting clarification by the Internal Revenue Service (IRS) and interpretation by the courts. Both the traps and the opportunities multiply when a company group operates in more than one country.

A company borrowing or investing outside its own country faces both 'exchange risk' and 'international taxation' problems, either of which it ignores at its peril. Tax planning, particularly *international* tax planning, must be treated as a branch of financial management. This is particularly true when we are dealing with the uncertainties of foreign exchange rate risk and interest risk.

The four main forms of tax fragmentation are explained below in general terms. The actual tax principles at work in each country are explained in more depth in the relevant country chapters.

1. Non-symmetrical treatment of assets and liabilities

This is the most extreme form, and is peculiar to the United Kingdom. A company borrows $12 million when the pound is $2.40, and buys a US asset. A few years later, the pound being $1.20, the asset is sold for the same $12 million, and the loan is repaid, with neither gain nor loss. The UK Inland Revenue will assess on the basis that the *asset* was acquired for £5 million and disposed of for £10 million, a chargeable capital gain of £5 million. No relief is available for the exactly corresponding capital loss on the *liability*. There is a tax charge of £1.5 million even where there is no economic gain. In 1976, the UK government stated that it would cost £1,500 million to correct the anomaly; a measure of how much business had lost. It is still uncorrected; see Chapter 10.

2. Capital gain v. ordinary income

A more widespread source of tax fragmentation arises from the relationship between interest and foreign currency risk. These are closely related through the forward market. If dollar interest rates are 12 per cent while Deutschmark rates are 6 per cent, the market is expecting, and the forward market is offering, a 6 per cent appreciation in the Deutschmark over the year. These 'interest arbitrage' relationships were explained in Chapter 2, but in this context there is a vital difference. The relationship holds in pre-tax terms; if the two balancing parts of the transaction are taxed differently then there can be an after-tax profit or loss of a whole percentage point or more.

The investor in Deutschmarks is forgoing six points of yield in the hope of six points of currency gain. The borrower of Deutschmarks is saving six points of interest – but will probably have to 'pay' for this with an equivalent currency loss. If the investor was sure that the currency gain would be taxed (as a capital gain) more lightly than the interest, he can *systematically* obtain a significant tax advantage by investing in Deutschmark bonds. He would forgo six points of interest, which would otherwise be taxed at 50 per cent, leaving three points, and (if the market expectations are right) eventually cash in a six-point capital gain worth 4.5 points after tax at 25 per cent. Similarly, the corporate borrower able to deduct interest at regular income rates but able to deduct exchange losses only against capital gains correspondingly loses (or expects to lose) in after-tax terms by borrowing the currency with the lower interest rate structure.

In dealing with fragmentation of types (1) and (2) we have to ask whether a foreign exchange gain is a capital gain or regular income. In general, current *assets* denominated in foreign currencies are treated for tax purposes in the same way as any other short-term assets. If goods are sold in the normal course of business at a price denominated in a foreign currency the amount that will eventually be taxed will be this foreign currency converted into domestic currency at the date of the transaction. Similar rules apply to liabilities; and hedging transactions in forwards and futures will *normally* be symmetrically taxed, but may sometimes still enjoy (or suffer) special tax treatment.

In other cases, as with the treatment of long-term liabilities and branch profits, it is *not* simple. Those who have based their financial planning on the assumption that it was obvious that tax would be levied (or tax relief given) on the basis of the actual profit made or loss sustained have been seriously misled. Lack of precision in the law often violates symmetry and works against the taxpayer. A taxpayer may attempt to set up a transaction so that it receives capital gains treatment on a gain. He may fail in this aim if there is a profit – but succeed only too well if there is a loss! This is perhaps the commonest relevant tax trap, and one which the good currency tax planner must avoid or (even better) turn into an opportunity.

3. Timing

We also have to ask *when* a gain or loss is recognised. This only affects the timing of tax payments but at present rates of interest this can be important. It may be possible to arrange matters so that year-end losses on currency exposure can be recognised in the current year while profits can be carried forward.

Tax law and practice may in fact be slightly *favourable* to the taxpayer here. At a 10 per cent rate of interest, one-year's postponement reduces the effective tax rate from (e.g.) 35 per cent to 31.5 per cent. The aspect of the subject, while complicated, is not particularly difficult to anyone who has mastered the elements of discounting, and is really an extension of the principles applied to inventory valuation.

4. Double tax relief

Double tax relief, whether given unilaterally or by treaty can be distorted by foreign exchange fluctuations. For instance, profits earned in a foreign branch will typically be subject to tax in more than one country, each of which will make the calculation in its own currency. The planning implications of this are contained more in the arithmetic than in the law, but some legal points are relevant. How are the profits of a foreign branch computed? Must we translate all transactions into home country currency, or will the home tax authorities accept the foreign currency computation, translating only the resulting profits? Must translation be at average or closing rates? How do we calculate double tax relief? What rate of exchange is appropriate?

Turning to the arithmetic of a simple general case, consider a merchanting branch with no fixed assets and no inventory. It turns over 100,000 pengoes per annum for a profit of 5,000 pengoes. Its only asset

Table 4.1 BRANCH TAXATION: EFFECT OF CURRENCY MOVEMENTS ON TAX COMPUTATION

Tax rates
Pengovia 50.00%
Homeco 50.00%

	Homeco computation (pengoes)	Homeco computation				
		($)	($)	($)	($)	($)
Opening exchange rate		2.00	2.00	2.00	2.00	2.00
Closing exchange rate		2.00	2.25	1.75	3.00	1.50
Average exchange rate		2.00	2.125	1.875	2.50	1.75
Sales	100,000	50,000	47,059	53,333	40,000	57,143
Profit	5,000	2,500	2,353	2,667	2,000	2,857
Opening receivables	10,000	5,000	5,000	5,000	5,000	5,000
Closing receivables	(10,000)	(5,000)	(4,444)	(5,714)	(3,333)	(6,667)
Taxable profit (ave. rate)	5,000	2,500	2,908	1,952	3,667	1,190
Pengovian tax	2,500	1,250	1,111	1,429	833	1,667
Homeco tax (before DTR)		1,250	1,454	976	1,833	595
Homeco tax (net of DTR)		0	343	0	1,000	0
Total tax (dollars)		1,250	1,454	1,429	1,833	1,667
Net profit (dollars)		1,250	1,454	524	1,833	(476)
Total tax (pengoes)		2,500	3,272	2,500	5,500	2,500
Net profit (pengoes)		2,500	1,728	2,500	(500)	2,500
Effective tax rate (dollars)		50.00%	50.00%	73.17%	50.00%	140.00%
Effective tax rate (pengoes)		50.00%	65.44%	50.00%	110.00%	50.00%

is 10,000 pengoes of debt due from customers, who are allowed one month's credit and who take a little more. Local tax at 50 per cent is 2,500 pengoes. Its profits are also subject to tax at 50 per cent in its home country, but with relief for foreign tax paid. Table 4.1 shows, not surprisingly, that with stable exchange rates the total tax charge is 50 per cent.

If the pengo falls in value, there will be a Homeco tax charge on the dollar appreciation in the value of the receivables. Given that the business remains intact, the parent has 5,000 pengoes of profit, but pays a total of 3,272 pengoes (64.4 per cent) in tax.

If the pengo rises in value, there is a dollar loss, leaving a translated profit of only $1,952. Pengovian tax translates at $1,429 on 73.2 per cent. In effect, the company pays 50 per cent tax as calculated in the stronger currency (whichever it is) but a higher rate in the weaker currency – the worst of both worlds.

Subsidiaries

Gains and losses in a foreign *subsidiary* will, in the first instance, be taxed under host country rules, which will have its own traps and opportunities. This is not the end of the story. The gain may ultimately be taxed (or the loss relieved) when there is a dividend distribution or when the subsidiary is wound up or sold.

There are a lot of planning points here, apart from those involving foreign exchange. Tax at parent company level is (generally) postponed so long as profits are undistributed. If they are distributed as a dividend to the parent there will, again generally, be a credit for tax paid, including 'underlying tax' on the profits out of which the dividend is paid. (This component is referred to in the United States as 'indirect credit'.) In many cases this will mean *no* extra tax at parent level.

Take the case of a US company with a Dutch subsidiary, which earns $1,000 of profits and pays $350 tax. If the Dutch company pays a dividend of $650 there will be a withholding tax of 5 per cent, leaving $617.50 received in the United States. The Dutch rate (effectively 38.25 per cent) exceeds the US rate, so no US tax is payable.

The withholding tax could be postponed by not paying a dividend, and it might be thought that it could be avoided altogether by winding up or selling the Dutch company with the benefit of its accumulated profits. Not so; this will often result in unrelieved double taxation. In the example above, the US parent will have a capital gain of $650. Dutch withholding tax of $32.50 will be avoided, but at a cost of a capital gains tax of $221. Net proceeds will be only $329.

This is a simple, but sometimes overlooked, point. Another complication is that the calculation of the tax due on the dividend will not
necessarily tie up with the calculation of the underlying tax relief. The
United States, in particular, has formal rules for calculating underlying
tax which may differ from the actual assessment in the host country.
There will be dramatic effects, calling for 'planning' rather than
'compliance' treatment, where a tax shelter available to the subsidiary is
ignored at the level of the parent. Foreign exchange movements can also
complicate the calculation: do we translate foreign tax for credit
purposes at the rate ruling when the dividend was paid, when the tax
was payable, an average rate for some year, or on some other basis?

The United States has, in principle, an 'overall limitation' basis for
calculating double tax relief, although this has been substantially
modified in recent years. Profits may be treated for this purpose as
'foreign source', even though no foreign country is claiming tax
jurisdiction. There are planning opportunities here, and we need to ask
two questions. Is a gain domestic or foreign source? Is a loss to be
allocated against domestic or foreign-source income? Under Section 904
of the US Internal Revenue Code (which limits credit for foreign taxes
paid), there is a presumption that the gain on the sale or exchange of
capital assets outside the United States is domestic source regardless of
where title passes. The effect of this can be to restrict the denominator
of the 'overall limitation' calculation, and treatment will not be
symmetrical.

Controlled foreign corporations

There is a major exception to the 'postponement' rule. Some countries
(the United States, the United Kingdom, Canada, France, West
Germany and Japan) have, and others (e.g. Australia and New
Zealand) are introducing, legislation 'deeming' the profits of controlled
foreign companies to arise at parent level. These mainly, but not
exclusively, concern low tax subsidiaries.

Is a currency gain or loss realised by such a subsidiary to be treated as
apportionable profits, 'sub-part F' income, or its equivalent? If it is, it
will be immediately taxable at parent level. There is no corresponding
provision for relieving a loss. This is another danger of non-symmetrical
treatment against the taxpayer.

Even if the gain is not sub-part F equivalent income, and is not
subject to taxation at parent level until there is a distribution, how is the
gain treated for the purpose of tax credit relief? Where foreign taxes are
paid by a company which subsequently pays a dividend what exchange

rate is to be used in calculating the deemed paid credit? The answers are not simple, and most companies leave these questions to be sorted out in negotiations with the Revenue after the event. This may be to miss important tax planning opportunities, particularly in arranging efficient international financing structures.

Planning for long-term risk

Given these problems and opportunities, how does one actually deal with long-term exposures? Analysis must come before prescription, and the first step must be to calculate, and calculate properly, what these exposures are.

The starting point for any calculations *must* be the 'implicit forward exchange rate'. As with shorter-term hedging the analysis takes place in stages:

Step one is to schedule the forward exposure of the group. For each taxable profit centre we need to know the real exposures analysed by currency *and date*. We have to take into account financial and contractual assets and liabilities. Remember that a ten-year foreign currency bond is not just a liability to repay in ten years. We have to take into account all the intermediate coupon payments, which in 'present value' terms may cost twice as much as the final payment. There is no real substitute for a yield curve analysis, but a table of yields to duration (better than yields to maturity) might be an acceptable approximation.

Step two is to prepare all consolidated figures and calculations on the basis of the actual or implicit forward exchange rates derived from the market. Are the decisions you have taken internally consistent with these?

Step three is to decide whether you like these forward rates or whether you would prefer to feed some other assumptions into the model. Then, and only then, comes step four: study how to hedge and cover your exposures. This is the stage to look for opportunities, and avoid traps thrown up by tax fragmentation and by exchange control and market anomalies.

There might also be lower administrative, legal and intermediation costs associated with a particular form of transaction. There may be exchange control, tax or related advantages. The impact on artificial accountancy standards may be different; an important point for those still bemused by the conventional 'bottom line' figure. One hedging technique rather than another may make it easier to take a financially sophisticated view of foreign exchange exposure without distorting final accounts or unnecessarily alarming the chairman. Other 'players', such as Japanese investment institutions who need to enhance bottom line accounting yields to feed the 'earning multiple' bubble machine, or British local government authorities bemused by the charm of commission-hungry bankers, may be moving the prices of financial instruments away from their rational level. These give opportunities which can be exploited more confidently if we know how they arise.

After that, step five. Back to the beginning and recalculate everything on different assumptions. How sensitive is the enterprise to future exchange rate changes? At what combination of circumstances is its very survival at risk? How can we *immunise* our strategy against the unforeseen?

Although the market place does not usually offer a free lunch, and although one technique of hedging rather than another will not usually provide a magically cheaper method of solving a particular financial problem, there are opportunities. That apart, it is certain that a company which does *not* make the calculation will find different departments acting on different assumptions – a *very* expensive procedure.

5

Implicit forward exchange rates

Our first attempt to look at the exchange risks implicit in foreign currency borrowing simply involved calculating the break-even exchange rate below which sterling could not fall without turning a 'cheap' borrowing into an expensive one. We frightened one company away from a Euro–Swiss bond issue suggested by its bankers, and *persuaded* them to make a rights issue instead.

The pound was then Sw Fr 10.30, and the borrowing looked cheap. We simply asked the finance director whether he was prepared to bet that the pound would not fall below Sw Fr 9 within ten years. He replied 'I am not a betting man', and we suggested that he should therefore not gamble the solvency of the company. The advice saved the company some £20 million.

This technique was explained in the *Financial Times Tax Newsletter* for September 1972. Readers of this article were forewarned about, and *careful* readers were saved from, the tax trap into which so many companies subsequently fell. Briefly, if the dollar spot exchange rate is Sw Fr 2.00, and the company can borrow francs at 5 per cent or dollars at 10 per cent the break-even exchange rate in five years is Sw Fr 1.58. If, and only if, the dollar is stronger than this when the loan is repaid in five years is the Swiss franc cheaper.

This simple technique has two limitations. It gives an accurate answer if the currency rate follows a smooth curve with a constant rate of change from the present spot rate to the assumed future rate, and if each country has a *flat term structure of interest rates*.

We needed something more precise, and found that 'implicit forward exchange rates' could be calculated from the yield and term structure of international bond markets. This concept was originally developed as a tool for assisting companies to make internally consistent financial and commercial decisions for periods beyond that for which a formal

Table 5.1 IMPLICIT FORWARD EXCHANGE RATE AGAINST US DOLLAR CALCULATED AT 31 MARCH 1989

31 March	United Kingdom	West Germany	Japan
1989	1.6850	1.7000	131.50
1990	1.653	1.656	126.5
1991	1.636	1.613	121.5
1992	1.635	1.571	116.3
1993	1.632	1.535	111.5
1994	1.636	1.503	106.9
1995	1.626	1.472	102.5
1996	1.614	1.445	98.2
1997	1.611	1.417	94.2
1998	1.612	1.390	90.4
1999	1.615	1.366	86.7

Table 5.2 IMPLICIT FORWARD EXCHANGE RATE AGAINST US DOLLAR CALCULATED AT 31 OCTOBER 1985 WITH ACTUAL RATES AND DEVIATIONS

31 October		United Kingdom	West Germany	Switzerland	Japan
1985	(spot)	1.44	2.62	2.15	211
1986	(implicit)	1.40	2.55	2.06	210
	(actual)	1.18	2.45	2.04	191
	(deviation (%))	15.7	(3.9)	(0.1)	(9.1)
1987	(implicit)	1.39	2.44	1.98	205
	(actual)	1.74	1.71	1.42	138
	(deviation (%))	(25.2)	(29.9)	(28.3)	(32.7)
1988	(implicit)	1.38	2.39	1.91	200
	(actual)	1.77	1.78	1.50	126
	(deviation (%)	(29.2)	(22.9)	(18.0)	(36.7)
1989		1.37	2.31	1.83	199

forward exchange market exists, but is now being applied to international bond portfolio management and swap analysis. Table 5.1 gives the figures as calculated on 31 March 1989. These figures are *not* forecasts but simply a guide to action. We calculate them weekly.

Table 5.2 compares the implicit forwards calculated in a previous book (Chown, 1985) with the outcome three years later.

The financing decision – an example

Exchange gains and losses

Interest arbitrage shows that the market *expects* (usually wrongly but no matter) that the borrower of a 'cheap' currency will suffer an exchange loss on repayments. The two factors are *expected* to cancel out – in pre-tax terms. This is where the fun begins.

Table 5.3 BORROWING ALTERNATIVES – UK COMPANY, END 1986

	Currency			
	£	$US	DM	Yen
A Data available				
1. Borrowing rate	10.68%	5.97%	4.60%	4.79%
2. Spot exchange rate	—	1.4745	2.8617	234.6
3. Break-even 12 mths forward rate	—	1.4118	2.7045	222.1
B Outcome				
4. Spot exchange rate (31.3.1981)	—	1.8715	2.9598	231.1
5. Actual sterling cost of borrowing (no tax)	10.68%	16.51%	1.13%	6.36%

Given that (at the time of writing) a UK company cannot in general claim relief for *capital* losses on *long-term* liabilities, but can claim relief for interest, *where a UK company is borrowing on capital account, it should borrow the most expensive of the available currencies.* This does *not* mean taking a view of exchange rates, but merely recognising a tax anomaly. The company is still free to choose its *world-wide* exposure position. If the switch in the borrowing caused the company to deviate from this, it could change its weight either by switching its assets or by altering its exposure in a third-country affiliate. An example will show the possible conflict between good currency planning and good tax planning. The date was deliberately chosen; the earlier book (Chown, 1985) used an example based on March 1980.

At the end of 1986 a British company was presented with the information given in Part A of Table 5.3. It could have borrowed various currencies for twelve months at the rates of interest shown in line 1. Which should it choose? The dollar, the Deutschmark and the yen were all 'cheap' in interest cost, but there was the risk that they would strengthen against sterling. Line 3 shows the 'break-even' exchange rate – if you thought that sterling would be above Y521 in twelve months, borrow yen. (Calculations assume all interest payable on maturity *and – at this first stage – ignore tax.*) Part B of Table 5.3 shows the outcome. Borrowing dollars for the year would have involved a profit rather than a cost!

Now let us put tax into the calculation. We generally advise on tax grounds that if a UK company borrows on a *capital* liability (no tax relief on the currency loss) it should avoid borrowing a low interest rate foreign currency.

Best *currency* advice is to borrow dollars, while best *tax* advice is to borrow sterling – is there a conflict? Not really. Assuming the borrowing would be on capital account two 'obvious' strategies, and their outcomes, are:

Strategy 1 (tax adviser)

Borrow sterling (£1 million)

Interest cost (10.68% on £1 million)	£106,800
Less tax relief (35%)	37,380
Net interest cost	£ 69,420

Strategy 2 (currency prophet)

Borrow dollars unhedged

Borrowing : $1,474,500 = £1 million at 31 December 1986

Interest cost (5.97%) $88,028 =	£47,036
Less tax relief (35%)	16,463
	£30,573

Sterling equivalent of:

Borrowing	£1,000,000	
Repayment (at $1,8715)	787,871	
Gain on exchange (tax free)		£212,129
Net cost (*negative*)		(£181,556)

Strategy 2 therefore beats Strategy 1 by over £250,000. These profits come from taking a risk. In many periods such a strategy would have been disastrous. Part of the benefit comes as a tax free 'gain on exchange'.

Strategy 3

There is a third and better strategy available but it is likely to be spotted only by those who take an *integrated* approach to tax and currency. The treasurer, wearing his 'currency' hat, sees the opportunity to borrow dollars, but also knows that it is better tax planning to borrow sterling. He therefore borrows £1 million sterling. At the same time he sells $1,530,000 (the principal, plus the interest he would have had to repay if he had made the dollar borrowing) forward at $1.4118 in a tax neutral way. The position could, in the event, have been closed at $1.8715.
Then

Net interest cost	£ 69,420
Gain on exchange	£266,197
Net cost (*negative*)	(£196,777)

This is (*after* tax) better even than Strategy 2 – a 'free lunch' derived from tax currency dynamics! Note that the strategy would have been better than actually borrowing dollars whatever had happened to the exchange rate. If the treasurer had guessed wrongly, and the dollar had strengthened to $1.35, Strategy 2 would lose his company £65,185 while Strategy 3 would limit the loss to £49,838. A useful shifting of the odds! Note also that the principles are the same, regardless of whether the treasurer actually needs Deutschmarks rather than sterling, i.e. if Strategy 2 is the 'neutral' and Strategy 1 is the 'uncovered' strategy.

6

The tax treatment of interest

The tax treatment of interest is very closely related to that of foreign exchange gains and losses. Where a company borrows money for the purpose of its business, we have to examine the three following tax questions:

1. Is the interest deductible in computing taxable profits?
2. Will the payment of interest affect the computation of tax credit relief?
3. Is the interest payment subject to the deduction of withholding tax at source?

This chapter deals in general with the first and second of these questions. Country rules are examined in more detail in the appropriate chapters. Withholding tax is discussed in Chapter 7.

Interest or distribution?

In the simpler past, companies financed themselves in three ways as follows:

(a) equity (ordinary or common) shares, the return on which varies with profits;
(b) preference (preferred) shares carrying a fixed rate of dividend;
(c) debt, including bond issues and bank borrowing.

Preference shares and bonds both offer the investor the same type of fixed, priority, return. The nature of the security is different but the most important distinction is in the tax treatment.

Interest will *in general* be a deduction from taxable profits. *Dividends*, including preferred dividends are, again *in general*, a distribution out of net-of-tax profits. Tax law has to draw a border-line between the two and companies and their advisers have used considerable ingenuity in trying to get their financing on one side or the other of this line. For instance how are 'convertible loan stocks', 'income debentures' and other hybrid securities to be treated? Most countries have anti-avoidance provisions covering these, which can affect international financing. The general treatment of 'debt versus equity' raises significant domestic tax issues which are not discussed here. Information can be found in standard textbooks such as Brealey and Myers (1981 and 1984) and Franks (1985).

Where to take a deduction?

In the old simpler days, it was probably safe to assume that each company within a group would borrow 'local' currency. A US parent would borrow dollars and a UK parent would borrow sterling, for general purposes. Each of the subsidiaries would borrow the appropriate local, domestic currency. This is no longer true, especially with the extraordinary growth first of Euromarkets and, later, of swaps and other derivatives. This question, 'where to take a deduction?', is now separate from, but closely related to, another: 'which currency to borrow?'

An international group of companies will, where there is a choice, prefer *profits* to accrue in that group company having the *lowest* effective rate of tax. The obvious corollary, sometimes overlooked, is that charges *against* income, such as interest, should be taken in a country having a *high* rate of tax. It is better to take a *profit* in Bermuda than in West Germany – but better to charge interest as a *deduction* against German, rather than Bermudan, profits. There are anti-tax-avoidance rules designed to prevent the blatant switching of profits by intra-group interest, but a company needing capital to expand abroad may be able to choose between borrowing via the parent company or arranging for the foreign subsidiary to borrow locally. If it borrows at parent level it may be possible to make an interest bearing inter-company loan to the subsidiary. These choices will have different tax consequences. The group may borrow through a third country. Financing subsidiaries in Luxembourg or Bermuda obviously offers no direct *tax* advantages; they can give a measure of flexibility. The choice of where (within the group) to borrow is logically distinct from the choice of what currency to borrow.

The choice of where to take the deduction depends on much more than a comparison of nominal tax rates. A company with most of its activities abroad may have insufficient profits taxable at 'parent' level to support major borrowings; it should finance at subsidiary level. A new project in a new country is unlikely to generate taxable profits for some years, especially where there are tax holidays or accelerated depreciation. There may then be 'timing' restrictions on carry-forward losses. Parent company finance will then be more appropriate, or it may be possible to arrange 'net of tax' financing. Leasing, in a form which surrenders some fast tax write-offs to a taxpaying counterparty may be attractive; leasing has been, and in some cases still is, a powerful technique for tax efficient financing, and is discussed in a little more detail below.

Borrowing at parent level

Some countries, such as the Netherlands, disallow interest paid on money borrowed, whether from domestic or foreign sources, *specifically* to make foreign acquisitions. The Dutch argue, logically enough, that since income from overseas subsidiaries is in general exempt from Dutch tax (although it may be taxable elsewhere), it is unreasonable for interest on the money borrowed to be charged against the Dutch profits of the parent. However, money is fungible, and in such countries the taxpayer will try to structure loans so that they appear to be for allowable domestic purposes.

Other countries, in the cause of 'capital export neutrality' may have been over-generous in giving interest deductions for borrowings which generate income on which the host country gets the first, and often the only, bite of tax.

Even if interest is deductible at parent company level, we may have to take into account the possible impact on the double tax relief calculations. Industrial countries typically enter into double tax agreements, one provision of which is that local taxes paid on profits earned abroad can be taken as a credit against tax due on the same profits at parent country level. This sounds simple in principle, and is, just occasionally, simple in practice.

There are other questions arising from interest paid by the parent company. In the United States, for instance, although the interest is deductible, a proportion of it may have to be allocated against foreign source profits as restricting the credit relief.

This aspect has become even more complex and important since the Tax Reform Act of 1986. In the United Kingdom and other 'imputation' countries the so-called 'ACT trap' can penalise UK companies which have to pay dividends out of profits which have borne foreign rather than UK tax (see Chapter 9). British multinationals faced with this trap needed to pay tax in the United Kingdom rather than abroad. One technique was to switch their borrowing (and therefore their interest deductions) from UK parent to foreign subsidiary levels. Following TRA 1986, US parents must also pay more attention to planning to reduce foreign taxes, and will do well to learn from European experience.

Borrowing at subsidiary level

It will thus often be appropriate to arrange borrowings at subsidiary level, and to claim deduction of interest against the subsidiary's taxable profits. Subsidiary borrowings can be as follows:

(a) from an unconnected lender in local currency without parent guarantee;
(b) from an unconnected lender in the parent country of a third country currency;
(c) from the parent; or
(d) from a third party lender but with parent guarantee.

All these raise the same general tax questions (but from the point of view of the subsidiary's country of residence) as parent country borrowing. In addition, the last two raise new problems, 'thin capitalisation', and 'arm's length'.

Local exchange control regulations may also restrict the scope for borrowing, including (a) and, where relevant, need to be considered as part of the analysis. A few years ago any analysis of financing and risk management techniques would have included a major section on exchange controls; these are, happily, no longer a constraint in most of the industrial world.

Thin capitalisation

Where the interest charge can be offset against overseas profits, the local tax burden could in principle be reduced by setting up a subsidiary with a small equity capital, the greater part of the funds being made available as interest bearing debt. The funds could come from local bank loans, bond issues from local investing public, or Euromarket loans from the parent as intra-company loans. This is attractive only if the particular subsidiary has, or is likely in the near future to have, sufficient otherwise taxable profits for some years which will normally be financed by parent equity, or by local leasing or 'net financing'.

The host country may not welcome this erosion of tax base. It may well typically have 'thin capitalisation' rules disallowing the deduction of interest and treating the payment as a distribution of taxed profits if certain ratios are not met. In some cases a 'swap' transaction or a 'back-to-back' loan via a bank may be treated differently from a direct loan from a parent. This problem will certainly arise in 'third world' and other capital importing countries, but in these cases it does not interact so closely with the multinational tax aspects of international financing.

Again, a 'political' perspective is useful, but the practical guidance in the country chapters which follow may be of more immediate relevance.

The arm's length principle

If the parent company, Company A, pays a low rate of tax (or, which can amount to the same thing, has a tax loss carry-forward) while the subsidiary, Company B, has a high rate of tax, it obviously makes sense to charge the highest possible rate of interest on any loan from Company A to Company B. If the situation reverses (perhaps Company B starts incurring losses) it is better to charge the lowest and preferably a nil rate of interest on the loans. Better still, if both are taxpaying, can Company A borrow at home, claiming a deduction, lend the money interest free to Company C in a tax haven and have Company C lend to Company B at the highest possible rate of interest?

Most countries have general rules governing 'transfer pricing' permitting the tax authorities to examine the prices used on transactions between related companies and, where appropriate, to adjust the tax liability by substituting arm's length prices. The general rules may be defined more precisely in bilateral double tax agreements. An obvious problem can arise where both countries seek to make an adjustment in opposite directions leaving the taxpayer with unrelieved double taxation.

The general principles covering transfer pricing are discussed in the OECD Report. There are also specific rules in most countries (they also concentrate on the pricing of goods, particularly part-finished goods), which raise obvious valuation problems. There is little typically of interest as such, although the general principles will normally disallow interest which differs materially from market rates. The 1988 US White Paper on transfer pricing has reopened this whole issue. Another aggressive initiative by the United States will, like that of 1962, initially result in multinationals erring on the side of paying too much to Uncle Sam. This forces other countries to look to their defences, leading to a destructive and time-consuming allocation war.

Generally it can be assumed that there is no longer much scope for manipulating taxes by the use of artificial interest rates, although this still leaves plenty of opportunity for designing an optimum financial structure based on market rates. There have, in the past, been opportunities for manipulating 'safe harbour' rules intended to refer to one currency by seeking to interpret them to apply to another currency with a different interest rate structure.

The 1979 OECD Report

The OECD Report *Transfer Pricing and Multinational Enterprise*, published in 1979, is the classic study on the general problems of arm's length pricing. It is now supplemented by a 1984 follow-up *Transfer Pricing and Multinational Enterprises – Three Taxation Issues*. The second of these three issues, banking, is relevant to our subject.

Chapter V, 'Loans' of the 1979 report points out that debt servicing within a group can provide opportunities for profit shifting depending on whether the lender charges an excessive or an inadequate rate of interest, and discusses various situations that are met in practice.

The first task in this connection is to distinguish between a loan and an equity contribution (thin capitalisation). The report describes the US rules (since abandoned) for determining this, which take into account several factors. Of these, the debt–equity ratio was considered in the past to be the most important and a ratio in excess of 3 to 1, computed on the basis of all debt over the fair market value of all assets less liabilities, was generally taken as evidence of a debt instrument. But in recent years the debt–equity ratio has not been given greater weight than other factors and the courts now recognise that high debt–equity ratio may be normal for some industries.

As things stand today there is a distinct possibility that the same financial transaction can be treated as a loan by one country and as an equity contribution by another, and the report expresses the view that it would be desirable to move towards international agreement as to the appropriate tests to be used. The 1979 report concludes:

191. It is generally recommended that a flexible approach should be adopted in which the special conditions of each individual case would be considered, although it is realised that such an approach would call for sufficient qualified staff to carry out a somewhat sophisticated analysis and could, if cases were numerous, thus raise problems for some tax administrations. A hard and fast debt–equity rule would, however, not be appropriate for the solution of problems raised by the determination of the nature of a financial transaction. Financing practices differ too widely from one country to another, and, within a given country, between different categories of enterprises. Most of the countries whose practices are described in the previous paragraphs, distinguished a loan from an equity contribution. On the same reasoning, it is considered that a rule

based on the fact that the owner of the shares was non-resident would not be appropriate for general adoption either.

This view was endorsed at the International Fiscal Association (IFA) Congress at Montreal in 1982 which, *inter alia*, proposed that

Individual cases should be decided on a case by case basis after taking all circumstances into consideration. Fixed ratios of debt to capital and the incidental normal interest rates should not be laid down, but should only have the character of a 'safe havens' clause. The ICC in a Statement drafted in 1984 endorsed these views and stressed the danger that measures against tax avoidance can easily 'distort normal credit transactions and competitiveness, leading to further distortion of the free flow of capital.

On this the Report states:

192. Once it is established that an intra-group loan exists, the general principle is that the loan should bear interest if interest would have been charged in similar circumstances in a transaction between unrelated parties.

Sometimes this would not be so. For example, as regards trade credits, it is recognised that interest would often not be charged by an unrelated party on outstanding balances and in such circumstances interest should not be required to be charged within a multinational enterprise (MNE).

Another case where interest is often not charged within an MNE is in start-up situations. This, however, is not regarded by the Report as a reason for a loan to be free of interest unless an unrelated lender would have waived payment of interest in the same circumstances. Again, occasions may occur where an intra-group loan is made in order to help a borrower overcome financial difficulties and in these circumstances the lender may waive or defer interest. Once again it is suggested that this should be acceptable for tax purposes only if an unrelated lender would have acted in the same manner.

The *rate of interest* should be determined by reference to the conditions in financial markets for similar loans, and in deciding what is a similar loan it is necessary to take into account the amount and maturity date of the loan, its nature and purpose, the currency or currencies involved, the security given and the credit standing of the borrower. On this point national governments, and the United States in particular have been spurred by the high interest rates ruling since the OECD Report was published to move towards an increasingly sophisticated approach.

The European Economic Community attitude

If it matters to a company group borrowing at 'parent' or 'subsidiary' level, it matters even more to the tax collecting authorities. It should be a key issue in harmonising European taxes.

Neither the Convergence Report of 1980, nor the proposed Directive on tax base (1988) have much to say on debt interest specifically, even though the subject is such an important one for taxpayers and taxgatherers alike.

Paragraphs 5–7 of the Introductory Memorandum to the 1975 Draft stated specifically that 'the Commission believes that in the long run it is better that the choice of means of financing should *not* depend on taxation considerations'. The Commission suggested that one argument favouring the imputation over the classical system was that it did not distort the choice between loan and equity financing. More recently this point has been brought home in the United States. As discussed in Chapter 13, the US Tax Reform Act of 1986, based on the classical system, worsened these distortions and led to a rash of leveraged buy-outs.

Within a fiscally harmonised Community there should be, from the company's point of view, nothing (except possibly for small variations in tax rate) to choose between borrowing in one country rather than in another. As the EEC would be regarded effectively as a single 'domestic' market, the most effective financial arrangement would be for Head Office to undertake at least all the longer-term borrowing on behalf of the group.

At present, in an unharmonised community the 'where to borrow' question remains an important one, fraught with traps and planning opportunities. A group of companies will not normally change physical investment or product sourcing decisions in response to minor tax changes. It will, if well advised, react very quickly to adjust its financing structure.

This immediately raises a serious problem from the point of view of the member states. Take the case of a UK parent with activities of roughly equal size in the United Kingdom itself and in France, which earns 12 million currency units pre-tax in each country. If it is entirely equity financed, the Draft Directive would ensure that the UK and France each tax the locally earned profits, and would also ensure that each country bears its due share of the cost of granting the imputation credit to shareholders, wherever those shareholders may live. If, however, the company decides to finance part of its operations by borrowing 10 million units at 10 per cent at parent company level, the

1 million units interest charge would completely wipe out the UK tax liability, but would still leave the French Revenue with 500,000 units of tax less (presumably the whole of) any imputation credit that was granted on company dividend.

This question remains unaddressed. Meanwhile, there are planning opportunities and traps for EEC resident companies and for US, Japanese, Canadian, Australian and other parents.

Net financing

Interest is generally deductible, while preference dividends are treated as a distribution of taxed profits. Companies have used some ingenuity to characterise what are really variable 'equity' profits as deductible interest. Against this, inter-company dividends are typically exempt from tax on the reasonable enough grounds that tax has already been paid at one level. Companies which are not currently taxpaying may find it advantageous to dress up interest as dividends even on bank 'borrowings'. This is a battleground between taxpayer and taxcollector; the most interesting case study is in Canada (see Chapter 18).

Deep discount bonds

If 'interest' is taxable to the recipient at full rates, while 'capital gains' are taxed, if at all, at lower rates, it is obviously attractive to the investor to buy a 'discount bond'. But what if a company issues an original issue discount bond? Will it get a deduction for the extra amount payable?

Most countries now have more or less symmetrical treatment as between borrower and investor.

The rules are dealt with in the appropriate country chapter. There are still interesting financing opportunities using deep discount bonds across frontiers.

7

Withholding tax on interest

Chapter 6 discussed whether interest paid was deductible in calculating taxable profits. There is another, closely related, question. Payments, such as dividends, interest and royalties, made to non-residents, are generally subject to withholding tax in the country of source. Withholding tax is normally at a flat rate, and historically is intended to compensate the Revenue authorities for the tax they would have collected if they were in a position to make an assessment on the recipient.

Most major countries have concluded bilateral double tax agreements to prevent a single item of income being taxed twice. These may provide for a reduced rate of withholding tax in the country of source, a credit for withholding tax in the country of residence, or a combination of the two. The right to tax certain categories of income may rest exclusively in the country of source; several treaties contain such provisions on real property connected income, sometimes including mortgage interest.

Capital exporting countries typically *exempt* interest paid to treaty partners; the exemption may be limited for hybrid instruments such as convertible bonds, or denied for real property loans.

Most capital importing countries do seek to impose withholding taxes. Indeed they endeavour, not always successfully, to ensure that any benefit paid to foreign investors is taxed, whether it flows as dividends, profit shares, interest, royalties or management charges. The Appendix to this chapter sets out some 'non-treaty' and 'treaty' rates of withholding tax on interest.

(Detailed information on withholding taxes on dividends, interest and royalties are obtainable on the *Interfisc Tax Treaty Service* published by Professional Publishing Limited, 7 Swallow Place, London W1R 8AB. This is kept updated by J. F. Chown and Company Limited.)

The original logic of this approach was to provide a simple and equitable system of dealing with normal cross-frontier investments while collecting tax at source on investments made from non-treaty countries (typically 'tax havens') or by those who, legally or illegally, are not paying tax on the income in any country of residence.

This logic fell apart when faced with the enormous post-war growth of the Eurocurrency and (specifically) Eurobond markets. The more important parts of the 'country' chapters are concerned, not with treaty provisions, but with specific exemptions afforded by borrowing countries to facilitate access to these markets.

Eurobond markets are markets in tax-free yields. The typical Eurobond investor is *de facto* based outside any taxing jurisdiction. If he can obtain 10 per cent tax free on a US dollar Eurobond, he will want 13.33 per cent gross on a bond in the same currency subject to a 25 per cent withholding tax:

	Euro		*Domestic*
Gross interest	10.00%		13.33%
Withholding	—	(25%)	3.33%
	10.00%		10.00%

In this context, the tax incidence really falls not on the foreign investor but on the domestic corporate borrower seeking access to international capital markets. Over the years this point has been recognised by many countries. It is still causing muddled thinking, particularly at the level of the European Community.

Many countries, including the United Kingdom, Australia and Canada, solved this problem by introducing exemptions for certain types of borrowing. In the United States, characteristically, it was originally solved by private enterprise. Ways were found of dealing with the problem within existing tax legislation. Also typically, not of the United States as a whole, but of Capitol Hill, Congress for years debated, on the one hand, measures to close the loopholes and, on the other, concessions to make them unnecessary. The position was partly resolved in 1984 with the repeal of withholding on certain categories of portfolio interest. (For a detailed discussion of the legislative history see Alan Granwell, 1984.)

The European Community is, more recently, attempting a backwards step. It is committed to abolishing exchange control, at least between member states. This is equivalent to total abolition, given that some members no longer favour exchange control. The French (who, one suspects, would prefer to impose ring fence controls around Fortress Europe) insist that a uniform withholding tax should be imposed. The only effect of this would be to drive business outside the EEC altogether; see Chapter 21.

The strategic use of tax credits

Where withholding tax cannot be avoided, it may be possible to arrange for it to be credited against otherwise taxable income, perhaps in a third country. This being a politically delicate subject, the point is best illustrated historically.

When a taxpaying company receives interest from abroad, can withholding tax collected in the country of source of the interest be credited against domestic tax? There have, in the past, been some interesting planning opportunities, and the principles may still find occasional application.

Certain capital importing countries, notably in Latin America, impose a withholding tax of gross interest payments at a rate of, say, 25 per cent. If the nominal rate of interest on the loan is 10 per cent, the lender would receive only 7.5 per cent. The question is whether the 2.5 points are treated for tax purposes in the lender's own country as a credit or a deduction. This is not a simple one, either at the practical or the 'public policy' level. It makes a lot of difference.

If the tax is merely treated as a deduction and the cost to the lender of funding the loan is 7 per cent, there will be a taxable profit margin of 0.5 per cent:

Gross interest	10
WHT	2.5
Net interest	7.5
Cost of funding	7.0
Net profit	0.5
Tax at 40%	0.2
Profit	0.3

If, however, it is treated as a credit there would be a three-point taxable spread on which tax would be, say, 1.5 points but with a credit of 2.5 points.

Gross interest	10.0
Cost of funding	7.0
Gross margin	3.0
On which tax at 40%	1.2
Tax credit	2.5
Tax recovery	1.3
Net profit	1.8

The after-tax profits would be 1.8 points clear of tax, 0.5 of margin after withholding tax plus 1.3 points effectively offset against other taxable income, subject to certain limitations. On this basis it would clearly be better to make the loan out of a taxable centre, such as the United States or the United Kingdom, rather than out of a tax haven such as the Bahamas where the profit would only be the 0.5 points.

In the past, some banks and other lenders had quoted on the basis of a net rate and treated the tax advantage as a bonus. As a result of competitive pressures and increasing sophistication of borrowers, the position has changed. The lender has to accept the terms in my example, even though his cost of funding is 8 per cent. If he only gets a deduction, he is 2.5 points down even before he begins and he needs the 'credit' treatment to make any profit at all.

Section 901 of the US Internal Revenue Code permitted a taxpayer, at his option, to treat as a credit, any 'income, war profits, and excess profits taxes paid or accrued during the taxable year to any foreign country or to any possession of the United States'.

Section 903 extended the concept to certain foreign taxes paid in lieu of such taxes. However, where the taxpayer elects for this treatment, he cannot treat *any* such taxes as deduction (Section 275(a)(4)).

In about 1978 the Internal Revenue Service began taking a much harder look at withholding taxes of this nature and thus what constitutes a creditable tax for the purposes of Section 901. Its attitude (which had some logical basis) is that where a tax is a tax on gross receipts rather than on net profits it should be regarded as more analagous to an *excise* tax than to an *income* tax.

In 1978, the Internal Revenue Service ruled (Revenue Ruling 78–235) that the 5 per cent tax (5.75 per cent including surcharge) imposed by the Federal District of Mexico in addition to the 21 per cent Federal tax is not a creditable tax. There has been a similar ruling in respect of Mexico State.

Brazil was even more adventurous than Mexico; it imposed withholding tax, but most of this was refunded to the Brazilian borrower as a subsidy under the Central Bank of Brazil Resolution No. 335 of 5 August 1975. This clawed back the benefit of the tax anomaly for Brazil. Lenders would fix their rates, taking account of the subsidy, and get credit for tax which was only notionally paid. United States Revenue Ruling 78–258 blocked this route for US lenders. In the case of loans made prior to 17 March 1978, the full 25 per cent withholding tax would be creditable on interest accrued or received prior to 1 January 1980. On all subsequent payments (all payments on subsequent loans) only 3.75 percentage points would be creditable.

Other countries have taken corresponding steps to protect their tax base, but it may occasionally be possible to find a gap in their defences.

Tax sparing loans

Developing countries sometimes offer tax holidays to encourage foreign investment. Much of this investment comes from countries such as the United States, the United Kingdom, West Germany and Japan which tax foreign source income, but with a credit for foreign tax paid. Subsidiary A, in Australia, earns $100 profit and pays $40 tax. There is no further tax on dividends to the US parent. Subsidiary B, set up to take advantage of tax incentive legislation in Indonesia, earns $100 tax free. Dividends to the US parent enjoy no credit, and suffer full US tax. The net return from the two investments is more or less the same. Where is the incentive? The tax deliberately forgone by Indonesia only benefits the US Internal Revenue Service.

To deal with this, some countries, including the United Kingdom but not the United States, concede a 'deemed paid' or 'tax sparing' credit so that the benefit of the tax relief does flow through to parent level. The economic implications of this are fascinating but take us beyond the scope of this chapter, or indeed this book. This principle has been extended to loan interest, and has, at least in the past, produced tax planning opportunities far beyond what was intended.

Interest rates being 10 per cent and tax rates, say, 50 per cent (they were actually 52 per cent at the time), a British bank could lend funds to a project in a suitable country at 8 per cent, and actually make a profit:

	£	£
Interest received		80
UK tax	40	
Less deemed paid credit	(40)	—
Income after tax		80
Cost of funding		100
Less tax relief/against other income		50
Costs after tax		50
Net profit after tax		30

The scope for this was limited by the Finance Act 1982 (Section 65, now Section 798 ICTA 1988). The 'gross up' is treated as part of the income and relief is limited to 15 per cent of the net cash interest.

Extract from typical double tax agreement

The following extracts from Article 18 of the Double Tax Agreement (DTA) with Singapore give an example of the type of provision which has been used:

(4) For the purposes of paragraph (3) of this Article, the term 'Singapore tax payable' shall be deemed to include any amount which would have been payable as Singapore tax for any year but for an exemption or reduction of tax granted for that year or any part thereof under –

(i) Parts II, III and IV of the Economic Expansion Incentives (Relief from Income tax) Act (1970 Edition) of Singapore (hereinafter referred to as 'the Act') so far as they were in force on, and have not been modified since 21 July 1975 (being the date of signature of the Protocol and amending this Agreement), or have been modified only in minor respects so as not to affect their general character; or

(ii) any other provision which may subsequently be made granting an exemption or reduction of tax which is agreed by the competent authorities of the Contracting Governments to be of a substantially similar character, if it has not been modified thereafter or has been modified only in minor respects so as not to affect its general character.

Provided that where the relief is a relief accorded under Part IV of the Act this shall be taken into account for the purposes of this paragraph only (i) if the enterprise qualifying for the relief could have been declared to be a 'pioneer enterprise' under Part II of the Act or an 'expanding enterprise' under Part III of the Act, and (ii) to the extent that the relief is given in respect of income arising within the 'tax relief period' as defined in Part II or Part III of the Act, as the case may be:

(5) For the purposes of paragraph (3) of this Article, the term 'Singapore tax payable' shall also be deemed to include–

(a) in the case of approved interest to which paragraph (2) of Article 7A applies, an amount not exceeding a sum equivalent to tax at a rate of 15 per cent in respect of Singapore tax which would have been payable but for an exemption or reduction of tax granted under Part V of the Act; and

(b) in the case of approved royalties to which paragraph (2) of Article 8 applies, an amount not exceeding a sum equivalent to tax at a rate of 15 per cent in respect of Singapore tax which would have been payable but for an exemption or reduction of tax granted under Part VI of the Act.

Rates of withholding tax on interest paid to non-resident companies

Source country	General rate	Treaty rate – recipient in			
		United Kingdom	United States	Switzerland	Netherlands
Argentina	11.25	G/R	11.25	G/R	G/R
Australia	10	10	G/R	10	10
Austria	Note	0	0	0	0
Barbados	Note	15	G/R	G/R	G/R
Belgium	20	15	15	10	10
Bolivia	30	G/R	G/R	G/R	G/R
Brazil	25	25	15	G/R	G/R
Canada	25	15	15	15	15
Chile	40	G/R	G/R	G/R	G/R
Cyprus (A)	42.5	10	10	G/R	G/R
Denmark	0	0	0	0	0
Egypt	32	15	15	G/R	G/R
Finland	30	0	0	G/R	0
France	25	Note	10	10	0
Germany (F/R)	Note	0	0	0	0
Gibraltar	40	G/R	G/R	G/R	G/R
Greece	43.4	0	9	G/R	10
Guernsey (A)	20	G/R	G/R	G/R	G/R
Hong Kong	15	G/R	G/R	G/R	G/R
India	71.75	Note	G/R	G/R	G/R
Indonesia	10	Note	G/R	G/R	G/R
Ireland	35	0	0	0	0
Israel	Note	15	17.5	G/R	15
Italy	20	20	G/R	12.5	20
Jamaica	Note	12.5	12.5	G/R	G/R
Japan	20	20	10	10	10
Jersey	20	G/R	G/R	G/R	G/R
Kenya	20	15	G/R	G/R	G/R
Korea (S)	25	Note	12	10	Note
Liberia	30	G/R	G/R	G/R	G/R
Luxembourg	Note	0	0	G/R	0
Malawi (A)	50–55	0	G/R	0	0
Malaysia	Note	15	G/R	10	G/R
Mexico	Note	G/R	42	G/R	G/R
Netherlands	Note	0	0	0	—
Netherlands Ant.	0	0	G/R	G/R	10
New Zealand	15	G/R	G/R	10	10
Nigeria	45	G/R	G/R	G/R	G/R
Norway	0	0	0	0	0
Pakistan	55	G/R	G/R	30	20

Source country	General rate	Treaty rate – recipient in			
		United Kingdom	United States	Switzerland	Netherlands
Panama	20–50	G/R	G/R	G/R	G/R
Portugal	30	10	30	10	G/R
Puerto Rico	20	G/R	G/R	G/R	G/R
Singapore	40	15	G/R	10	10
South Africa	10	10	G/R	10	10
Spain	15	12	G/R	10	10
Sweden	0	0	0	0	0
Switzerland	35	0	5	—	0
Taiwan	20	G/R	G/R	G/R	G/R
Thailand	25	Note	G/R	G/R	G/R
Trinidad	30	10	15	10	G/R
United Kingdom	—	—	0	0	0
United States	30	0	—	5	0
Venezuela	18–50	G/R	G/R	G/R	G/R
Zambia	30	10	G/R	G/R	10
Zimbabwe	10	10	G/R	G/R	G/R

Notes to Appendix 2

G/R: the general rate applies. Either there is no DTA, or no interest article in the current DTA.

(A): in some countries with historical UK connections the payer of interest is treated as the agent of a non-resident for the discharge of the non-resident's tax liability, and is entitled to retain that tax out of the interest payments at a rate notified to him by the tax authorities. Where the recipient of the interest is a company, the rate would generally be the company tax rate. This is the rate shown in the tables.

Austria: a 10 per cent tax applies to interest on convertible or profit sharing bonds. The UK Double Tax Agreement eliminates this tax.

Barbados: 40 per cent, but may be reduced to 12.5 per cent where Commissioner directs.

France: 25 per cent rate for interest on state loans and negotiable bonds generally of French public and private bodies (including companies); 45 per cent general rate for other interest, from 1 January 1983. The UK, Netherlands and Swiss DTA stipulate a maximum rate of 12 per cent for interest on bonds issued in France before 1 January 1965, and 10 per cent for other interest.

West Germany: a 25 per cent tax is levied on interest on certain fixed-interest bonds only. The tax treatment of interest in West Germany is the subject of political debate; see Chapter 21.

India: the UK DTA limits rate to 10 per cent for interest paid to banks, whatever the date of the loan, and to 15 per cent for other interest where the loan or debt was first created after 21 October 1981. Otherwise the rate is general rate.

Indonesia: the UK DTA limits rates to 10 per cent for interest paid to banks, whatever the date of loan, and to 15 per cent for other interest where the loan or debt was first created after 21 October 1981. Otherwise rate is general rate. A new agreement was due in 1988. Indonesia gave notice of termination in April 1984, but the existing treaty will continue in force until a new one is negotiated.

Israel: 25 per cent rate applies to bond interest; rate for other interest is 61 per cent (income tax and company tax)

Jamaica: 12.5 per cent but 37.5 per cent where Commissioner directs that the 12.5 per cent rate does not apply.

Korea: DTA limits rates to 10 per cent for interest on loan/debt claims for periods exceeding two years, for the UK, and seven years for Netherlands. Otherwise the rate is 15 per cent.

Luxembourg: a 15 per cent rate applies to interest on profit sharing bonds.

Malaysia: there is no tax on 'approved' (development) loans, and loans for three or more years. Otherwise the rate is 15 per cent.

Mexico: 15 per cent on interest paid to foreign banks registered with the Secretariat of Finance. 21 per cent where money is lent for the purchase of plant and machinery to be used in Mexico, or the interest is paid by Mexican banks. 42 per cent on other interest.

Netherlands: a 25 per cent tax is levied on interest on profit-sharing bonds only.

Panama: 20 per cent–50 per cent rates depend on amount of interest (company tax rate slice scale). A 5 per cent rate applies to interest on negotiable securities.

Thailand: UK DTA limits rates to 10 per cent on interest paid to banks, etc., 25 per cent in other cases.

8

Modern financial instruments

This chapter deals in outline with some fairly recent developments in financial instruments: futures, options, swaps, caps, cylinders and the like. There is also a brief look at leasing, now in decline, as a method of tax efficient international financing. These developments are part of a world-wide upheaval in financial markets, known in London as 'Big Bang'.

The demarcations between banks and brokers, and between brokers and jobbers have disappeared. We operate in an international world without frontiers, in which a dealing book may be passed on from London to New York to Tokyo to give a twenty-four-hour market service. Debt is increasingly securitised; formal and informal markets in futures and options have expanded the opportunities, and dangers, of risk management and risk transfer.

Unfortunately, tax law is having a hard time keeping up with these changes. There are still many grey areas and uncertainties, and with today's slim margins a relatively minor mistake in tax planning can turn a small profit into a large loss. Why does this concern the practical treasurer or banker? He employs accountants and lawyers to worry about such matters. A few banks (but many more oil companies) actually have an international tax specialist of world standing on the staff. Most do not. In today's world, tax is too important to be left to the specialist; general management, particularly financial and treasury management, should at least have a working knowledge of the main issues.

Futures

It has been possible to deal 'forward' in foreign exchange for as long as there has been a modern banking system and, indeed, as far back as the mediaeval trade fairs.

There have also, for many years, been 'futures' markets in commodities: wheat, cocoa, tin, pork bellies and the like. Some years ago Chicago began trading currencies in the same way. The tax system has in the past not distinguished between the two, but most of the anomalies have now disappeared. In the US Hoover case the judge muddled his terms and said 'futures' when he meant 'forwards'. This did not affect his conclusion, but misled some of the commentators on the case.

Interest rate futures offered new risk management facilities, not previously available from banks, although they now also have parallels in the over-the-counter bank market. A company which expects to have to raise a bond issue in six months' time can in effect lock in the rate by buying whatever futures contract is a suitable proxy for its requirements. If interest rates rise, the profit on the contract will compensate for the extra cost. If they fall, there will be a loss on the contract, offset by cheaper than expected borrowings.

Generally, a non-financial trading company which simply borrows money for the purpose of its business will incur interest expense, which will be deductible in computing its profits. In the modern world, the 'cost of money' in terms of economics or business common sense has to be calculated after adding or subtracting swap fees, option premiums, compensatory payments under forward rate agreements or caps and differences in the settlement of futures transactions. These payments arise from treasury transactions designed to adjust the maturity structure of debt, to transfer the risk of unanticipated interest rate movements, or to some combination of both.

Problems have arisen from historic distinctions between 'capital' transactions and 'regular income', between 'investors' and 'traders', between 'short-term' and 'long-term' gains and (in the UK) between 'short interest', 'annual interest', and 'annual payments which are not interest'. The attempt to apply these categories to modern financial techniques can produce perverse and unacceptable results; a US example is the attempt to apply anti-straddle rules to currency swaps.

Options

If futures are the simplest means of locking in a price, options are the classic method of insuring against uncertainty over what that price will be. An option is a contract which gives the right, but not the obligation, to buy or sell an asset at a fixed price: the 'strike price'.

Options are available on a wide range of financial instruments: those on individual share prices have a very long history. Philadelphia pioneered trading in currency options, but these are now widely available both on specialist financial markets (using standardised contracts) or tailor made 'over the counter' from banks. Options are now available on virtually every instrument for which there is a futures contract, notably including a wide variety of short- and long-term interest rates in different currencies.

The buyer (giver of option money) limits his risk of loss, while retaining, or obtaining, the hope of gain if the price moves in the way expected. This is not cost price: the seller or writer (taker of option money) demands his premium. On the whole, option writers make money by accepting the risks. It follows that option buyers, collectively, lose – on their option transactions. This does not mean that they lose overall. They profit from being able to accept, and lay off commercial risks that they would not otherwise be able to afford to take.

Many other instruments are merely variations on the option theme. 'Caps', 'collars' and 'cylinders' and old-fashioned convertible bonds can all be analysed using an option pricing model. It is often cheaper to buy the separate components rather than the package. The tax treatment of options was, in many countries, a jungle but most of the traps have now disappeared.

Swaps

In principle, swaps enable a borrower who is (for example) in a relatively favourable position to raise long fixed-rate US dollar funding but in fact wants floating-rate term yen to marry his requirements with another borrower of relatively higher standing in the yen market, but who does not have the same access to long-term fixed-rate dollars. The benefit arises from trading out market imperfections, and broadening the access of borrowers to international lending markets. More generally, they assist the treasurer to manage his *liability* portfolio using techniques long developed by fixed-interest *asset* managers – perhaps such as his own pension fund.

During the life of a swap periodical 'fees' are paid reflecting interest rate differentials. In the case of a 'fixed to fixed' currency swap the fee payable on each occasion can be calculated in advance. In practice many transactions are either interest rate swaps (fixed versus floating) in a single currency or 'mixed swaps' where one side is a floating rate loan, and the other is either a fixed or floating rate loan in the same or another currency.

Although the 'fee' may be small in the first year or two, the tax problems have to be measured by possibly very substantial future fee levels. Both parties have to ensure that the payment is deductible and (if the payment is cross-frontier) not subject to a non-creditable with-holding tax. At extreme figures (either way) the tax exposure could become serious.

It is particularly important to remember that the outcome flow of funds may be the reverse of what is originally assumed. However, it is inconceivable, knowing the nature of the beast, that the tax authorities would allow the receipt of a swap fee to escape taxation. If the payer is denied relief or is forced to withhold tax which cannot be recovered or credited by the payee there will be a tax penalty which is likely to far exceed the intended benefit of the swap. If this problem is *perceived* (and no way round it can be found) the parties will simply not enter into the transaction. If it is *not* perceived and a retrospective claim for tax is made, the consequences could be disastrous.

International tax specialists agree that tax law relating to currency risk in general, and swaps in particular, is irrational, uncertain and confused. Wherever there is uncertainty as to the outcome of a transaction there is always a danger that the tax treatment will not be *symmetrical*. The taxman's share of the upside potential may be greater than his share of the downside risk, which is a serious distortion of the odds. The good tax planner is aware of these dangers and will try to ensure that the Revenue's share of the downside is at least as large as its share of the upside. In currency risk management we can live with a 50 per cent or even 60 per cent tax charge – provided that we enjoy equivalent deduction for losses. But if the revenue authorities stand to take a higher (even slightly higher) proportion of the gains we will be cleaned out just a surely as the gambler is cleaned out by the zero on the roulette wheel.

Swaps are a powerful tool in the right hands, but are not always approached with the necessary care. In the early days of swaps, *practitioners* initiated them where appropriate to *solve* tax or exchange control problems. The transaction arose naturally from a problem-orientated, analytical approach to the overall financial and fiscal requirements of the client company. It was very hard work indeed to explain the concepts in those days. Now it has achieved the status of 'buzzword' and 'financial product' actively promoted by banks. This is both good news and bad news. The good news is that some treasurers (or their boards) who could not be *persuaded* by analysis into doing what they needed to do are being effectively *pushed* by salesmanship. The bad news is that they are not always being pushed in the right direction.

If a bank sets up a 'swaps' department and tells a group of high-salaried young men to 'go out and sell swaps' they will do just that.

Instead of starting with the problem and ending with a solution, they start with a solution and go out to look for problems. This is a much more dangerous procedure. The wise treasurer should rely on his professionals, in-house or external, for *advice*, and treat the bank offering services with the same friendly caution as he treats someone trying to sell him a computer system. Specifically, he will ask the following questions:

1. First, why do differential credit ratings persist? Why are they not arbitraged out and why cannot the company approach the alleged comparative advantage market directly? Are the intermediaries, deliberately or not, actually perpetuating a fragmented market place?
2. Second, the profit for the bank on the case presented looks modest. How can it afford to pay such high salaries to swaps specialists and to divert so much of the time of such high-salaried people on sales promotion? Is there a catch in the mathematics?
3. Third if the ultimate counterparties are both corporates, why pay toll to a bank in the middle? Surely the whole object of the concept of swaps is to cut out the middle man – to 'disintermediate'.

To some extent the third question has had a tax answer. Banks paying or receiving swap payments are generally symmetrically treated for tax purposes and are unlikely to have problems as principals in the transaction. It is the non-bank participants who have the problems. Generally the tax position is far clearer when swaps are intermediated through banks than when they are negotiated directly between non-financial corporations. This may be because most applications for clearance have been made by or on behalf of banks who have an obvious interest in perpetuating their role; in the United Kingdom, pressure by the Association of Corporate Treasurers has removed one of the artificial requirements that banks should be needed as intermediaries.

The United States and Canada, as do the United Kingdom, favour free competitive markets in financial services. The British government in particular is seeking to remove tax anomalies which discriminate in favour of financial intermediaries.

Banks enthuse about swaps; international tax specialists regard them as a major source of tax traps and fragmentation. There is said (by banks) to be a volume of some $150 billion. Should company treasurers be impressed, or should they ask the old Wall Street question: 'Where are the customers' yachts?'

There have been exciting developments in capital markets which help to make the treasurer's role a profit centre rather than a cost centre, and life more interesting for treasurers and those who advise them. Some of these 'products' need treating with caution, particularly where the tax aspects have not been properly analysed by the sponsoring banks.

The dangers arise not with known and deliberate tax ploys, but in cases where the tax dimension is *not* obvious. Banks have had considerable scope for managing their tax exposure by leasing, net loans, tax spared lending, 'transfer pricing' on transactions within a group, and by the judicious use of offshore financial centres. On the whole they have known what they were doing at technical level, although some seemed unaware of the broader issues and of political reaction, and have been unnecessarily taken by surprise by changes in the law. The difficulties are with unperceived tax traps where the tax treatment seems obvious.

It sometimes seems to professionals that banks have not researched the tax angles of their products properly. In the old days of 'relationship banking', someone, somewhere within the bank looked at the transaction from the point of view of the customer. Today the banker at the sharp end is a product specialist knowing that his promotion prospects and his bonus depend on his ability to 'sell' options, collars, swaps, Eurobond issues, or whatever. Like the life assurance salesman of old he wants to pocket his commission and move on to the next transaction. He has no patience with the tax adviser who may actually hold up the deal for as long as forty-eight hours while the more detailed implications are being examined!

Cross-currency swaps have been aggressively sold by banks to corporate treasurers, but have always worried international tax specialists. Against this, banks often claim that a particular 'window' will only be open for a day or two. The way forward is surely to take *professional* advice in advance of the opportunity, and to be ready for it when it comes. The trap comes at the end – perhaps five or ten years out (see Greenwell 1984).

'Back to plain vanilla?'

This is the title of a *Festschrift* essay by Professor Leif Muten (1989) now of the International Monetary Fund (IMF), who wrote his thesis at Uppsala University on the tax treatment of discount bonds. This was at the time a recherché subject which only later became fashionable.

His later paper suggests that the wheel may now have gone full circle. The financial community, understanding the time value of money and the basis of pricing option, while the Revenue authorities did not, invented financial instruments with remarkable tax advantages. Many of these have now been rumbled. Muten concludes:

(1) Sophisticated accounting theorists, and Sven-Erik Johansson among them, have advanced our thinking with respect to the evaluation of income streams beyond the narrow concepts prevailing at the time income taxation was first applied and present income tax laws were conceived.

(2) The basic condition for equitable taxation, that equals should be treated equally, will take on another, deeper meaning, inasmuch as we evaluate what is equal not in formal terms, based on narrowly defined legal concepts such as interest, or simplistic evaluations of income and cost amounts, regardless of the time at which they fall due, but rather in terms of economic equivalents, where yield is yield, regardless of under what label it is realized, and the time value of money makes it a relevant element in what period money earned is available and money spent is actually disbursed.

(3) Once we arrive at this type of sophistication, if we are successful, the tax system will be neutral *vis-à-vis* different investments with equal yield. The upshot should be not only a higher degree of equity and justice in taxation, but also a simplification of the actions of taxpayers, who will not have to safeguard their interests by resorting to intricate tax planning schemes but can return to the plain vanilla types.

True, but we are many years away from that goal. Meanwhile the close study of tax anomalies will continue to be rewarding.

Leasing

One of the devices which was used in the early 'flavour of the month' period is leasing, a powerful financing technique and at one time the most widely used technique of tax efficient company financing. The international angles were particularly interesting, enabling a 'double dip' or two separate depreciation allowances to be obtained in two different countries. Tax law in most countries has been changed to check the most blatant forms of tax avoidance. Much leasing business is now undertaken on commercial considerations and is no longer tax driven. However, no comprehensive treatment of tax efficient financing can ignore leasing, and some general principles are discussed below. This subject is not discussed in the 'country' chapters. There have been too many, and too complex changes. Nothing and too few really useful practical angles remain.

First principles

A business wishing to acquire a new piece of equipment can buy it for cash, relying if necessary on general borrowing powers, or it can use an asset-based financing technique. The three ways in which this can be done are credit purchase, hire purchase or leasing. With credit purchase, the equipment is acquired by the purchaser in return for an obligation to make a series of payments over a period of time. The vendor has then disposed of his interest in the equipment but would have a claim on the owner for the purchase price. Under a leasing contract, the user of the machine would not have title to it but would have the right to use it in exchange for a series of rental payments. The *lessor* would have legal ownership and would be entitled to a series of cash payments over the life of the contract.

Leasing contracts are of many kinds, including short-term leases where the full cost is *not* recovered against the initial lease, and the lessor bears the risk of obsolescence.

A *financial* lease is normally entered into on terms which commit the user or lessee to making a series of payments over a period of years (probably approximating to the useful life of the machine), designed fully to recoup the lessor for his capital investment and financing charges. At the end of the period the machine may revert to the lessor, there may be an arrangement by which the lessee can purchase it for a small sum, or the lessee may then have the right to pay a much lower rental for the balance of the life of the machine, however long this may be. Where the lease is tax driven, the aim may be to assimilate the contract as far as possible to a straight loan, with the lessee rather than the lessor bearing the economic risks of ownership.

Historically, a hire purchase transaction is a lease with an option to purchase, although from a practical point of view it is usually equivalent to a credit sale. In the United Kingdom, a hire purchase contract, where it is envisaged that the user will ultimately purchase, is treated for tax purposes as an immediate sale. The 'buyer' gets the depreciation write-offs and the payments are apportioned into capital and interest elements. (If the purchase is not completed, the tax is recomputed on a 'leasing' basis.) It may be possible to set up the transaction so that it is treated as a credit sale in the law of one country and as a lease in the law of another.

From the tax planner's point of view the important point is which party enjoys the benefits of tax depreciation. If a machine has a useful life of ten years during the whole of which it is equally profitable, arguably one would write off the cost at the rate of a 10 per cent per annum straight line. If the cost was £1,000 and the estimated scrap value at the end of ten years was £200, one would only have to write off £80 per annum. In many countries depreciation has been at a far more generous rate, as an incentive to re-equipment and as a royal justice counter to the distortions of inflation. This is now less common, but tax accounting and economic depreciation will still often differ from each other.

If, and only if, the terms of a leasing transaction exactly coincide with the rate at which a machine can be written off for tax purposes, the tax consequences of leasing would be no different from those of any other method of finance. The differences offer a planning opportunity which is now well understood.

Going back into history the United Kingdom at one stage granted an 'investment allowance' permitting 130 per cent of the cost to be depreciated. This was extraordinarily attractive to partnerships of individual taxpayers, then subject to tax at 83 per cent. As the late Professor Ash Wheatcroft explained, ('Claus S.' 1962) the purchase of a capital asset even of no value to the business (provided it is intended to be profitable) can show an after tax profit:

	£
Cost of asset	100
Value of tax allowances	
(against other income) 83% of 130	107.9
after tax 'profit'	7.9
equal to gross income of	46.5

Leasing companies could use this as a tax shelter, but of course the lessee was denied the benefit; instead he enjoyed cheap finance. If the lessee was a non-taxpayer, including local government agencies, or a foreigner, the full rate could be charged.

Double dip leasing

There was an obvious development. If the UK lessor could obtain the tax benefits on a lease to a foreigner, could the foreigner also claim tax advantages in his own country? There were many variations on this theme, some of which survived when countries began restricting relief on assets used outside the country of ownership.

The UK benefits were based on ownership. If the asset was used in the United States the lessee could well be eligible there for the investment tax credit. It was possible for a West German lessor to set up an asset-based tax shelter (often, there, a limited partnership of high tax bracket individuals) and lease to a UK intermediate leasing company. If the terms were drawn up correctly the contract would be a 'lease' in West Germany but a 'hire purchase contract' under UK law. The UK company would also be regarded as an 'economic owner', could claim the double dip and could re-lease to the ultimate user.

The concept was easier between lessees in countries such as the United States, Japan, West Germany, Netherlands which use an 'economic ownership' test, and those, such as lessors in countries that rarely, if ever, make such distinctions – Switzerland, France, Sweden, and the United Kingdom.

Leveraged leasing

Leasing, looked at from a tax perspective, is a method of transferring tax reliefs between taxpayers in different tax positions. The logical next question is why this transfer needs to be associated with the provision of finance.

The answer was leveraged leasing, typically an arrangement between three parties: lessee, lessor and a long-term lender. The lessor would enjoy the tax benefits, such as capital allowances. The lessee would obtain cheap finance. The lender would have the cash flow of the asset as security but would have no recourse to the lessor. These could be international and double dip variations.

Leasing techniques such as those described above constituted a major tax avoidance industry. Its wings were clipped by specific anti-avoidance legislation, but also by the 'broader base lower rate' thrust of recent tax changes. The tax treatment is not discussed in the country sections. A brief discussion would add little to the above summary, while anything comprehensive would require a separate volume and would detract from the central theme.

Part Two

The United Kingdom

9

The general tax system

Since 1979 there have been major changes in UK taxation. The first Conservative Government brought down the top rates of personal tax – from 98 per cent to 75 per cent! The 1984 package, phasing out accelerated depreciation but reducing the rate of corporation tax from 52 per cent to 35 per cent, anticipated the US 1986 Tax Reform. It has brought in more revenue even than its supporters hoped, and has paved the way for the 1988 Budget which rationalised personal tax, reducing the top rate to an internationally competitive 40 per cent. There are now only two rates of personal income tax: a 25 per cent 'basic' rate and a 40 per cent 'higher' rate. The position is complicated by national insurance contributions which have grown up into a secondary tax system. This subject is outside our terms of reference, but national insurance planning is a major preoccupation for labour intensive industries, including the financial services industry.

The imputation system was introduced in the United Kingdom in 1972. Profits were taxed at 52 per cent (a rate which remained unchanged until 1984; it is now 35 per cent), but dividends were eligible for an imputation credit at a rate equal to the basic rate of income tax. This was then 30 per cent, but has been reduced, in stages, to 25 per cent. *Distributed* profits thus suffered a 'true' corporation tax of 31.43 per cent, now reduced to 13.33 per cent.

	December 1984	1988–9
Profits	£100.00	£100.00
Corporation tax	£ 52.00	£ 35.00
	£ 48.00	£ 65.00
Imputation credit	£ 20.57	£ 21.67
Grossed up dividend	£ 68.57	£ 86.67
True CT	31.43%	13.33%

or, expressed differently

Profits	£100.00	£100.00
Less true CT	£ 31.43	£ 13.33
	£ 68.57	£ 86.67
Less income tax 30%	£ 20.57	
25%		£ 21.67
Net after tax	£ 48.00	£ 65.00
(Basic rate)		

The basic rate taxpayer is assessed at 25 per cent on the gross amount, but the tax liability is already met by the imputation credit. A '40 per cent' taxpayer would have to pay an extra 13 per cent, while a tax-exempt investor, such as a pension fund, can reclaim the imputation credit.

The imputation system of taxing companies and shareholders reduced economic distortions at the *domestic* level, but increased or perpetuated them at the *international* level. Specifically a new 'prejudice' was created against UK-based companies investing abroad. This arises from an important feature of the system. At the time of payment of the dividend, the company must pay the Revenue 'Advance Corporation Tax' (ACT) an amount equal to the imputation credit. This ACT can be credited against the imputation credit and is *normally* simply a pre-payment of tax. It is an extra burden where there is no mainstream liability, perhaps when a company incurs losses and continues to pay dividends out of reserves, but most notably when dividends have to be paid out of foreign source profits.

This is known as the 'prejudice problem' and is the most widely criticised aspect of the imputation system.

The internationally accepted principle of credit relief is that if a UK company has paid foreign tax through a branch or subsidiary abroad, the foreign tax should be allowed as a credit against UK tax. If the foreign tax rate was 52 per cent (now 35 per cent) no further UK tax is payable at *corporate* level.

There was a major and important concession built into the system. The 'attribution' rules permit a company paying dividends to allocate its ACT *first* to profits which have borne UK tax and only then to slices of profit which have enjoyed a greater degree of credit relief and against which ACT cannot be fully offset. This is considerably more favourable than an averaging system. A company is only 'prejudiced' if it cannot meet its dividends out of *UK* taxed profits.

Amidst all the changes, one running sore remains. This is the main subject of this book: the irrational treatment of foreign exchange transactions, particularly of foreign currency liabilities. Many UK companies have been unfairly taxed because of the lack of symmetry in the legislation. This has caused resentment, has soured taxpayer compliance and attitudes, and has discouraged some companies from expanding internationally at all.

Other companies, still a minority but now a growing one, are finding tax saving opportunities because of this lack of rationality in the legislation. In such circumstances there is always a danger that the Inland Revenue authorities will act swiftly to close what they perceive as 'loopholes' while dragging their feet on anomalies adversely affecting the taxpayer.

Capital gains tax

Capital gains tax is levied on individuals. The rules are different from those of income tax, and are laid down by separate legislation, now the Capital Gains Tax Act 1979. Until 1988 capital gains were taxed at 30 per cent; they are now taxed at full rates, but subject to indexation and to an annual personal exemption. Companies are liable to 'corporation tax on capital gains' assessed under the same rules. The anomalies of these are a main cause of 'tax fragmentation', the main subject of Chapter 11.

This book is concerned with corporate treasury management, and only incidentally with the tax treatment of investors. There have been a number of UK tax changes during the last few years which, taken together, have materially changed the climate for UK fixed interest investors, and, therefore, for corporate borrowers. Some of these were designed to relieve investors, some to prevent tax avoidance. Others were deliberately designed to stimulate the then moribund UK corporate bond market. These included the deep discount proposals, where the detailed provisions fell short of what was needed. The domestic corporate bond market still refuses to take off; the problems may now be institutional rather than fiscal. Not so long ago government borrowing 'crowded out' industrial borrowers, particularly for longer-term money. The new phenomenon of a 'negative PSBR' opens new opportunities, which have yet to be fully exploited.

Once more, history is particularly revealing. In the United Kingdom, capital gains were tax free until 1962, when a tax was introduced on short-term gains. In 1965 a general capital gains tax was introduced. Government securities (gilts) were exempted from this tax. They remained liable to the short-term tax and when this was abolished were subject to tax only when held for less than a year.

The 1984 Budget extended the tax concessions on government securities to holders of 'qualifying corporate bonds' defined as bonds issued after 13 March 1984 (Section 64(2)(a)), by a company 'if any share, stock or security of the company (but not necessarily the security referred to) is either quoted on a recognised stock exchange in the United Kingdom or dealt in on the Unlisted Securities Market and which is a debt which represents a "normal commercial loan"', defined as one which;

(a)   does not carry any right either to conversion into shares or securities of any other description or the acquisition of additional shares or securities; and

(b)   does not entitle the loan creditor to any amount of interest which depends to any extent on the results of the company's business assets or which exceeds a reasonable commercial return on the new consideration lent; and

(c)   in respect of which the loan creditor is entitled, on repayment, to an amount which either does not exceed the new consideration lent or is reasonably comparable with the amount generally repayable (in respect of an equal amount of new consideration) under the terms of issue of securities listed in the Official List of the Stock Exchange.

The interaction of inflation and capital gains tax produced an unintended 'wealth tax', at a higher rate and a far lower threshold than the explicit tax rejected some years earlier.

To deal with this, capital gains were granted an (initially less than perfect) indexation relief for inflation in 1982. This measure, though welcome, was criticised on several points of detail. First of all, it applied only to inflation subsequent to March 1982. This decision could be defended on practical grounds: it substantially reduced the cost of the concession, which might otherwise have had to wait until there was enough slack in the Budget to deal with the past.

The other two criticisms of the initial measure were more serious. The indexation calculation was made only from the anniversary of the acquisition of the securities with no relief for the first year of ownership. This still amounted to a 'wealth tax' or perhaps more strictly a 'transfer tax' amounting to 30 per cent of the rate of inflation every time an investor switched securities. We argued that it should apply from the date of acquisition *provided* that the securities had been held for twelve months. The proviso was important, as subsequent events proved.

The second criticism was that indexation could not produce a loss.

This was asymmetrical and discriminated against the investor (surely a desirable citizen) who had a well-spread portfolio of 'venture' securities, as compared to one whose portfolio tracked the index. We fought strongly for two amendments to be made.

The 1985 Budget contained these two amendments plus (unfortunately as it turned out) two more. Indexation can now produce a loss; gains and losses are symmetrically treated. Relief is calculated from the date of acquisition but *without* the twelve-month qualifying period we had suggested.

The problem arose from the interaction with another measure, directed at tax avoidance on government and other fixed-income securities. The two measures, considered separately, made sense. Taken together, they created problems.

A month earlier, in February 1985, the government had given advance warning of the introduction of an 'accrued income scheme' applying to investors in government securities and 'qualifying corporate bonds'. They would no longer be able to get a tax advantage by selling such securities 'cum dividend' so that the last six months' interest (and sometimes more) arose as a capital gain.

Gilts and 'qualifying corporate bonds' were already exempt from capital gains tax, provided that they had been held for over a year. It was possible to arrange to hold securities for a year and a day in such a way that only one half-yearly coupon attracted tax, the other half of the return accruing as a tax free capital gain. (There were also special opportunities in leap-year.)

This loophole having been closed, another was immediately opened. Had it persisted, some investors (notably life assurance funds) could have claimed indexation relief on their gilts by systematically selling *within* the year. Although they would be required to pay tax on their nominal interest they would get an offsetting loss at capital gains tax rates, equivalent to the real interest.

The indexation changes also went some of the way towards simplifying the identification rules for capital gains tax. With consistent treatment, all post-1982 acquisitions could go into a single pool. Securities purchased prior to the 'relevant date' (1 April 1982 for companies, 6 April 1982 for individuals) needed more calculations: one needed to know the basis cost *plus* the basis for indexation relief. Trouble came over the rules of identification. These were to be FIFO ('first in first out') rather than LIFO ('last in first out'), which meant that securities sold today were identified with old, and possibly pre-1965 purchases. The government had, it seemed, hoped to use this FIFO procedure as a means of eventually clearing up the past, but it had misjudged market reaction.

Eventually both problems were resolved. First the government announced that gilts and qualifying corporate bonds would be *exempt* from capital gains tax regardless of the holding period – one of the few examples in history where, by disallowing the allowable capital losses which would have been thrown up by indexation, the abolition of a tax brought in £150 million per annum of extra revenue! In the very last stages of the Finance Bill debate, the government also gave way on the FIFO issue and substituted LIFO.

In 1988, when the top rate of income tax was reduced to 40 per cent, capital gains tax rates (previously 30 per cent) were brought into line with income tax rates. The rules are still very different; the planning implication for individuals and companies are outlined at the end of Chapter 11.

International aspects

There are two major international tax problems affecting UK based multinational companies. The first is the 'prejudice problem' which distorts double tax relief and which has already been discussed. The second, the controlled foreign corporation rules, imposes current tax on income arising to certain foreign subsidiaries. Both interact closely with foreign exchange planning and with 'tax fragmentation'.

Controlled Foreign Corporations

The 'Controlled Foreign Corporation' (CFC) legislation came into force in 1984 after a long and acrimonious battle between the Inland Revenue and the international tax community. Complex enough in itself, it can interact in subtle, unexpected (and very occasionally profitable) ways with the tax treatment of foreign exchange. The main object of the legislation is to prevent the accumulation of tax-free profits in offshore money-box companies, but the provisions go well beyond the mere checking for blatant avoidance. They can adversely affect commercially normal transactions, and need treating with great care.

A UK parent company caught by the provision suffers immediate tax on the profits earned, but not distributed, by its CFC subsidiary. There are a number of let-outs in the detailed legislation designed to prevent this penalty applying to normal trading subsidiaries; the 'exempt activities test' mainly concern commercial transactions (such as actually operating tourist hotels in the Bahamas) and are unlikely to be available to a 'money box', 'captive bank', or financing type company. There is also a let-out for a company operating in an 'excluded country' but the list of exclusions, 'white list', is intended to exclude any country which has a low tax regime.

It might be thought that there is no longer any way for a UK parent to avoid tax by using an offshore money-box subsidiary. As a first approximation, this is true, but there *are* some angles which can save tax and usefully enhance the net return on investment. There are also traps: what appear to be straightforward financing or treasury management activities in a foreign subsidiary may fall foul of two sets of tax anomalies. The most obvious, though not the most dangerous, is that while profits in a CFC are fully taxed, *losses* are not relieved.

Two possible let-outs may be available, even to a pure financing subsidiary: the 'acceptable distribution test' and the 'lower level of taxation' test. There are three possible strategies. The first is simply to use a tax-free money box and let the Inland Revenue impose an apportionment on the parent company. The parent will then be assessed to tax on the whole of its 'chargeable profits' for the accounting period (Section 747(4) ICTA 1988). 'Chargeable profit' is defined (Section 747(6)(a)) as 'the amount of the total profits of the company for that period on which, after allowing for any deductions against those profits, corporation tax would be payable'. However, Section 747(6)(b) provides that 'chargeable profits' does not include 'chargeable gains'. This already gives us an advantage: using an offshore money box can *postpone* tax on capital gains, though not on income. The gains will build up the value of the subsidiary, which will be taxed if and when the subsidiary is itself sold or wound up.

The second strategy is for the CFC to avoid an apportionment by making an 'acceptable distribution' within eighteen months of the year end. If it is not a trading company, the distribution must be 90 per cent of its 'available profits' as defined. In principle, this would be 90 per cent of investment income, *but again not capital gains*. This is slightly better than an apportionment in that 10 per cent of income can also be deferred.

If the money-box company is set up as a trading company, it would be required to distribute only 50 per cent of its profits, but these profits would include what would otherwise be capital gains. (As a matter of arithmetic, 'investment' status is better if capital gains, as defined, exceed 44.4 per cent of total returns.)

The third strategy is to use the 'lower level of taxation' let-out. The rules require that 'the amount of tax [in this section referred to as 'the local tax'] which is paid under the law of that territory . . . is less than one half of the corresponding United Kingdom tax on those profits'

(Section 750(1)). The latter is defined (Section 750(2)) as 'the amount of corporation tax which, on the assumptions set out in Schedule 16 . . . would be chargeable . . .'. Section 750(3) appears to make it clear that the 'apportionment' principles would apply.

There are several jurisdictions where the tax rate is slightly in excess of half the UK rate, including Hong Kong and Jersey. The Hong Kong rate went up to 18.5 per cent the year it was announced that UK rates were coming down to 35 per cent. (The authorities in Hong Kong claim that this is a pure coincidence! Since then it has been reduced in stages to 16.5 per cent which is too low.) Neither taxes capital gains, so can shelter all capital gains and nearly half the income. As the test is on the actual computation rather than the nominal rates, and as the definition of 'capital gains' is different, the mix needs to be watched rather carefully. Hong Kong's 'source' basis is also an obstacle.

There are some subtle, and in one case unresolved, points on computation. For the purposes of apportionment, or the 'lower level of taxation' test, we have to calculate profits as if CFC were a UK resident company, but *leaving out of account* chargeable gains. The company is, subject to the right to certain transitional claims, treated as if it became resident at the beginning of the first year for which an apportionment was made.

However, the *acceptable distribution test* seems to follow different rules. A UK shareholding company can avoid a charge if the controlled foreign company distributes to UK residents by way of dividend at least 50 per cent or 90 per cent, as appropriate, of its 'available profits'. Chargeable gains are then eliminated by deduction rather than exclusion (Schedule 25 Paragraphs 3(1) and (3) ICTA 1988). There are in principle two ways, as follow, in which the profits could be calculated:

(a)   investment income as calculated *ignoring* capital gains;
(b)   accounting profits *less* capital gains.

It seems clear that (a) is correct for the apportionment and 'lower level of taxation' calculations. However, (b) *may* be relevant for the 'acceptable distribution' test. This could give a different answer, and suggests possible strategies for managing international financing.

Planning the investment of surplus funds

The rewards of investing surplus funds by a UK company can be taxed as follows:

(a)   as trading income;
(b)   as capital gain;
(c)   as 'nothings' not within the tax charge.

Both (a) and (b) are now taxed at the same 35 per cent rate. Capital gains are, however, subject to indexation relief and there are other distinctions which can be important.

Surplus funds can be invested via:

(a) a UK company not taxed as a 'dealer in securities' (the normal case);

(b) a UK company taxed as a 'dealer in securities' and assessable under Schedule D Case I on transactions which would otherwise be capital gain;

(c) a foreign subsidiary.

We then have to ask two related questions. Does the *instrument* in which we invest produce its return as income or as capital gain? Is the *entity through* which we invest eligible for capital gains treatment, or is it a 'dealing company' for which the distinction is irrelevant?

Interest (and dividends) on straight bonds (and shares) received by a UK company are taxed as income. So are discounts on bills. Gains on the sale of shares are clearly capital gains, provided that the entity is an investment company and not a trading company.

Bonds are much more complicated, thanks to the history discussed above. The gains on the sale of bonds are governed by a number of complex rules. They may fall one side or the other of the line, or may escape tax altogether.

The border-line between 'income' and 'capital gain' has moved against the taxpayer, and there is now much less scope for 'manufacturing' capital gains. Gains or losses on bonds have to be divided into the following categories:

(a) Amortisation, over the holding period, of original issue discount securities:

    (i) within Section 36 FA 1984 (corporate deep discount bonds issued after 12 March 1984);

    (ii) within Section 46 Finance Act 1985 ('stripped treasuries', etc., issued after 18 March 1985);

    (iii) outside both provisions, i.e. issued before the relevant date (note: these provisions now consolidated as Section 57 ICTA 1988).

(b) Accrued interest:

    (i) on securities disposed of after 28 February 1986;

    (ii) other cases not caught by the transitional provisions.

(c)   Gains on redemption of bonds bought at a 'market discount':

    (i)   on government securities and 'qualifying corporate bonds';

    (ii) on other securities.

(d)   Gains or losses from the purchase or sale of bonds, arising from interest rate movements:

    (i)   on government securities and 'qualifying corporate bonds';

    (ii) on other securities.

(e)   Gains or losses arising from foreign exchange movements.

Under UK domestic law (a) (i) and (ii), and (b) (i) now constitute income. Gains under (c) (i) and (d) (i) are exempt from tax. Gains under (c) (ii) (d) (ii) and (e) are taxable chargeable gains. Gains under (b) (ii) (if there are any) and (a) (iii) and (c) are *probably* capital; however gains on original issue discount securities held to maturity may well be assessed as income.

All this assumes that the company investing the money is taxed as an investor and not as a 'dealer in securities', It may well *suit* a company to set up a subsidiary as a financial dealer or in-house bank. If the company, on principal account, is too active, particularly in complex synthetic instruments, there is a danger that the Inland Revenue may assess the company as a dealer whether it suits the taxpayer or not.

The roots of the prejudice problem

The original concept of the UK tax system was 'deduction at source'. Going back far into history, companies paid tax at the individual standard rate and, when dividends were paid, this tax was treated as a pre-payment of the tax due by the individuals. This may all seem long ago, but many of the problems now bedevilling the UK tax system (and the tax planning opportunities opening out to readers of this book) have their roots in the past.

Most other countries began with the so-called 'classical' system of corporation tax, by which corporate profits were subject to tax at one level, while dividends were subject to a further level of tax at the individual level. In 1965 it was argued by the then UK Labour government that such a classical corporation tax would, by discriminating against distribution, promote saving and investment. The government introduced such a system, which remained in force from 1965 to 1972. The reasoning appeared to be based on little more than a statement in the minority report of the Royal Commission on Taxation, arguing that 'the market makes little difference in valuation for differences in the earnings cover of dividends if plainly adequate'. This was probably a fairly accurate observation of stock market behaviour in the immediate post-war period but, as it happened, the year in which the Commission reported (1955) was also the year in which the very serious undervaluation of stock market equities began to be corrected. This led to a sharp rise in stock exchange prices, and a period where investors certainly *did* look very closely indeed at underlying assets and earnings. The moral is that if you must travel using a ten-year-old Bradshaw it is a good idea to recheck the information before taking any decisions!

Against this, it was argued that the incentive to retain cash flow was given regardless of whether or not it was actually invested. 'It may become easier for some companies to finance growth out of retentions but it will become correspondingly more difficult for other companies to expand by raising new capital.' (Chown, 1965.) The classical system was abandoned in favour of an imputation system in 1972. The imputation system was felt to have the balance of advantage in contributing to a coherent system of international harmony. The issue was, however, complicated and obscured by the sharp rise in inflation (and fall in real returns on investment) in the late 1970s.

The prejudice problem has its roots in the way in which the 1965 change, and that which followed in 1972, affected and distorted the calculation of foreign tax credit relief. It may seem ancient history, but it is relevant and revealing.

The United Kingdom gave, and in principle still gives, comprehensive credit relief for foreign taxes, computing these on a 'slice by slice' basis so that each source of income received in the United Kingdom either suffers the UK rate (of income tax *and* profits tax) or the foreign rate, whichever is higher. Immediately prior to the 1965 changes, the combined rate was 56.25 per cent (41.25 per cent or, in the language of the day, 'eight and threepence in the pound' income tax, plus 15 per cent profits tax). Thus the company would pay a total of 26.25 per cent extra UK tax on income received from abroad which has borne 30 per cent foreign tax. If the foreign source had borne 60 per cent, no relief was available, directly or indirectly for the unused 3.75 points.

If the UK company paid a dividend to a UK taxpayer the benefit of the tax credit would in effect flow through. The dividend of 43.75 would be treated as being a gross dividend of 74.47 which had borne income tax at 41.25 per cent *regardless of whether that tax was actually paid to the United Kingdom or whether it represented tax, assessed but discharged by the claiming of a tax credit*. If, however, the dividend was paid to a non-taxpayer (most notably to a pension fund) the right to recover tax was limited to the 'net UK rate', i.e. the tax actually paid to the UK Inland Revenue. (The calculations were complex, the results often anomalous, and there turned out to be a major loophole in the draftmanship, but these are of no immediate concern to us.) From the point of view of foreign investors into the United Kingdom, the income tax was treated as an underlying, rather than a withholding, tax and the rate was not reduced by typical tax treaties. (The treaty with Ireland was an interesting exception.)

The 1965 Reform had an immediate and adverse impact on those UK companies deriving most of their income abroad. If the foreign tax rate was 50 per cent the benefit of the unrelieved 15 per cent would not be passed on to the shareholder. The effective rate of tax would then be 70 per cent, a serious extra penalty on foreign-source profits.

In answer to this criticism the 1965 Finance Bill was amended to concede 'overspill relief'. The company had to choose as a 'base year', one of the three years before the change of system. The calculation was then made of the difference between the actual relief available in that year (but only up to a maximum of 56.25 per cent), which happened to be the combined rate of income tax and profits tax in 1964–65 and the relief that would be due under the new rules at the rate of corporation tax applying in the relevant year. In principle, this amount would be paid to the company during each of the first three years of the new system. In year 4 only four-fifths of the relief was to be given and the relief was to be reduced by a further one-fifth in each successive year, disappearing altogether from year 8 onwards.

Following domestic criticisms of the '1965' system, a new Conservative government set up a Select Committee to discuss the relative merits of a German-type split rate, and a French-type imputation system (see Report from the Select Committee on Corporation Tax, 20 October 1971 – particularly Appendix 19).

The imputation system was introduced in 1972. Profits were taxed at 52 per cent (a rate which remained unchanged until 1984) but dividends were eligible for imputation credit calculated from a 30 per cent basic rate. *Distributed* profits thus suffered a 'true' corporation tax of 31.43 per cent, compared with 25.53 per cent pre-1965. From 1988, this was reduced to 13.33 per cent.

Although the new system reduced domestic distortions they actually increased those at international level in a way already discussed above. Overspill relief was extended but in a very restrictive way so as to give a 'prejudiced' company less than half the relief really needed. It was still calculated quite unrealistically with reference to a pre-1965 base year.

When this problem was discussed by the 1971 Select Committee it did seem that it would only affect a few 'resource' companies (e.g. Shell, RTZ), a couple of UK-based multinationals with an exceptionally low proportion of UK activities, such as British American Tobacco, and a rather larger number of specialist plantation and similar companies. Since then the picture has changed dramatically. The oil companies now *do* earn profits in the United Kingdom (North Sea) and the specialists obtained (as was expected) consent to emigrate to their country of operation.

Against this, many other companies who thought this problem was not for them, found themselves, by the late 1970s, joining the 'Prejudice Club'. These companies had typically earned two-thirds of their profits in the United Kingdom and one-third abroad, and therefore had no difficulty in meeting their dividends out of UK-taxed profit. Falling UK profitability left them 'fiscally starved' with the losses in the United Kingdom; they were paying overseas tax plus ACT.

10

The tax treatment of interest

Although UK companies can normally deduct interest in calculating taxable profits, the legislation is a little more complex, and needs more careful study than in the United States. There is a general principle that interest, like other deductible expenses, must be wholly and exclusively laid out or expended for the purposes of the trade profession or vocation (Section 74 (a) ICTA 1988); there is a further restriction on interest paid to a non-resident at 'more than a reasonable commercial rate'.

Until 1981 a deduction was denied where interest was charged to capital accounts. The 1984 Finance Act cleared up some anomalies on acceptance credits and on the 'incidental costs of raising loan finance' such as commissions and legal expenses (these provisions are now included in Sections 77 and 78 ICTA 1988). It also simplified the procedures for issuing Eurobonds (now Section 124(1)–(3) ICTA 1988).

(Individual taxpayers can, since 1974, no longer deduct interest from taxable income unless the money is borrowed for the purpose of a trade or for certain other qualifying purposes (Sections 353–368 ICTA 1988). Relief is given for interest paid on the first £30,000 of borrowing for house purchase or improvement.

There is an important procedural distinction between 'annual' and 'short' interest. 'Annual' interest has been judicially defined as interest on a debt which is in the nature of an investment, or which has a duration of at least one year. Thus, normal trade debts are not included. They fall under 'short' interest with all other interest that is not 'annual'. 'Short' interest paid on trading account is deductible. 'Annual' interest on trading account is deductible if paid to a UK bank. Other 'annual' interest is deductible for corporation tax purposes as long as the debtor company carries on a trade or holds investments. In the international context the distinction between 'short' and 'annual' interest is most relevant for determining liability to withholding tax. Where a company cannot obtain immediate relief for interest (generally because it has insufficient otherwise taxable profits) relief can be carried forward indefinitely against the profits of the same relevant trade (Section 393 ICTA 1988). Readers of the first part of this book will understand that 'present value' is a key tool of the fiscal planner. Tax postponed is tax saved, while relief postponed is relief.

Relief may also be surrendered to and set against the profits of another UK member of the same 'group' (Sections 402–413 ICTA 1988). A group comprises a parent and its '75 per cent subsidiaries'. Ownership may be traced through any number of sub-subsidiaries, *provided they are all UK resident.* There is no longer scope for creating artificial groups using special classes of shares. Two wholly owned direct UK subsidiaries of a foreign parent do *not* constitute a group, a major booby trap which has claimed some eminent victims!

Payment of interest to non-residents

Where a UK company borrows money from non-residents, whether by a publicly listed bond issue, an inter-company loan or otherwise, there are two separate but closely connected rules to be watched. Is there an obligation to deduct withholding tax on the interest payments? Is the interest deductible? In many cases the two are linked, but there are exceptions. Interest, paid gross under the provisions of a double tax agreement, can be granted relief, but the obligation to withhold is governed by separate rules.

Withholding tax

A non-resident of the United Kingdom who receives 'annual interest' from a UK 'source' is in principle liable to UK tax at the current basic rate of income tax (25 per cent for 1988–9). There are exemptions for specified UK government securities, and under double tax agreements. The provisions of these agreements are given in the Appendix to Chapter 7.

'Short interest' is not subject to tax but the non-resident may be assessible under Section 54 TMA 1970 if he has a trustee or agent in the United Kingdom. The 'branch or dependent agent' of a foreign company is assessable on its UK source profits including interest. In other cases the Inland Revenue does not have effective power and does not in practice seek to assess.

In the case of Eurobond loans it is essential to ensure that interest can be paid gross. Since 1984 this has been specifically permitted by what is now Section 124 ITCA 1988. Previously, the normal procedure, where the UK company was a direct borrower was to ensure that the loan had a foreign 'source'. Until the end of 1979 this could be achieved by a few simple precautions, including a provision that the loan was governed by foreign law (Bermuda law, being substantially identical to UK on this point, was often chosen). As it was public policy to encourage borrowings, the Inland Revenue took a relaxed view of this arrangement. As in the United States, there has been a conflict between different policy objectives.

With the abolition of exchange control the Inland Revenue changed practice and had been taking a much more stringent view of 'source'. It seemed to us that the Inland Revenue's grounds for concern were somewhat irrational, as is the more recent French EEC initiative discussed in Chapter 21. If a UK resident wishes to evade tax by failing to declare interest income received abroad he is far more likely to invest in non-UK obligations. Withholding tax on interest is not in practice a tax on foreign lenders but on domestic borrowers. The Inland Revenue announced its intention to require UK companies paying interest on Eurobonds to deduct income tax at the basic rate from such interest payments. They would be deemed to constitute Schedule D Case III income, unless shown not to be such income. The basis for the Inland Revenue's previous willingness to allow such interest payments to be made free of withholding tax was that they constituted income arising from securities or possessions out of the United Kingdom in terms of Schedule D Case IV or Case V. This change in practice has since been reversed by statute.

Deductibility of interest paid to non-residents

Charges, including interest, *paid* by a resident company are allowed as deductions against the total profits for that accounting period, provided that they are ultimately borne by the company, and are made under a liability incurred for a valuable and sufficient consideration (Section 338 ICTA 1988).

Section 338(3) defines such charges as:

(a)   any yearly interest, annuity or other annual payment and any other payments such as are mentioned in TA 1970, Section 52;

(b)   any other (*i.e. non-yearly*) interest payable in the United Kingdom on an advance from a *bona fide* banking business or from a member of the Stock Exchange or a discount house.

Where annual interest payments are made to persons not resident in the UK, one of four tests detailed in Sections 338 and 340 must be complied with if a deduction for tax purposes is to be obtained. These rules are of central importance in structuring international loans and Eurobond issues.

1. The borrower must have deducted withholding tax from the payment of interest made to the non-resident at the basic rate of income tax (now 25 per cent) unless this rate is reduced or eliminated under a double tax agreement (Section 338(4)(a)).

2. Interest is paid on quoted Eurobonds falling within Section 124 (Section 338(4)(b)).

3. The payment of interest must be out of income 'brought into charge to tax under Cases IV or V of Schedule D' (i.e. income arising outside the United Kingdom, including both branch profits and foreign source dividends and interest income, including income from subsidiaries) (Section 338(4)(d)).

4. The last test is a little more complicated, and three conditions must be met.

   First, under the terms of the contract under which the interest is payable, the interest may be required to be paid outside the United Kingdom.

   Second, the interest is, in fact, to be paid outside the United Kingdom.

   Third, *either* the liability to pay the interest must be incurred wholly or mainly for the purposes of activities of the company's trade carried on outside the United Kingdom, *or*,

   if interest is payable in a non-sterling currency, the liability to pay the interest must be incurred wholly or mainly for the purposes of activities of the company's trade *wherever carried on* (Section 338(4)(c) and Section 340).

The Inland Revenue has interpreted rule (3) rather generously. Take the case of a UK company which incurs the obligation to pay interest of $1 million per annum to a non-resident. It receives dividend income from its US subsidiary of £650,000 cash, after US withholding tax, for underlying Federal tax and for state tax. In total, these credits will exceed 35 per cent (the current UK corporation tax rate) and, therefore, no UK corporation tax will be payable. There is then £1 million of 'grossed up' UK income, which *permits* the £1 million interest to be deducted. There is no requirement that the interest be set off against that particular (US) income on which there is no UK tax liability.

Test 3 (the 1968 'Lever' amendment) made it possible to borrow foreign currency for *domestic* operations. This test does not permit a UK company to borrow foreign currency by means of a bond issue to form, acquire or expand a foreign subsidiary. Various 'roundabout' solutions were devised for the problem.

Interest paid to associated companies

Section 340(2) ICTA 1988 limits the general application of Section 340 so that interest paid in a foreign currency outside the United Kingdom will *not* be allowed as a charge on income if the trade:

(a) is carried on by a body of persons over whom the person entitled to the interest has control, or

(b) the person entitled to the interest is a body of persons over whom the person carrying on the trade has control, or

(c) the person carrying on the trade and the person entitled to the interest are both bodies of persons, and some other person has control over both of them.

(The reference to 'control' has the meaning assigned to it by Section 840 ICTA 1988.) Where either of the *second* and *third* tests of Section 248 is satisfied, then the interest so paid would qualify as a charge on income. However, there could still be an *obligation* to withhold tax under Section 54 unless either the *source* of the interest is outside the United Kingdom or a tax treaty overrides the withholding requirement.

As a general rule, therefore, interest paid to a foreign parent or associate is treated as a distribution of profits. The payment is not deductible in computing taxable profits, and the paying company must account to the Inland Revenue for ACT at the rate (1988–9) of one-third of the payment. Section 209, discussed below, treats payments of interest in certain situations as *distributions*. Sub-Section (2)(v) applies to a payment of interest by the UK company to a non-resident company where one is a 75 per cent subsidiary of the other, or both are 75 per cent subsidiaries of a third non-UK company. The section is often specifically overridden by a double tax treaty subject to a proviso that the exemption does not apply if the non-resident lender is itself controlled directly or indirectly.

Deduction or distribution?

Interest is a deduction from taxable profits, while dividends are a distribution out of such profits. The distinction is becoming less important, as the rate of corporation tax is falling closer to the level of imputation credit. When a company which suffered tax at 35 per cent, paid interest of £100, the after-tax cost was £65. If it paid a dividend of £75 net plus imputation credit of £25, the net cost (in terms of retentions forgone) would be £75. (The differentials were wider before the 1984 rate changes. Interest then cost £48, while a dividend cost £70.)

A taxpaying company might seek to have 'distributions' to shareholders characterised as interest rather than dividends. Many ingenious capital structures had been designed to achieve this end; Section 233 was designed to forestall them.

Section 209 ICTA 1988 (previously Section 233 ICTA 1970) extends the definition of 'distribution' to certain payments that might otherwise be treated as deductible interest. The relevant extensions are:

Interest on convertible securities. (s 209(2)(e)(ii)). There is an exemption for securities quoted on a recognised stock exchange or issued on terms which are reasonably comparable with the terms of such issues, and in practice interest on convertibles is deductible. Many UK companies have issued convertible Eurobonds, taking advantage of this exception.

Securities under which the consideration given by the company is to any extent dependent on the results of the company's business or any part of it, or under which the consideration so given represents more than a reasonable commercial return for the use of that principal. (s 209(2)(e)(iii)). This prevents companies claiming a deduction for profit sharing 'loan stocks' which are really equities.

Securities held by a foreign parent company (s 209(2)(e)(iv)) – (this provision is often overridden by a double tax agreement and its relevance for UK subsidiaries of foreign parents is discussed below).

Securities which are connected with shares in the company i.e. where 'in consequence of the nature of the rights attaching to the securities or shares, and in particular of any terms or conditions attaching to the right to transfer the shares . . . it is necessary or advantageous' (to hold acquire retain or dispose of the securities *pro rata* to shares) (s 209(2)(e)(v)). This effectively kills (in this context) the device of 'stapled stock' or 'Siamese twins'.

Net loans

In the United Kingdom, as in other countries, there is a tax distinction between *interest* on loan stocks and *dividends* on preference shares. *Interest* is treated as a deduction from taxable profits. Dividends are treated as a distribution of already taxed profits, but as 'franked income' in the hands of a corporate recipient.

A taxpaying company is generally better off paying *interest*, if the recipient is an individual, a foreigner, or a UK tax exempt entity such as a pension fund. The advantage can work the other way. A 'fiscally starved' company (not liable to tax, e.g. because of losses or double tax relief) will find it cheaper to pay dividends (or payments that can be characterised as dividends) to a corporate provider of finance, such as a bank.

'Section 233', now Section 209, was intended as an anti-avoidance section designed to prevent companies dressing up 'dividends' as 'interest'. Prior to 1982, the provision could be 'played backwards' to give a tax advantage to a fiscally starved borrower, which could arrange to treat a payment to its bank as a 'distribution' rather than as income.

What were then known as 'Section 233 loans' were drafted on terms which offered the lender some participation (usually nominal) in the profits of the company. This triggered the anti-avoidance provision (Section 209(2)(e)(iii) – see above), and the interest paid was then treated as a 'distribution'. It was disallowed as a deduction to the paying company but this did not matter because the company had no taxable income anyway. The point of the exercise was that the payment then constituted 'franked investment income' to the recipient. If both borrower and lender were taxpaying at 52 per cent, a 'Section 233' interest payment of £48 net (£68.57 gross) would be equivalent, from the point of view of the lender, to deductible loan interest of £100 gross.

Prior to 1982 such loans were made when the lender was not currently taxpaying. The cost of the normal loan would be £100; that of the 'Section 233' loan would be £48 net, but the taxpayer would have to account to the Inland Revenue for Advance Corporation Tax (ACT). At the 30 per cent basic rate then ruling this would bring the cost up to 68.57 per cent. The payment would be negotiated at a gross figure somewhere between 68.57 per cent and 100 per cent of the amount that would be charged on a normal loan.

The calculations at 1988–89 rates are shown below. If such loans had not been legislated against in 1982, their benefits would have been substantially reduced by the 1984 rate changes.

	Normal loan (£)	Net loan (£)
Borrower pays	100	65
plus ACT		21.67
Cost to borrower	100	86.67
Corporation tax deduction	35	—
ACT offsettable		21.67
Net cost	65	65
Lender receives	100	65
plus imputation credit		21.67
		86.67
Less corporation tax	35	
Less ACT on dividend paid		21.67
Net receipt to lender	65	65

The definition of 'distribution' in Section 233 was modified by Section 60 of the Finance Act 1982. This excluded from the definition 'interest or any other distribution' which is paid to another company which is within the charge to corporation tax *and* which is so paid in respect of securities of the borrower which fall into what are now Section 209(2)(e)(i), (ii), (iii) or (v).

Thin capitalisation

There are at present no formal guidelines in the United Kingdom on debt–equity ratios. The UK Inland Revenue has been showing increased interest in this subject. It has been suggested that the Inland Revenue was looking for a debt–equity ratio of between two and three to one and that equity should be equal to the fixed assets of the business. It is also suggested that it wanted to see a four times income cover for the interest. More recently it has been suggested that even a one-to-one ratio may not be regarded as a safe haven.

On 1 December 1987 the Inland Revenue issued a short press release commenting on the OECD paper on thin capitalisation (see p. 50). Comments were requested but no firm policy guidelines have yet been issued.

The interest clauses in certain recent double tax agreements may give the Inland Revenue effective power to impose a debt–equity ratio. For example, in the US/UK DTA full benefit of the interest article is denied 'where, owing to a special relationship between the payer and the person deriving the interest . . . the amount of the interest paid exceeds *for whatever reason* the amount which would have been paid in the absence of such relationship'.

Article 11(5), Section 15 Oil Taxation Act 1975 also limits Section 338 in relevant cases. Specifically, interest to an associated company is disallowed to the extent that 'the rate at which it was payable did not exceed what, having regard to all the terms on which the money was borrowed and the standing of the borrower, was a reasonable commercial rate'. The Inland Revenue does appear to interpret this as giving it power to impose debt–equity ratios.

The arm's length rule

Section 720 ICTA 1988, applies where 'the buyer is a body of persons over which the seller has control' (or vice versa) 'and the property is sold at a price less (or more) than the price which it might have been expected to fetch if the parties had been independent persons at arm's length'.

The Inland Revenue has the right to recompute tax liability substituting arm's length prices. The principle is extended 'with the necessary adaptations' to 'the giving of business facilities of whatever kind' and is in practice applied to non-arm's length interest.

Deep discount securities

The fashion for zero coupon bonds began in the United States. It became technically possible to issue them in the United Kingdom following an announcement by the Chancellor on 25 June 1982. Relevant tax legislation which, it was indicated, might follow US precedents, was to be included in the 1983 Finance Bill, and a Consultative Paper was issued in January 1983.

The election intervened, and the legislation was only introduced in 1984. Meanwhile there had been a series of consultations to try to reconcile the Treasury's desire to stimulate at least one section of the long-term corporate bond market with the Inland Revenue's fear of avoidance.

In the event there is some degree of deliberate asymmetry in favour of the taxpayer, but it has not proved sufficient to tempt many borrowers. The income taxable to the investor is calculated on the same basis as the amount deductible to the borrower, but while the company can deduct on an accrual basis the investor is taxed only on the redemption or sale.

The corresponding deduction is given to the borrowing company *each year* so that, from the point of view of the borrower, the tax treatment is exactly the same as a 'full coupon' bond with the same yield to redemption.

The difference in the *timing* of the tax treatment means that zero coupon bonds should cost about 1 per cent less (or yield correspondingly more) than full coupon bonds. Since 1984 a company issuing zero coupon (or other deep discount) bonds can obtain a deduction each year for the amount deemed to be in lieu of interest (Schedule 4, Paragraph 5 ICTA 1988).

A 'deep discount' bond is defined as one where the discount exceeds the lesser of 15 per cent, or 'half y per cent' where y is the number of complete years to redemption (Schedule 4, Paragraph 1 ICTA 1988). The amount is calculated on a compound interest basis, using the interest rate derived from the initial issue price. The notional price at any date, and the taxable or deductible amount accruing between any two dates, is thus pre-determined.

Although the company enjoys deductions on an accruals basis, investors pay tax only when they are actually redeemed (Schedule 4, Paragraph 1 ICTA 1988). The same predetermined figures are used. This 'timing' discrepancy offers a material advantage. For example, consider a ten-year bond yielding 10 per cent gross. The price would be £38.55, and the notional value would increase by 10 per cent per annum in accordance with the table.

	£
Cost	38.55
Proceeds on maturity	100.00
Gain	61.45
Tax 35%	21.51
Net proceeds	78.49

$$\text{Gain} = \frac{78.49}{38.55} = 2.036$$

$$= 7.37\% \text{ per annum}$$

The price realised by the investor might well not be the price on the schedule. For instance at the end of year 3 the notional price is £51.32. If interest rates had fallen to 9 per cent the price might be £54.70. The balance of £3.38 would be a capital gain, if interest rates rose. There would be an income gain and a capital loss. This asymmetry would have made it possible to 'round trip' between associated companies to prevent this.

Schedule 4, Paragraph 9 ICTA 1988 sets out the rules for transactions between associated companies. These apply 'where a deep discount security is owned by another company', which is:

(a)   an associated company (within the meaning of Section 416) of the issuing company; or

(b)   a member of a group of companies of which the issuing company is also a member.

In these cases any 'linked income element' (i.e. the income accruing while the securities are so owned) is not deductible on an accruals basis but only in the 'accounting period in which the security is redeemed' (Paragraph 3 modified, where appropriate, by Paragraph 5).

Further anti-avoidance provisions were introduced in 1985. These prevent the packaging of zero coupon bonds, i.e. issuing bonds eligible for an accruals basis deduction on the effective security of similar bonds where tax would (but for these rules) be levied only on maturity.

Indexed bonds

The UK government issues indexed securities, both the interest and principal of which is linked to a measure of inflation. These are attractive investments for pension funds and other investors with 'real' liabilities. The 1983 announcement suggested that it would be possible for corporate borrowers to issue indexed, as well as deep discount, bonds. This would be an attractive means of financing projects, such as, say, the Channel Tunnel, where real cash flows can be predicted more accurately than inflation rates.

This has not happened. The tax treatment is not satisfactory. The uplift of the principal would not be taxable to a UK investor (indexation relief) but it would not be deductible to the borrower. There is a possible solution. It is possible to structure the issue so that the indexation relief is rolled up to be paid on the maturity of the bond. The Inland Revenue appears to accept that 'the rolled up interest', when paid, will be given the same tax treatment, both for the borrower and the lender, as non-indexed interest. This is not altogether satisfactory.

11

Foreign exchange gains and losses

The tax treatment of foreign exchange gains and losses is still, in the United Kingdom as elsewhere, a mess. The problems are compounded when we come to deal with options, swaps and other modern financial instruments; see Chapter 12. It is impossible to deal rationally with these while there remain anomalies even on relatively simple foreign exchange transactions. The central problem of tax fragmentation has been a public scandal since 1976, and has been of concern to specialists since 1970.

Meanwhile the traps, and opportunities, remain. Treasurers cannot afford to ignore tax factors and the complicated instruments in which they deal, nor can they afford to be rushed into an ill-considered deal by bankers looking for a quick turn. If ever there was a case for seeking truly independent advice it is here. Even though the problems do not directly concern banks, the intelligent banker, looking to establish relationships with his customers, will seek to make sure that the deals he offers are indeed tax efficient.

Following the Marine Midland case, the Inland Revenue issued a Statement of Practice (SOP). This, it was pointed out, merely interpreted unsatisfactory law. While welcome, it was no substitute for a change in the law itself. The government conceded this point, and the Inland Revenue invited various bodies representing taxpayer interests to form a Working Group to recommend changes in the law. Following these initiatives, discussed in more detail below, a complete restructuring of the law may well be imminent. However, it is clear that, when changes are made, transitional provisions will necessarily be inadequate. They will not, repeat not, wipe the slate clean. Those who have borrowed in a tax inefficient way, or fallen into the 'swap trap' cannot expect retrospective relief from new legislation. On the other hand, those who in the time remaining take the trouble to make the anomalies work in their favour can expect to enjoy the benefits.

The problem of tax fragmentation in its present form goes back to the early 1970s. (The earliest letter on our own files advising a company against a foreign currency borrowing is dated December 1970.) It became serious during the 1976 collapse of sterling, when considerable pressure for new legislation was thwarted by the failure of the separate CBI and BBA working parties to liaise effectively.

Tax fragmentation

There are four main types of tax fragmentation. All are of serious concern to the international treasury manager. The first is the non-symmetrical tax treatment of foreign currency assets and liabilities. The United Kingdom imposes capital gains tax on gains (including foreign currency gains) realised on *assets*. There is no such tax (and no relief for losses) on *liabilities*. These are treated as 'nothings'. This produces a particularly virulent form of tax fragmentation which is peculiar to the United Kingdom.

A company borrows $12 million when the pound is $2.40, and buys a US asset. A few years later, the pound being $1.20, the asset is sold for the same $12 million, and the loan is repaid, with neither gain nor loss. The UK Inland Revenue will assess the company on a chargeable capital gain calculated as follows:

Disposal proceeds $12m. at $1.20 =	£10 million
Less cost of acquisition $12m. at $2.40 =	£ 5 million
Chargeable gain	£ 5 million
On which tax	£ 1.5 million

The hard-pressed taxpayer might well ask about relief for the exactly corresponding loss on the *liability*? Unfortunately, this being treated as a 'nothing', there is no relief and the result is a tax charge of £1.5 million even where there is no economic gain. This is not a hypothetical example: real cases have cost UK companies £1 billion or more.

The second type of tax fragmentation also applies on assets and arises from the relationship between interest and foreign currency risk. If sterling interest rates are 10 per cent while Deutschmark rates are 4 per cent, the market is expecting, and the forward market is offering a 6 per cent appreciation in the Deutschmark over the year. A treasurer who borrows Deutschmarks instead of sterling gets tax relief on the interest, but not on the capital loss. This is, in general, bad news.

Until fairly recently, most long-term foreign exchange exposures by UK companies were on the liability side of the balance sheet. Now, many have spare cash and have to face the 'mirror image' problem. A treasurer who invests surplus sterling to earn *interest*, will suffer tax at 35 per cent. If he buys a Deutschmark bond or other financial instrument, this may earn interest of 4 per cent, and is *expected* to produce a chargeable gain of 6 per cent. Since the 1987 Budget, chargeable gains are also taxed at 35 per cent. Given that both interest and chargeable gains are now taxed at the same 35 per cent rate, does it matter? The short answer is 'yes'. Chargeable gains are eligible for indexation relief. If the company invests £1 million for a year at 10 per cent interest, it pays tax on the whole of the amount. The return, after 35 per cent tax, is £65,000. If invested in such a way that it realises a 10 per cent capital gain the company will enjoy indexation relief, and will pay tax only on the real gain, after inflation. Assuming inflation at 5 per cent, the net return after tax will be £82,500. This is worth the equivalent of 2.7 percentage points on the gross yield on the investment.

In dealing with these two types of tax fragmentation it is important to be certain whether a foreign exchange gain is a capital gain or regular income. In some cases, it is *not* simple. Those who have based their financial planning on the assumption that it was obvious that tax would be levied (or tax relief given) on the basis of the actual profit made, or loss sustained, have been seriously misled.

Lack of precision in the law often violates symmetry and works against the taxpayer. A taxpayer may attempt to set up a transaction so that it receives capital gains treatment on a gain. He may fail in this aim if there is a profit – but succeed only too well if there is a loss! This is perhaps the commonest relevant tax trap, and one which the good currency tax planner must avoid or (even better) turn into an opportunity.

The third type of tax fragmentation, depends on *when* a gain or loss is recognised. This 'only' affects the timing of tax payments but at high rates of interest, or fine margins, it can be significant. Tax law and practice may in fact be slightly *favourable* to the taxpayer here. At a 10 per cent rate of interest a year's postponement can reduce the effective tax rate from 35 per cent to 31.5 per cent.

The fourth type, anomalies in the calculation of double tax relief, is more complex and is discussed at the end of this chapter. One variant of this involves the CFC legislation, already explained in Chapter 9.

The United Kingdom, in common with the United States, Canada, France, Germany and Japan, has legislation 'deeming' the profits of certain controlled foreign companies to arise at parent level. In the United Kingdom this does not apply to capital gains. Is a currency gain or loss realised by such a subsidiary to be treated as apportionable income? If it is, it will be immediately taxable at parent level. There is no corresponding provision for relieving a loss. This is another danger of non-symmetrical treatment against the taxpayer.

Capital or revenue?

The question of whether a gain or loss is to be treated under the capital gains tax rules or as being on trading account is still relevant for several reasons. Capital gains are indexed, but the rules for offsetting *capital* losses against other income are restrictive. Capital gains and losses on liabilities and on debts due which do not constitute a 'debt on a security' are 'nothings', neither taxed nor relieved. Two early cases indicate roughly where the border-line between capital and revenue was drawn. In those days, capital gains escaped tax altogether, and capital losses could not be set against ordinary income.

In the Imperial Tobacco case (*Imperial Tobacco Company (of Great Britain and Ireland) Ltd* v. *Kelly* 25 TC 292) the company had acquired dollars which it intended to apply to the purchase of Virginia tobacco. On the outbreak of war in 1939 it was instructed by the Treasury to cease further purchases and to surrender the balance of the dollars to the Bank of England. This resulted in a profit and this profit was held to be assessable. A foreign currency had been acquired with the intention that it should be exchanged in due course for stock-in-trade and it did not lose its revenue character merely because the original purchase had been frustrated and the currency disposed of.

In the Shell Company of China case (*Davies* v. *Shell Company of China Limited* 32 TC 133) the courts reached the opposite conclusion. The question arose from the practice of that company (UK resident but trading in China) of requiring its agents to make deposits by way of securities which were retained as long as the agency continued. When Japan invaded China in 1937, these deposits, which had been held in Shanghai banks, were converted into sterling and deposited with the UK parent company. When the deposits came to be repaid, the Chinese currency had depreciated substantially against sterling. The sterling profit was held *not* to be assessable on the grounds that the Chinese currency was not acquired for the purpose of effecting a transaction on revenue account.

The leading case on the effect of foreign exchange movements on capital gains tax is *Bentley* v. *Pike*. The facts of this case were unusual and quite different from the circumstances in which the judgment is currently applied. In December 1967 Mrs Bentley inherited land in Germany on the death of her father, who was domiciled in Israel. At the

time of his death the land was valued at DM132,780 equivalent to
£11,446 at the then ruling exchange rate of 11.6. On 6 July 1973, probate
having been granted, the land was sold for DM152,241. The exchange
rate was by then 6.57, and the sterling proceeds were £23,175. How was
the gain to be taxed?

The calculation could, in principle, have been made in either of two
ways:

	DM	*£*
Sale proceeds	152,241	£23,175
Costs	132,780	£11,446
Gain	19,461	11,729

Taxable gain

Basis 1
DM gain (DM19,461) converted at 6.57   £ 2,962

Basis 2
gain calculated in sterling   £11,729

Mrs Bentley argued that she should be taxed on Basis 1, i.e. the
difference between the market value in Deutschmarks at the date of
her father's death (when she acquired the land) and the sales proceeds
in Deutschmarks. This profit would then have been translated into
sterling at the rate ruling on the latter date, and would have eliminated
the currency element in the gain. The High Court upheld the Inland
Revenue's contention that the cost had to be converted into sterling at
the rate ruling at the date of death (Basis 2).

Mr Justice Vinelott, having considered a number of aspects specific to
the transaction, concluded:

while I feel some sympathy for Mrs Bentley, who is in large measure called on to
pay capital gains tax upon a gain resulting from the devaluation of the pound, I
can see no possible justification in the capital gains tax legislation for this [i.e.
Basis 1] approach . . . . The market value of the acquisition . . . as I see it, can
only be expressed . . . in sterling which is the only permissible unit of account.
In my judgment, therefore, this appeal fails.

The decision, on the facts, was not unreasonable. Mrs Bentley had
inherited an asset worth some £11,000 free of UK estate duty.
Subsequently, and mainly as a result of devaluation, she doubled her
windfall and was required to pay 30 per cent tax on the difference.

This conclusion is now followed by the Inland Revenue even where it
is much less reasonable. If Mrs Bentley had borrowed DM133,000 to
buy a second home, and sold it for DM152,000 a few years later, would

the judge then have accepted so readily that she be assessed to tax of £3,518 on a financial gain of only £2,962? What if the land was a business asset, and was sold as part of a German trade? Again it is assumed that the tax should be levied.

The problems, particularly on *debt*, came into prominence in 1976. Following pressure from industry, rules and practice were set out in an Inland Revenue Discussion Paper published on 6 October 1976. This gave useful guidance, and is still generally valid but has been overtaken by events.

Marine Midland

More recently the Inland Revenue did in fact lose one case (*Pattison* v. *Marine Midland Limited* 5 TC 540) involving tax fragmentation Type 1 – but on limited facts. Marine Midland Ltd, a UK Eurodollar bank with no sterling business, was partly financed by a $15 million subordinated loan from its US parent. These funds were never converted into sterling but were on-lent, in the normal course of business, in dollars. By the time the loan was repaid in 1976 the pound had fallen from $2.55 to $1.78. The value of the $15 million *asset* had gone up from £5.9 million to £8.4 million. The Inland Revenue sought to assess tax on this £2.5 million purely paper gain, while disallowing the exactly corresponding *loss* on the *liability*. It won in the first instance, but was roundly defeated in the higher courts.

The point at issue was whether the company was to be taxed on this translation profit. The sum at stake was £1.25 million, but much larger amounts depended on this test case. The Court of Appeal (and later the House of Lords) found for the company, reversing a decision of the High Court. The case is explained in more detail in Appendix 1. Another recent case is of more limited relevance. In *Van Arkadie* v. *Sterling Coated Materials Ltd* 1983 STC 95 (exchange loss on repayment of a loan linked with the purchase of plant) SCM originally agreed to purchase some plant from a Swiss company, for Sw Fr 3 million, in ten half-yearly instalments starting in 1974. The Swiss vendor needing immediate finance, SCM entered into a loan agreement to borrow Sw Fr 3 million from a Swiss bank, which was immediately paid to the Swiss company. SCM agreed to repay the Sw Fr 3 million to the bank over the same ten half-yearly instalments.

In the event, SCM paid the originally agreed instalments for two years and then paid off the balance. Because the Swiss franc had appreciated the total sterling cost was more than if the total payment had been made in a lump sum. SCM claimed first year capital allowances on the extra expenditure. The Inland Revenue disallowed the extra FYA claim arguing (following the case of *Ben-Odeco Ltd*) that the expenditure was attributable to the provision of finance, not the cost of the plant. The High Court held that the extra expenditure was directly connected with the provision of plant and that the expenditure was incurred when the instalment payments were made. The loan agreement was regarded as being at one with the original contract.

The statement of practice

The Marine Midland case had let some of the banks, but typically not the corporate borrowers, off the hook. Following this case, the Inland Revenue published a *Provisional Statement of Practice* followed by a *Draft Statement of Practice* and, in early 1987, a definitive version (Appendix 1). Those consulted told the Inland Revenue that the guidance (discussed below) was quite inadequate and that the Statement was no substitute for urgent new legislation. To our surprise, we were invited to Somerset House, told that ministers 'did not rule out' a legislative solution and were sent away to form a Working Group. The text of its report is given in Appendix 2.

Previous initiatives in 1976 had broken down because of differences of approach between the banks and commercial borrowers. The Working Group therefore endeavoured to find an agreed solution which would deal with the main problem of tax fragmentation while not being unacceptably expensive to the Inland Revenue. Inevitably, the transitional provisions and the 'options' available for the future had to be limited; the aim was to provide a rational basis for future treatment. Some companies who understood the anomalies and how to profit from them were naturally reluctant to agree to any change. Nevertheless the final document (Appendix 2) represents the consensus of those actually taking part in the discussions. There are still some difficult points, notably on 'accruals on realisation' (Paragraphs 11–13) and on the 'matching' elections (Paragraphs 19–21).

Meanwhile the Statement of Practice (SOP) (Appendix 1) is our best guide to the present state of the law. The non-specialist needs to read the document with care. A statement that 'there is no exchange gain or loss for Case I purposes' must be read, not as a reassurance, but as a *warning* that there *is* probably a serious capital gains tax trap.

The basis of SOP is 'matching'. In certain circumstances a gain on an asset will be matched against a loss on a liability (or vice versa) but *only* for *Case I* purposes.

Generally, SOP does not give relief for *capital* transactions. The old problem remains. Paragraph 14 specifically permits long-term monetary assets to be matched against current liabilities in the same currency. This appears to be intended as a new relief but may well, in practice, turn out to be a new *restriction*.

Paragraphs 16–20 set out the basis of computation. They accept that the extent of matching will fluctuate within the accounting period but assume 'that the extent to which currency assets and liabilities are matched during an accounting period is reflected in the size of the net exchange difference debited or credited to the profit or loss account *or in some circumstances to reserve*'.

Paragraphs 28–30, dealing with 'roundabouts', were new and represented a reversal of long-standing Inland Revenue practice. It was argued that SOP will make roundabouting (in this specific sense) unnecessary. This is incorrect.

SOP confirms the fears of specialist professionals that cross-currency swap transactions often involve a long-term tax trap. This aspect is discussed in the next chapter.

Tax credit relief

The last type of tax fragmentation is the most complex, but still deserves close study. Foreign exchange fluctuations distort the calculation of credit relief. The United Kingdom, like the United States, grants credit relief for underlying tax (indirect credit) on dividends received by corporations from foreign corporations in which there is a 'substantial' interest, but there are two important respects in which the UK rules differ from those in the United States.

First, the UK credit is separately calculated with respect to each source of income. There is no concept of 'overall limitation' (or even 'per country limitation') and an excess credit from a high tax source cannot be offset against income from a low tax foreign source. *Second*, the relief extends to tax paid by a remote sub-subsidiary regardless of the length of the chain of intermediate companies provided that each company in the chain has the requisite 10 per cent interest in the next company. There are circumstances in which a smaller interest is acceptable, if this has resulted from the involuntary dilution of a 10 per cent plus interest. There has been some scope for 'mixing' sources of income through an intermediate holding company. These procedures are probably compatible with the 'controlled foreign corporation' provisions of the 1984 Finance Act, but in the atmosphere of uncertainty generated by *Furniss* v. *Dawson* such transactions need treating wth caution. The Inland Revenue has been making some difficulties with profits paid out of pre-merger profits when a subsidiary is involved in a merger in an overseas territory.

Credit relief is given unilaterally by Section 790 ICTA 1988 or by double tax agreements made under the general provisions of Section 788.

Where relief for underlying tax is available (generally on a 10 per cent plus holding, but smaller holdings sometimes qualify), Section 799 provides that 'the tax to be taken into account shall be so much of the foreign tax borne on the relevant profits of the body corporate paying the dividend as is properly attributable to the proportion of the relevant profits represented by the dividend'. This simple statement raises some questions particularly from the point of view of our subject. One such – the definition of the accounting period – is dealt with by sub-Section (2) which states:

The relevant profits are
(a) if the dividend is paid for a specified period, the profits of that period;
(b) if the dividend is not paid for a specified period, but is paid out of specified profits, those profits, and
(c) if the dividend is paid neither for a specified period nor out of specified profits, the profits of the last period for which the accounts of the body corporate to be made up which ended before the dividend became payable.

Are realised capital gains (including currency gains so treated by local law) to be taken into account? Where these are taxed at a lower rate or exempted from tax altogether, the effect of including them would be to reduce the tax charge as calculated and restrict the extent of credit relief. The decision in *Bowater Paper Corporation Limited* v. *Murgatroyd* was that the relevant profits are the profits available for distribution as shown by the accounts. The Inland Revenue's interpretation of this is that capital profits were available for distribution and therefore part of 'relevant profits', even though the gains were credited directly to capital reserve. The Inland Revenue says it will accept submissions, backed by evidence including relevant minutes of meetings, that dividends *were* paid out of specified profits, and it may be important to invoke this procedure (or to ensure that no suspect distribution takes place) in any period for which there are potentially distributable profits which have not borne a full measure of tax.

From July 1978 UK Inland Revenue practice changed on *unrealised* gains on currency realignments. These are now treated as *not* available for distribution unless the unrealised gains are in fact used for a dividend or credited to a general reserve. *Realised* gains *are* treated as available for distribution.

In calculating credit relief it is important to determine what denominator is to be used in the calculations. The company's accounts may well show the profits after tax as being profits *before* tax *less* tax actually payable and *less* deferred tax. However, only tax *paid* and not *deferred* tax can be taken into account for the *numerator* in the calculation. Should the *denominator* be gross profits, or accounting net profits plus tax actually payable? The UK Inland Revenue in practice (and in contrast with the US treatment) accept the latter view, which normally gives the more favourable answer for the taxpayer.

Another important question is to determine the rate of exchange at which foreign tax liabilities have to be converted in determining credit relief. In *Greig* v. *Ashton* (1956) 36 TC it was held that the appropriate rate of exchange to be applied to any foreign withholding tax is the rate of exchange ruling at the date the withholding tax was paid.

The question is less simple in the case of underlying tax, or subsidiaries of foreign subsidiaries, or for foreign tax borne by foreign branches of UK companies. Not all foreign tax liabilities are paid before or at the same time as the UK tax liability on that same income. Inland Revenue practice has often been helpful in accepting the same rate of exchange for foreign tax as the rate used to convert the foreign income. Conceptually the following five different exchange rates could apply; the strict legal position is not clear:

(a)   the rate on the date the foreign tax became payable;
(b)   the rate on the date the foreign tax was actually paid;
(c)   the year-end closing rate;
(d)   the average rate for the year;
(e)   the rate used in the company's accounts.

It is often worthwhile calculating the effect of the alternatives before finalising accounts or even before investment decisions. This can, if no more, indicate the gain from the best, and the downside risk of the worst, outcome.

UK Revenue Statement of Practice

Date: 17 February 1987

Exchange rate fluctuations

Introduction

1. The Revenue has been asked for its views on the treatment under current tax law of profits and losses arising from exchange rate fluctuations following the judgment of the House of Lords in Pattison v. Marine Midland Limited [1984] AC 362. This Statement of Practice attempts to deal with some aspects of this problem. It is put forward as a practical guide to facilitate the preparation and agreement of tax computations of *trading taxpayers*. The general rules it contains may need to be modified in the way in which they are applied in particular circumstances, for example, where the local currency (as defined in paragraph 4 below) of an overseas trade is a currency other than sterling.

Marine Midland: a summary

2. A UK resident bank carried on business in international commercial banking. For the purpose of making dollar loans and advances in the course of its banking business, it borrowed 15 million US dollars in the form of subordinated loan stock, redeemable in ten years. As a result of exchange rate fluctuations, the sterling value of the loans to its customers increased, but so also did the liability in sterling terms of the loan stock. Its general aim was to remain matched in each foreign currency and for the most part the dollar borrowings remained invested in dollar assets. After five years the loan stock was repaid out of existing dollar funds and at no time was any of the 15 million dollars converted into sterling.

3. Each year in the accounts, the monetary assets and liabilities denominated in a foreign currency were valued in sterling at the

exchange rate at the balance sheet date but to the extent that currency liabilities were matched by currency assets, no profit or loss was shown for accounts purposes. The Court of Appeal and the House of Lords held that in these circumstances no profit or loss arose for tax purposes. On the other hand the company brought into its profit and loss account any increase or decrease in the sterling value of excess dollars – i.e. to the extent that it was in an *un*matched position – and this had been accepted as a profit or loss for tax purposes. Lord Templeman said that this practice 'reflected the success or failure of the company in acquiring and holding excess dollars which could be converted into sterling'. He noted without disapproval the Revenue's acceptance of the practice and said it was '. . . not inconsistent with the company's submission that no profit or loss was attributable to dollar assets equal in dollar terms to dollar liabilities'.

Definitions

4.   In this Statement:

(a)   *translation* into sterling is regarded as the valuation of a foreign currency asset or liability in terms of sterling at a particular date;

(b)   *conversion* into sterling is the exchange of that asset or liability for sterling;

(c)   *local currency* is the currency of the primary economic environment in which the trade is carried on and net cash flows are generated.

The recognition of exchange differences: accounts treatment and tax consequences

5.   It has long been the general practice in the case of trading companies to bring exchange translation adjustments, other than those in respect of capital items, into account for tax purposes where they have similarly been brought into account in arriving at the accounting profit or loss. By contrast, it has been the practice in some circumstances – mainly in the case of certain overseas trading activities dealt with for accounts purposes on what is now generally referred to as the 'closing rate/net investment' basis – to translate the net profit or loss for tax purposes (the so-called 'profit

and loss account' basis). In the Revenue's view, the decision in Marine Midland does not make it necessary to abandon either of these practices, although it may of course affect the issue of what adjustments should be made for capital items (see below).

Translation and Conversion

6. Some commentators, including some of those who accepted the invitation to comment on the Provisional Statement of Practice, have suggested that judicial dicta in the Marine Midland case can be interpreted as indicating that translation profits or losses should be ignored for tax purposes on the grounds that they have not been realised or incurred, and that exchange profits and losses should be taken into account for tax only on conversion of the relevant currency into sterling.

The Revenue view

7. The Revenue does not subscribe to this view as a general proposition. The Marine Midland case was decided in the context of its own very special facts. In deciding whether account should be taken of translation profits and losses in calculating the annual profits of a business for tax purposes, it is necessary to consider the wider body of case law indicating that generally the calculation of annual profits and gains for tax purposes should start with a consideration of the accounts drawn up in accordance with the correct principles of commercial accounting.

8. In general, the Revenue view is that if the accounts of a business have been compiled in accordance with the Companies Acts and generally accepted accountancy principles and have taken account of *translation* profits and losses then those profits and losses should normally also be taken into account for tax purposes unless there are particular reasons relevant to the case in question, including whether they are in respect of capital items, for taking a different view.

9. It is clear too that any attempt to deal with exchange profits and losses only where there is *conversion* into sterling would in many cases present substantial problems of identification and follow-up for both taxpayers and their taxation advisers and the Revenue. In deciding what is generally accepted accountancy practice for this purpose regard will be had in particular to Statement of Standard Accounting Practice 20: Foreign Currency Translation (SSAP 20) and to published accounting practices of particular industries.

Application of conversion basis

10.   Where, exceptionally, a taxpayer considers that a different basis –
      including a 'conversion' basis – would result from the application
      of the relevant case law to his particular facts, it will be necessary
      for him to make out his case to the Inspector.

Capital and current liabilities

11.   In computing trading profits for tax purposes the question whether
      a loss or profit on exchange on a foreign currency loan is
      respectively an allowable deduction or assessable receipt is
      determined by the nature of the loan and whether it is to be
      properly regarded as a capital or current liability. The distinction
      between capital and current liabilities is based on principles well
      established in tax case law. The distinction is essentially between
      loans providing temporary financial accommodation and loans
      which can be said to add to the capital of the business. The answer
      in any particular case must turn on its facts and circumstances,
      which have to be considered in detail.

12.   The Court of Appeal and the House of Lords did not find it
      necessary to decide whether the borrowing by Marine Midland was
      a capital or current liability; the House of Lords indicated that it
      would have needed further evidence and argument to decide the
      issue. The Commissioners and the High Court, however, agreed
      with the Revenue's view that the borrowing was a capital liability.
      The Revenue remains of the view that the liability in question in
      the Marine Midland case was of a capital nature.

Matched assets and liabilities

13.   The Court of Appeal and House of Lords judgments in Marine
      Midland indicate that where foreign currency borrowings are
      matched by assets in the same currency, the capital or current
      nature of the borrowing will no longer be relevant in determining
      whether adjustments are to be made for the purposes of computing
      trading profits or losses for tax. In these circumstances exchange
      differences, whether profits or losses, arising on long-term
      borrowings are not to be distinguished and adjusted in computing
      trading profits or losses for tax.

Same currency

14.   Liabilities and assets of the same trader are regarded as matched in
      the way described in paragraph 13 above to the extent that foreign

currency denominated monetary assets are equalled by liabilities in the *same currency* and a translation adjustment on one would be cancelled out by a translation adjustment on the other. In general, therefore, where there are transactions in more than one foreign currency the question of matching must be considered separately for each currency (see paragraph 21 below). However, it is possible for assets and liabilities in different currencies to be regarded as effectively matched when hedging transactions, such as forward foreign currency contracts, are taken into account (see paragraphs 22–24 below).

Matching of capital assets in foreign currency with current liabilities

15. There may be circumstances where foreign currency *assets*, which for tax would be treated as capital assets, are matched with current liabilities in the same currency – the reverse of the situation in Marine Midland. This may arise in the case of certain monetary assets, e.g. where loans to subsidiary companies, which for tax would be treated as capital, are matched by short-term currency borrowings, which for tax may fall to be treated as current liabilities. The Revenue takes the view that the Marine Midland matching principle applies in such circumstances, with the result that again exchange differences arising on the assets or liabilities are not to be distinguished and adjusted. Cases where, exceptionally, non-monetary capital assets are treated as foreign currency assets for accounts purposes will need to be considered by reference to their particular facts.

Assets and liabilities not matched

16. In general, an adjustment is required to the tax computation of trading profits in respect of exchange differences that have been debited or credited to the profit and loss account in respect of capital items. It will be for the trader to demonstrate matching of capital currency liabilities, or assets, by reference to the position both during and at the end of the accounting period; and where such liabilities or assets are wholly or partly matched, to show the effect if any on the tax computation. Where exchange differences relating to assets or liabilities not matched, or not completely matched, are taken to reserve, the nature of the assets or liabilities will need to be considered to determine whether or not a tax adjustment is required.

17. However, in practice, the extent to which currency assets are matched with currency liabilities will in most cases fluctuate in the

course of an accounting period, so that it would be impracticable to measure and take account of such fluctuations on a day-by-day basis in determining what adjustment is required in the tax computation to the net exchange difference debited or credited in the profit and loss account. Instead the practice outlined in paragraphs 20 and 21 below may be adopted, provided it is applied on a consistent basis from year to year.

A practical approach

18. In essence the practice offered at paragraphs 20 and 21 below assumes that the extent to which currency assets and liabilities are matched during an accounting period is reflected in the size of the net exchange difference debited or credited to the Profit and Loss account or, in some circumstances, to reserve. The rules suggested for determining the adjustment to be made for tax purposes in respect of the exchange difference arising on capital assets or liabilities which are unmatched, or only partly matched, are based on the premise that capital liabilities are matched primarily with capital assets in the same currency. Any capital liabilities not matched by capital assets in the same currency are regarded as matched by current assets of the same currency only to the extent that the current assets exceed the current liabilities in that currency.

19. Where this practice is not adopted capital liabilities and assets will be regarded as matched only to the extent that this can be demonstrated by reference to the trader's currency assets and liabilities during the accounting period.

20. Under the practice referred to in paragraph 18 the first step will be to ascertain the aggregate of exchange differences, positive and negative, on capital assets and liabilities in the profit and loss account figure.

    a.   If there are no such differences then no tax adjustment is necessary.

Example 1

A company normally trading in sterling incurs a liability on a trade debt of $600,000 when $1.5 = £1. The liability is entered in the books in sterling at £400,000. By the accounting date sterling has fallen to $1.25 = £1, so that the sterling value of the liability has increased to £480,000. The exchange loss of £80,000 is charged to the Profit and Loss Account.

There were no capital exchange differences. No adjustment is required for tax purposes because the transactions are wholly on revenue account.

b. If the net exchange difference on capital items is a loss and the net difference in the profit and loss account is also a loss, the smaller of the two figures is the amount to be disallowed in the tax computation as relating to capital transactions.

Example 2

A trading company borrows $600,000 on long-term capital account when $1.5 = £1. It retains $150,000 as current assets and converts the balance of $450,000 to £300,000. The books will then show the following entries:

Capital loan ($600,000)	£400,000	Current assets ($150,000)	£100,000
		Cash on hand	300,000
	£400,000		£400,000

By the accounting date when sterling has fallen to $1.25 = £1 these become:

Capital loan ($600,000)	£480,000	Current assets ($150,000)	£120,000
		Cash on hand	300,000
		Exchange difference to Profit & Loss Account	60,000
	£480,000		£480,000

The exchange difference on capital account is £80,000 (£480,000 – £400,000) but the tax adjustment is limited to the amount charged to the Profit and Loss Account so that £60,000 is disallowed. This reflects the fact that $150,000 of the liability is matched with $150,000 assets. The whole of the exchange difference £60,000 is attributable to the excess currency liability on capital account, the value of which has increased from £300,000 to £360,000.

Example 3

A trading company incurs a liability by way of overdraft on current account of $300,000 and borrows $600,000 on capital account when $1.5 = £1. It retains $150,000 as current assets and converts the balance of $750,000 to £500,000. The books then show the following items:

Capital loan ($600,000)	£400,000	Current assets ($150,000)	£100,000
Overdraft on current account ($300,000)	200,000	Cash on hand	500,000
	£600,000		£600,000

By the accounting date sterling has fallen to $1.25 = £1 and the book entries are then:

Capital loan ($600,000)	£480,000	Current assets ($150,000)	£120,000
Overdraft on current account ($300,000)	240,000	Cash on hand	500,000
		Exchange difference to Profit & Loss Account	100,000
	£720,000		£720,000

The net exchange loss of £100,000 in the Profit and Loss Account is made up of £120,000 loss on the liabilities and £20,000 profit on the assets. The exchange difference on capital account is £80,000 (£480,000 = £400,000). This is less than the Profit and Loss Account figure so the £80,000 is disallowed for tax purposes. This reflects the matching of the $150,000 current assets with $150,000 of the current liabilities. The capital liability is therefore wholly unmatched.

c. If the net exchange difference on capital items is a profit and the net difference in the Profit and Loss Account is also a profit, then the smaller of the two figures is the amount to be deducted in the tax computation.

Example 4

A trading company incurs a liability by way of overdraft on current account of $150,000 and borrows a further £300,000 as a capital loan when $1.5 = £1. It converts the £300,000 to $450,000 and makes a loan (not in the course of trade) of

$600,000 to an associated company. The books show the following entries at this point:

Overdraft on current		Capital assets	£400,000
account ($150,000)	£100,000	($600,000)	
Capital loan	300,000		
	£400,000		£400,000

By the accounting date sterling has fallen to $1.25 = £1 and the book entries are as follows:

Overdraft on current		Capital assets	£480,000
account ($150,000)	£120,000	($600,000)	
Capital loan	300,000		
Exchange difference to			
Profit & Loss Account	60,000		
	£480,000		£480,000

The net exchange profit of £60,000 in the Profit and Loss Account comprises £80,000 profit on the assets and £20,000 loss on the liability. The net capital exchange difference is £80,000 (£480,000 – £400,000) but the adjustment for tax purposes is limited to the figure in the Profit and Loss Account of £60,000. This reflects the fact that $150,000 of the assets are matched with the dollar liability. The non-taxable exchange profit is attributable to the excess capital assets, whose sterling value changed from £300,000 to £360,000.

d. Where the net exchange difference on capital items produces a loss but the net difference in the Profit and Loss Account is a credit entry, then no tax adjustment is required. Similarly no adjustment is necessary where there is a profit in respect of exchange differences on capital items but a net loss on exchange is debited to the Profit and Loss Account.

Example 5

A trading company borrows $900,000 on capital account and raises a further sterling loan of £200,000. It converts the £200,000 to $300,000 and makes a loan (not in the course of trade) of $750,000 to an associated company. At this time $1.5 = £1. The balance of $450,000 is retained as a current asset. The books show the following entries at this point:

Capital loan ($900,000)	£600,000	Capital assets ($750,000)	£500,000
Capital loan	200,000	Current assets ($450,000)	300,000
	£800,000		£800,000

By the accounting date the exchange rate alters to $1.25 = £1 and the book entries become:

Capital loan ($900,000)	£720,000	Capital assets ($750,000)	£600,000
Capital loan	200,000	Current assets ($450,000)	360,000
Exchange difference to Profit & Loss Account	40,000		
	£960,000		£960,000

The Profit and Loss Account entry for the net exchange profit of £40,000 is made up of £160,000 profit on the assets and £120,000 loss on the liability. The net capital exchange difference is a debit of £20,000, i.e. (£720,000 – £600,000) – (£600,000 – £500,000) but the Profit and Loss Account shows a net credit of £40,000. No adjustment is therefore required for tax purposes. This reflects the matching of the net capital liability of $150,000 with part of the dollar current assets. The taxable exchange profit of £40,000 is attributable to the balance of the dollar current assets, whose value increased from £200,000 to £240,000.

e. It follows that normally the amount of any tax adjustment is limited in each case to the credit or debit for net exchange differences in the Profit and Loss Account.

More than one currency

21. Where there are transactions in more than one currency, the same principles will apply but each currency must be considered separately. In such circumstances the exchange difference in the profit and loss account is the aggregate of the net exchange profits and losses arising in the various currencies and the tax computation adjustment is determined by comparing the aggregate exchange difference on capital assets and liabilities in a particular currency with the exchange difference for that currency in the profit and loss figure (but see paragraphs 22–24 below where hedging transactions are involved).

Example 6

A trading company borrows $900,000 on long-term capital account and DM300,000 on overdraft when £1 = $1.5 = DM3.0. It makes a loan of $600,000 to an associated company (not in the course of trade) and converts $300,000 into DM600,000. It loans DM500,000 to another associated company (not in the course of trade) and retains the balance of DM400,000 as a current asset. The books show the following entries:

Capital loan ($900,000)	£600,000	Capital assets ($600,000)	£400,000
Overdraft (DM300,000)	100,000	Capital assets (DM500,000)	167,000
		Current assets (DM400,000)	133,000
	£700,000		£700,000

By the accounting date sterling has fallen to £1 = $1.20 = DM2.5 and the book entries are as follows:

Capital loan ($900,000)	£750,000	Capital assets ($600,000)	£500,000
Overdraft (DM300,000)	120,000	Capital assets (DM500,000)	200,000
		Current assets (DM400,000)	160,000
		Exchange difference to Profit & Loss Account	10,000
	£870,000		£870,000

The net exchange difference of £10,000 comprises £50,000 loss on the Dollar assets and liabilities offset by £40,000 profit on the Deutschmark assets and liabilities. The Dollar exchange loss is entirely on capital account and should be added back to the tax computation. The Deutschmark exchange difference comprises £60,000 profit on the assets and £20,000 loss on the liability. The net capital exchange difference on Deutschmark assets and liabilities is a profit of £33,000, i.e. (£200,000 – £167,000) so the adjustment for tax purposes is limited to £33,000. This reflects the fact that the overdraft is matched with Deutschmark current assets and the Deutschmark capital assets are unmatched.

Thus the overall adjustment to the tax computation is an addition of £17,000, i.e. (£50,000–£33,000).

Hedging transactions

22. In considering whether a trader is matched in a particular currency, *forward exchange contracts* and *currency futures* entered into for hedging purposes may be taken into account, provided the hedging is reflected in the accounts on a consistent basis from year to year and in accordance with accepted accounting practice. For example, where a trading transaction is covered by a related or matching forward contract, under SSAP 20 the transaction may be translated using the rate of exchange specified in the forward contract. Alternatively, the forward contracts open at the balance sheet date may be shown as assets or liabilities, valued on a 'mark to market' basis or by reference to the difference between the contracted forward exchange rates and the spot rate on the balance sheet date.

23. Where a trader enters into a *currency swap agreement* to exchange borrowed currency for an equivalent amount of another currency (including sterling for a fixed period, the two transactions in the original currency should be treated as matched, so that the underlying liability in the first currency is effectively converted into a liability in the second currency for the duration of the swap. If, when the swap is terminated, the currencies are swapped back at the spot rate of exchange prevailing at the commencement of the swap there will be for Case I purposes no exchange loss or profit in terms of the original currency (but the capital gains consequences of unwinding the swap will need to be taken into account).

24. In the Revenue's view, where currency assets or liabilities are hedged by transactions in *currency options* no matching can be said to have taken place and such transactions are unaffected by the Marine Midland decision.

Example 7: Hedging

The facts are those of example 3 above in the subsequent accounting period at the start of which the book entries are:

Capital loan ($600,000)	£480,000	Current assets ($150,000)	£120,000
Overdraft on current account ($300,000)	240,000	Cash on hand	500,000
		Exchange difference b/f	100,000
	£720,000		£720,000

Three months from the end of the accounting period (there having been no transactions in the meantime affecting the assets and liabilities referred to in the example), when $1.18 = £1, the company enters a forward contract to purchase $600,000 at $1.20 = £1 in six months' time, to hedge the capital loan which is repayable on the date the forward contract matures. By the accounting date, when $1.0 = £1 the books show either:

Capital loan ($600,000)*	£500,000	Current assets ($150,000)	£150,000
Overdraft on current account ($300,000)	300,000	Cash on hand	500,000
		Exchange difference b/f	100,000
		Exchange difference to Profit and Loss Account	50,000
	£800,000		£800,000

*translated at forward rate $1.20 = £1

or:

Capital loan ($600,000)	£600,000	Current assets ($150,000)	£150,000
Overdraft on current account ($300,000)	300,000	Cash on hand	500,000
		Forward contract	100,000
		Exchange difference b/f	100,000
		Exchange difference to Profit and Loss Account	50,000
	£900,000		£900,000

Because the forward contract specifically hedges the capital loan the net exchange loss on capital items on either basis is £20,000 (£500,000–£480,000; or £600,000–£480,000 less £100,000 profit on forward contract). Because this is less than the overall exchange loss of £50,000, the capital loss of £20,000 is disallowed for tax purposes.

Overseas branches and trades

25. Where a trade carried on wholly abroad, or an overseas branch of a trade, has a local currency other than sterling, accounts will

normally be drawn up in the local foreign currency and translated into sterling using the 'net investment/closing rate' method (SSAP 20 paragraphs 25 and 46). In such circumstances the Revenue will accept computations based on:

a) accounts prepared in the local currency, with the adjusted profit before capital allowances etc. translated into sterling at either the average or the closing exchange rate for the accounting period; or

b) the sterling equivalent of accounts prepared in local currency, translated into sterling using the 'net investment/closing rate' method; or

c) sterling accounts produced by the 'temporal method' described in paragraphs 4 to 12 of SSAP 20;

but whichever method is adopted must be applied consistently from year to year. The method adopted in a particular case will affect only the determination of the Case I profit adjusted for non-taxable and non-allowable items, but before capital allowances and stock relief are taken into account. Capital allowances and other statutory reliefs and charges will be calculated in sterling in the same way under either approach.

26. The principles outlined in this Statement of Practice should be applied in considering to what extent an adjustment for tax purposes should be made to the profit figure to be translated into sterling in respect of an exchange difference in the local foreign currency accounts.

Assets held on the 'realisation' basis

27. Some financial concerns hold assets, the profits on the disposal of which are treated for tax purposes as receipts of their trade but which are not stock in trade. Such profits are assessable only when the assets are disposed of (the 'realisation' basis). Nevertheless it may be the practice for accounting purposes to revalue the assets to reflect exchange rate fluctuations. Where the resulting exchange differences are either taken to Profit and Loss Account or set off against exchange differences on liabilities as part of the matching process, with the result that the profits or losses on realisation are recognised for accounts purposes effectively net of exchange differences, the Revenue will normally be prepared to follow the accounts treatment for tax, provided that this is applied consistently. The following example shows how this works. The treat-

ment which is appropriate in any particular case will need to be agreed with the Inspector by reference to all the relevant circumstances.

Example 8

A financial concern borrows $600,000 on capital account and raises a further sterling loan of £200,000. It converts the £200,000 to $300,000 and buys financial assets (realisation basis) for $900,000. At this time $1.5 = £1. The books then show the following entries:

Capital loan ($600,000)	£400,000	Cost of financial assets ($900,000)	£600,000
Capital loan	200,000		
	£600,000		£600,000

At the accounting date the rate of exchange is $1.25 = £1 so the entries are as follows:

Capital loan ($600,000)	£480,000	Financial assets ($900,000)	£720,000
Capital loan	200,000		
Exchange difference to Profit & Loss Account	40,000		
	£720,000		£720,000

Since the capital exchange difference is a debit of £80,000 (£480,000–£400,000) and there is a net loss of £40,000 overall, no tax adjustment to the £40,000 is needed. At the end of the next accounting period the rate of exchange has altered to $1.2 = £1 and the assets are sold so the entries become:

Capital loan ($600,000)	£500,000	Cash proceeds of sale of financial assets ($1,200,000)	£1,000,000
Capital loan	200,000		
Exchange difference for Year 2 to Profit & Loss Account £10,000			
Exchange difference for Year 1 brought forward 40,000			
*Profit on realisation of assets 250,000	300,000		
	£1,000,000		£1,000,000

*Sale proceeds $1.2 m. less cost $0.9 m. giving a profit on realisation of $0.3 m. or (at $1.2 =£1) £250,000. The exchange profit from holding the $900,000 assets while the exchange rate moved from $1.5 = £1 to $1.2 = £1 has already been taken into account in the exchange differences.

The capital exchange difference is a loss on the loan of £20,000 (£500,000–£480,000) but there is a profit of £30,000 in respect of current assets, i.e. £750,000 ($900,000 at $1.2 = £1) – £720,000. Thus, there is no adjustment to the figure in the Profit and Loss Account for the exchange difference.

Roundabout loan arrangements

28. In exchanges of views with certain representative bodies following the decision of the House of Lords in *W. T. Ramsay Ltd* v. *CIR, [1982]* AC 300, the Revenue indicated that they would not regard that decision as applying to arrangements involving long-term borrowing in foreign currency by banks and other concerns with related short-term loan facilities (often described as exchange roundabouts). This view was subject to reconsideration when the Marine Midland case was final.

29. Since it is accepted that Marine Midland leads to the conclusion that no Case I tax adjustment arises where currency assets and liabilities are matched (see paragraph 13 above) it seems much less likely that roundabout arrangements will be used in matched situations. Where roundabouts are employed this is likely to be in respect of unmatched or partly matched transactions and in the Revenue's view these loan arrangements may, applying the *Ramsay* principle, fall to be treated for tax purposes by reference to their composite effect. Whether or not a contention based on these decisions is invoked will depend on the facts of particular cases.

30. The Revenue regard this amended view as applying to roundabout arrangements entered into and to existing arrangements where they are re-negotiated after the date of this statement.

Non-trading companies

31. The Marine Midland decision and the practice outlined above have no application outside the trading context. In non-trading companies the capital gains tax rules will apply to the acquisition and disposal of foreign currency chargeable assets (except where the transactions give rise to profits assessable under Case VI of

Schedule D) and exchange fluctuations will generally have no tax consequences outside the capital gains field.

Groups of companies

32. The principles and working rules outlined in this Statement of Practice apply only to individual trading companies and are not applicable to a group of companies seen as a whole, or in a way which recognises 'matching' between assets and liabilities of different companies in a group.

Capital gains

33. The decision in *Bentley* v. *Pike*, 53 TC 590, established that a gain or loss on an asset should be computed by comparing the sterling value at the date of sale of the sale consideration with the sterling value at the date of acquisition of the acquisition cost. The principle is not affected by the Marine Midland decision which is concerned only with the computation of trading profits.

Assessments open for earlier years

34. The practice set out in this statement will normally be applicable to years of assessment/accounting periods for which the assessments have not become final and conclusive. Where, however, it involves a change from a previously agreed basis, including the practice described in the Provisional Statement of Practice SP3/85 (Provisional), the transitional arrangements will depend on the facts of the case, and will be subject to negotiation with the Inspector.

(The Inland Revenue Statement of Practice reproduced in this appendix is Crown Copyright and is reproduced with the permission of the Controller of Her Majesty's Stationery Office.)

Report to the representative bodies from the working group on the taxation of exchange rate fluctuations: proposals for legislative change

Terms of reference

1. At a meeting on 27 February 1987 the nine representative bodies listed below were asked to explore the extent to which they could reach agreement on proposals to change the law on the tax treatment of foreign exchange differences.

2. This report represents a consensus reached by a working group of nine, each nominated by one of the representative bodies. The representative bodies have received and accepted the report and support its recommendations. The members of the working group were:

A. E. Willingale (Chairman)	Confederation of British Industry
J. E. Brewster	Association of British Insurers
J. F. Chown	Association of Corporate Treasurers
P. R. Tipping	British Bankers' Association
R. J. G. White	Institute of Chartered Accountants in England and Wales
W. K. Evans	Institute of Directors
J. Clark	Institute of Taxation
T. L. Halpern	International Chamber of Commerce
M. Mathews	The Law Society
S. M. Thornhill (Secretary)	British Bankers' Association

Minimalist approach

3. The working group strongly recommend that urgent action be taken to deal with the serious anomaly that 'capital' gains and losses on foreign currency borrowings are neither taxed nor relieved. Differing views as to the right approach technically have been subordinated to the need for an agreed solution. In

accordance with the terms of reference, we examined, but rejected, several wider-ranging approaches to the question and, in particular, do not recommend removing the distinction between 'capital gains' and Case I. Specifically, permanent investment denominated in a foreign currency would continue to be treated as chargeable assets. We have tried to keep the number of elections to the minimum: some remain in paragraphs 13, 16, and 21.

4. It is accepted that any new legislation must be symmetrical, i.e. gains on borrowings must be taxed on the same basis as losses on borrowings are relieved. It would also have to take account of, and give parity of treatment to, the differing requirements of investment holding companies, commercial trading companies, financial trading companies and close companies. We have not considered the position of sole traders and partnerships.

Matching

5. Matching, as an overall concept, seems to be of little interest to many taxpayers. The working group therefore recommends that, in general, gains and losses on foreign currency borrowings should be taxed or relieved without regard to the nature and tax treatment of the assets financed.

6. However, as outlined later (see paragraphs 19–21) there may be a significant problem for what we believe will be a small number of taxpayers: those for whom a currency borrowing is economically matched by that taxpayer with a foreign currency asset, which need not be a monetary asset. We therefore recommend that there should be an election for matching in prescribed circumstances.

Capital gains or Case I

7. We have considered whether gains and losses on borrowings should be brought exclusively within the scope of capital gains tax legislation. This was rejected, and would probably have been rejected even without the Budget proposal to bring the rates into line.

8. We also considered whether it was practicable to assimilate foreign exchange gains and losses on borrowings to interest. The proposal had little support. Specifically, we considered and rejected the suggestion that we could amend Section 130(f) to permit exchange losses on loans denominated in a currency other than sterling to be deducted as if they were interest. The complex special rules

governing interest, particularly the distinction between short and long interest, could not, in our view, be adapted without undue complexity.

9. We therefore recommend that, in general, foreign currency gains and losses arising in respect of borrowings should be taxed or relieved under the provisions of Case I of Schedule D, subject to the limited exceptions set out in paragraph 17.

10. Exceptionally, as outlined in paragraph 21, where a company has borrowed currency to fund fixed assets whose value is denominated in foreign currency, there may be an election for matching foreign exchange profits or losses on borrowings to be converted to chargeable gains.

Accruals or realisation?

11. We have considered whether gains and losses should be taxed on an accruals or a realisation basis. There are strong practical arguments against taxing unrealised profits on capital assets, and these arguments would be equally valid against a proposal to tax the notional fall in value of a long-term borrowing in a 'weak' currency.

12. It is accepted that a tax imposed on a 'realisation' basis may give the taxpayer some scope for precipitating losses while running unrealised profits forward into a future period.

13. We recommend that gains and losses on borrowings should, in general, be taxed on a realisation basis. We accept that there will have to be exceptions to protect both the Revenue and the taxpayer and believe that taxpayers should have the right to elect for an accrual basis. We also recognise that the definition of what does, or does not, constitute a realisation will need to be drafted carefully.

Transitional provisions

14. The working group accepts, reluctantly, that it is unrealistic to expect more than limited relief for the past. We therefore recommend that all existing borrowings should be translated at the exchange rate ruling on the effective date of the new legislation. On a realisation, or other taxable event, the gain or loss would be calculated with respect to this exchange rate. Pre-'D-day' gains or losses would remain as 'nothings' in accordance with prior law.

15. This provision, strictly applied, could cause hardship to taxpayers who might subsequently be taxed on a post-'D-day' gain where there was an overall loss. Some transitional relief will be required. Several possibilities were considered, but our preferred solution is set out in paragraph 16.

16. We recommend that the relief could take the form of a limited 'kink' provision to avoid tax being levied on a notional gain in excess of a real economic gain. Companies would be able to elect for this relief on an 'overall group' rather than a 'loan-by-loan' basis and would have to accept that the election applied equally to restrict, to real economic loss, any losses arising only be reference to the exchange rate applicable on the appointed day.

Companies not taxed as trading companies

17. Since there can be no adjustments to an existing Case I computation, and Case VI assessments are unacceptable to many groups of taxpayers, special consideration will need to be given to such categories as investment, investment holding and life assurance companies. Alternative solutions exist, such as treating foreign exchange losses as additional management expenses, and gains (over otherwise allowable management expenses) as a species of taxable income, perhaps Case I. Another possibility is to allow such companies to fall entirely within the capital gains structure. The answer is not altogether clear at present, but is capable of resolution within the framework of the general solution finally adopted on exchange gains and losses.

Close companies

18. Although close companies are in general no longer subject to apportionment on trading income, there are penalties on non-trading close companies which receive investment or Case VI income. Furthermore Paragraph 3A, Schedule 16, Finance Act 1972 provides that interest paid by a close company will be apportioned unless one of the exclusions of sub-paragraph 3A(2) applies. Case VI income does not qualify for exclusion under 3A(2)(c)(ii). It is particularly important for close companies to ensure that any reliefs or assessments do not have adverse effects on the computation of apportionment either of income or of interest expense.

Election for matching

19. One key problem is that, whether an accrual or a realisation basis is adopted, there will be anomalies affecting any company that borrows, say, dollars to finance a dollar fixed asset which is then held as a permanent investment. If the dollar was strong the company might be able to claim relief on the loss on the liability while the corresponding gain on the asset is postponed indefinitely. Conversely, if the dollar (or other currency borrowed) was weak over an accounting period, the taxpayer would risk having a currently taxable profit which could not be offset, for tax purposes, against an unrealised loss. Unless there are special provisions, the tax charge could be distorted from one year to another.

20. We recognise that the Inland Revenue will want even-handed treatment in connection with any approach which looks forward. In particular we are not seeking to produce an option for the taxpayer which gives any ability to obtain a systematic advantage. We do want to enable taxpayers to elect for an administratively simple procedure so that they can find a practical solution to their own foreign exchange exposure problems in a manner which achieves certainty and consistency for both the taxpayer and the Revenue.

21. We therefore recommend that there should be provisions enabling a company to designate borrowings in a foreign currency as qualifying for special treatment because the company regards these borrowings as being associated with capital assets whose value is determined by reference to that currency. Where this irrevocable election was in force, any gains or losses on the borrowing would be 'ring-fenced'. No tax would be levied on any gain or loss either on an accruals basis, or on what would otherwise be a realisation on reorganising or rolling over the borrowing, until such time as the asset was disposed of. On disposal of the asset the same tax treatment would be accorded to the gain or loss realised or accrued up to that date on the borrowing as would be applicable to the asset in respect of which the election is made.

Summary of recommendations

22. a) Urgent action should be taken to enable capital gains and losses on foreign currency borrowings to be taxed or relieved whilst leaving the distinction between capital gains and Case I.

   b) Any new legislation should allow parity of treatment between different groups of taxpayers and must be symmetrical in its treatment of gains and losses.

c) In general, gains and losses on foreign currency borrowings should be taxed or relieved without regard to the nature and tax treatment of the assets financed. However, there should be provisions enabling matching in prescribed circumstances.

d) Normally, foreign currency gains and losses arising in respect of borrowings should be taxed or relieved under the provisions of Case I of Schedule D on a realisation basis. However, special consideration will need to be given to companies not taxed as trading companies.

e) All existing borrowing should be translated at the exchange rate ruling on the effective date of the new legislation. Transitional provisions would be required.

12

Financial instruments

The general problem

Exchange rates risks can be hedged, or deliberate foreign exchange speculation undertaken, in many different ways. Chapter 11 dealt with the general tax problems arising from changes in the actual value of currency assets and liabilities.

Some years ago, the commodity markets began offering futures and, a little later, option contracts in foreign currencies. More recently, a wide range of specially created 'financial products' have been invented. These have made it much easier for the treasurer to analyse and hedge his exposures; unfortunately, the tax aspects have not always been properly understood. The problems of tax fragmentation discussed in Chapter 11 have been compounded by these new instruments. It is impossible to deal rationally with their tax treatment until the general anomalies have been removed.

Interest rate risk

Similar instruments have been developed for interest rate risk, and these have created similar problems. Generally, a non-financial trading company which simply borrows money for the purpose of its business will incur interest expense, which will be deductible in computing its profits. In the modern world, the 'cost of money' in terms of economics or business common sense has to be calculated after adding or subtracting swap fees, option premiums, compensatory payments under forward rate agreements or caps, and differences in the settlement of futures transactions. These payments arise from treasury transactions designed to adjust the maturity structure of debt, to transfer the risk of unanticipated interest rate movements, or to some combination of both.

With a 'comparison of net worth'-type tax system all these payments and receipts would simply be brought into the general tax computation. The problem, in the United Kingdom, arises from historic distinctions between 'revenue' and 'capital' transactions, between 'trading' and 'investment' companies, and between 'short interest' 'annual interest', and 'annual payments which are not interest'. The attempt to apply these categories to modern financial techniques can produce perverse and unacceptable (or, with foresight, profitable) results.

The financial techniques discussed in this chapter divide into two groups. The first, interest rate futures, swaps and forward rate agreements (FRAs), enable the treasurer to pre-detemine, or amend, his maturity structure within existing market conditions. The second, interest rate options and their 'package' variants, such as caps and collars, enable him to protect himself, at a price, from adverse changes in interest rates. In economic terms, all relevant costs should be deductible. Although it may be impossible always to agree a clear border-line between 'capital' and 'revenue', at least the category of 'nothings' should surely disappear.

Futures

The simplest and oldest form of risk management instrument is the futures contract. In the currency market this is now an alternative to very much older 'forward' markets. Interest rate futures offered new risk management facilities, which now also have parallels in the over-the-counter bank market. A company which expects to have to raise a bond issue in six months' time can in effect lock in the rate by buying whatever futures contract is a suitable proxy for its requirements. If interest rates rise, the profit on the contract will compensate for the extra cost. If they fall, there will be a loss on the contract, offset by cheaper than expected borrowings.

From 6 April 1985, profits from futures dealings, and gains from *traded* options and futures, are taxed either on a Case I basis as normal trading income, or as capital gains. Previously such gains were caught under Case VI of Schedule D: 'Annual profits or gains not falling under any other Case of Schedule A, B, C or E'. Where this applied, profits were taxable at full rates, but losses were quarantined and not available for offset. Against this there is a new and more general source of uncertainty; the Inland Revenue might use the *Furniss* v. *Dawson* principle to *deem* certain gains to be taxable, without the taxpayer being able to play it backwards to claim his losses.

Although the 'heads I lose, tails the Inland Revenue wins' trap of Case VI is (in this context) no more, there remain uncertainties as to whether a particular transaction is on capital, or revenue account. These are compounded by the increasing sophistication of hedging techniques.

Options

If futures are the simplest means of locking in a price, options are the classic method of protecting, for a price, against uncertainty over what that price will be. The Case VI problem, discussed under 'futures', above, seriously limited their commercial use until 1985. There has been another trap. When capital gains tax was introduced in 1965 options were treated as 'wasting assets'; the allowable cost of options *sold* (not exercised) before the expiration date was deemed to waste away on a straight-line basis over the life of the option. This meant that disposal of such an option during its life at a commercial *loss* could actually give rise to a chargeable capital *gain*, and that no relief was available on abandonment on expiry. This was a notorious example of tax fragmentation deliberately imposed.

The rules were somewhat modified, initially by the 1980 Finance Act. This provided that where an option lapsed, the tax treatment depended on whether or not the option was or was not a 'quoted option' or a 'traded option' to which 'wasting asset' treatment did not apply. Initially, a 'traded option' was one quoted on a recognised stock exchange (e.g. Philadelphia Stock Exchange, London Stock Exchange) or on LIFFE. The concession was extended, by Inland Revenue order dated 19 December 1986, to the Chicago Mercantile Exchange the Philadelphia Board of Trade and the New York Mercantile Exchange.

Section 81 Finance (No. 2) Act 1987 removed the distinction between traded and over-the-counter options both for 'Case VI' and 'wasting asset' purposes. It substituted the concept of 'qualifying options'. The terminology of the Section was designed to coincide with definitions in the Financial Services Act (FSA). The Section in fact only came into force, with the FSA, on 29 April 1988.

Options used to protect a company from forex exposure on trading activities will normally themselves be taxed as trading transactions. The computations should be straightforward. Option premiums will be deductible and gains on exercise are taxable. What if the company can show that the option was used to hedge a capital transaction, e.g. purchase of a fixed asset? Will the Inland Revenue accept that capital gains treatment is available? What if a currency option is initially purchased to hedge a capital transaction, which is aborted? There are other border-line questions paralleling those relating to futures and indeed to currency hedging generally.

Capital v. revenue

This is the only major point of difficulty remaining on straightforward futures and options. It was dealt with in the Inland Revenue's Statement of Practice on foreign currency gains and losses. Futures will normally be matched but options will not. Paragraph 24, states:

In the Revenue's view, where currency assets or liabilities are hedged by transaction in *currency options* no matching can be said to have taken place and such transactions are unaffected by the Marine Midland decision.

The point was considered in more detail in a Draft Statement of Practice by the Inland Revenue on the *Tax Treatment of Transactions in Financial Futures and Options* published 13 April 1988, the text of which is appended to this chapter. Generally this Draft adopts the concept of 'matching' and recognises that the economic effect of a hedge is not, and the tax treatment should not be 'dependent upon the form of the eventual disposition of the position'.

The example in Paragraph 8 deals with cases where the taxpayer would normally wish the hedge to be treated as giving rise to capital gains or losses and is generally satisfactory for this purpose. However, it will be recognised that taxpayers and the Inland Revenue will have similar but opposite incentives to seek to characterise transactions with reference to whether they have, after the event, resulted in a gain or a loss. This can produce uncertainty and these uncertainties can be greater in the kind of transaction considered in Paragraph 10 where 'the underlying transaction or motive falls away'. In these cases it does seem that for the avoidance of doubt, we should consider giving the taxpayer the right, or possibly the obligation, to designate in advance whether a transaction is to be treated as on capital or on trading account.

Paragraph 9 is the most difficult. From the point of a view of a Treasurer, all costs included in borrowing money should normally be regarded as a trading expense. This will apply in the case of options and losses on futures designed to lock in an interest rate. We would regard the type of transaction given in the first example of Paragraph 9 as being appropriate to trading treatment. Against this, it will be argued that the short-term hedging cost can give rise to a long-term benefit where it enables a long-term issue to be fixed at a lower interest rate. It may be preferable to ensure that all costs associated with, or in anticipation of, borrowing are afforded Case I treatment.

Swaps

Most of the other instruments with which we are concerned can be reduced analytically to a combination of 'futures' and 'options' contracts. However, in addition to the problems discussed above, there are several types of payment associated with these instruments which do not enjoy symmetrical, consistent and rational tax treatment. Swaps are a classic case where tax law does not provide a solution in accord with common sense and economic reality.

Is there a risk that companies are walking into a tax trap on the scale of the 'foreign currency borrowing' trap of the 1970s? Certainly, cross-currency swaps have been aggressively sold by banks to corporate treasurers, but have always worried international tax specialists. An examination of the Inland Revenue's attitude, as set out in SOP, confirms these fears. Treasurers must check out their whole currency exposure for tax efficiency before entering into any such transaction. Banks often claim that a particular 'window' will only be open for a day or two. The way forward is surely to take professional advice in advance of the opportunity, and to be ready for it when it comes. The trap comes at the end – perhaps five or ten years out. British companies who are already a party to swaps should take advice immediately, before disaster actually hits.

The overall lesson is clear. Foreign currency transactions in general, and swaps in particular, involve company treasurers in a tax minefield. It is essential that any transaction is analysed within or on behalf of the company by a treasury analyst who has some understanding of tax *and* of a tax adviser who understands modern financial instruments. This raises another problem. There are two separate approaches to analysing financial problems. Auditors use, and have to use, 'generally accepted accountancy principles'. Unfortunately, these are based on the assumption that 'a pound is a pound is a pound' and have proved difficult to adapt to the real world where a pound in 1985 can be a very different animal from a pound in 1975. The accountancy profession, collectively, has found it difficult to adapt to the realities of inflation and currency fluctuation and many practitioners are still not even really at ease with the idea that money due in a year's time is worth less than money due today. American companies, in particular, fell into currency planning traps because of the notorious innumeracy of the now superceded FAS 8.

The alternative approach, used by financial analysts, based on 'net present value' is often dismissed by 'practical men of business' as theoretical mumbo jumbo churned out by business school professors. It is, however, the only sensible and internally consistent way of approaching modern financial instruments and, indeed, financial decision making (as opposed to financial reporting) generally.

For instance most published examples on swaps, ignore the shape of the yield curve and assume that 'the' rate of interest ruling a particular currency is (say) 10 per cent. This is not typically true and it is certainly not true at the end of 1988 when we have the interesting phenomenon of the dollar yield curve sloping in one direction and the sterling yield curve sloping in the other. In one case in our experience a bank mispriced the terms on which a swap could be unwound by some £500,000 – in favour of our client. It is always worth working out the arithmetic very carefully indeed.

Swap fees

Swap fees are not treated as 'interest', but *are* 'annual payments' made 'not out of profits or gains brought into charge to income tax (Section 350 ICTA 1988, previously Section 53 ICTA 1970). In principle, where this applies the paying company would have to deduct 25 per cent withholding tax. The payment would then be deductible from taxable profits (Section 233 ICTA 1988, previously Section 248 ICTA 1970). The (UK resident) recipient would be liable to tax as income under Case III Schedule D, but would be able to credit the withholding tax against tax otherwise due, or, if appropriate, claim a refund. There would then be a 'timing' disadvantage which would have to be costed into the overall deal.

The swap fee is not an 'annual payment' if it constitutes a normal trading receipt in the hands of the recipient. The Inland Revenue accepts that the fee may be paid gross where it is paid to a UK bank (or approved UK branch of a foreign bank) in the ordinary course of the bank's business. Similarly, fees paid by such a bank in the ordinary course of its business may be paid gross. The test of 'pure income profit' was discussed in *Re Hamburg, Gorniskey* v. *Hamburg* (38TC 588). See also *Moss Empires Ltd* v. *CIR* (21TC 264).

Where swap fees are eligible to be paid gross to a bank, then a UK trading company may claim them as a trading expense and a UK investment company (defined in Section 130 ICTA 1988, previously Section 304(5) ICTA 1970) may claim them as a charge on income under Section 233 ICTA 1988 (previously Section 248 ICTA 1970).

Section 74(b) ICTA 1988 (previously Section 130(f) ICTA 1970) prohibited a deduction on Case I of Schedule D in respect of 'any capital withdrawn from or any sum employed in or intended to be employed as capital in the trade profession or vocation that says that this paragraph shall not be treated as disallowing the deduction of any interest'. It appears to follow that if a bank enters into a swap as principal as part of an operation designed to provide long-term funding, a deduction may be disallowed and the bank's only remedy will be a charge against income under Section 233 ICTA 1988.

Banks, including *bona fide* branches of foreign banks, can pay swap fees free of withholding tax to foreigners as well as UK residents, subject to the procedures described above. Otherwise, withholding tax can be a real burden on the transaction when one of the parties is resident outside the United Kingdom. In some cases, but not in most, the recipient may be able to credit the withholding tax against his own domestic tax liability. Even then, there is likely to be a 'timing' disadvantage. If the other party is resident in a treaty country, the relevant treaty article will not be the interest article. There is no underlying loan behind the swap fee which is not treated as interest. It will be necessary to consider the treaty article on 'other profits' or possibly the 'business profits' article. We understand that this will normally be the case in practice, subject to the usual 'effectively connected with a permanent establishment' proviso.

We understand that the UK Inland Revenue does not accept that swap arrangement fees meet the 'wholly and exclusively' test of Section 74(a) ICTA 1988 (previously Section 130(a) ICTA 1970). UK companies claiming a tax deduction under that head will meet firm resistance – justifiable or not. The provision in Section 77 ICTA 1988 (previously Section 38 Finance Act 1980) allowing a tax deduction for the incidental costs of raising loan finance is of no help, as no loan has been obtained. Furthermore, Section 77(7)(a) specifically denies relief 'for any sum paid in consequences of, for obtaining protection against losses resulting from the changes in the rate of exchange between different currencies'.

Generally, therefore, swap transactions *require* the intermediation of a bank if tax penalties are to be avoided. This is unsatisfactory from a public policy point of view.

The swap trap

The real problem comes on the maturity of the swap. Take a hypothetical, but highly probable, example, which was discussed with the Inland Revenue during consultations on the Statement of Practice.

Company A is a UK corporation which needs to raise sterling funds for UK trading operations. A bank suggested that it can achieve a saving in interest by borrowing $150 million on a five-year fixed coupon bond and swapping the proceeds ($150 million) with 'Bank' in exchange for £100 million (the spot rate of exchange then being $1.50). The agreement provides, *inter alia*, that, on the unwinding of the swap in five years, 'Bank' will repay $150 million, and Company A will repay £100 million, using the original exchange rate. Assuming that the exchange rate at the time is $1.25, the company would realise a profit of £20 million on disposing of the dollars received on the maturity of the swap. In accordance with the original intention, the dollars are in fact applied in repaying the dollar loan.

The economic effect of this is that the swap washes out, and Company A has effectively borrowed £100 million sterling at LIBOR minus X, repaying £100 million sterling at the end of the period.

The 'tax fragmentation' terms: on maturity Company A receives a gain of £20 million on the unwinding of the swap, and an equal loss in sterling on repaying the dollar borrowing. Both transactions are on capital account. *Prima facie* the gain on the swap would be subject to capital gains tax, while the loss on the repayment of the bond would not be deductible.

The benefit of the swap may have been 15 basis points after expenses – or £15,000 per annum before tax. The accumulated benefit after tax over five years would be nearly £60,000. The cost of the tax trap would be, on the assumptions, £7 million!

How does the Statement of Practice deal with this? Paragraph 25 begins with the words:

Where a trader enters into a *currency swap agreement* to exchange borrowed currency for an equivalent amount of another currency for a fixed period, the two transactions in the original currency should be treated as matched, so that the underlying liability in the first currency is effectively converted into a liability in the second currency for the duration of the swap.

On a casual reading this *seems* to permit us to match a dollar borrowing with the dollar leg of the swap, although this is not in fact so.

The Draft version continued:

If when the swap is terminated the currencies are swapped back at the spot rate of exchange prevailing at the commencement of the swap there will be no exchange loss or profit *for Case I* purposes.

In the course of discussions, the Inland Revenue was asked what this meant, using the above example. There *is* no exchange loss or profit for

Case I or any other purpose on the unwinding of the *swap*. However, there is a gain or loss on the disposal of the dollars. If this currency is used to repay the borrowing is it intended that they should be treated as matched?

The Inland Revenue confirmed our fears that this paragraph was not meant to cover the *capital gains tax* consequences. There *would* in its view, be a charge to capital gains tax on the swap (asset) leg of the transaction without a deduction for the loss on the bond (liability) leg. The final version of SOP concedes our point on clarity (but not on substance) by adding the words:

but the capital gain consequences of unwinding the swap will need to be taken into account.

Forward rate agreements

A forward rate agreement (FRA) enables a company which wishes to deposit or borrow a sum of money (in domestic or a foreign currency) at some future date to obtain a pre-determined rate of interest. It can be compared to a single-period interest rate swap, or to an interest rate futures transaction.

The FRA is a transaction independent of the actual deposit or loan. At the end of the period a net payment is made between the parties. A borrowing company may receive a payment to compensate it for higher interest payable, or may have to pay the counterparty if interest rates fall. The commercial effect is to pre-determine the total effective cost of borrowing: if this is fixed at (say) 10 per cent and the actual borrowing rate is 11 per cent, the difference will be refunded by the FRA counterparty.

Again, the transaction may not have the appropriate tax consequences. As with swap payments, the payment does not constitute 'interest' for UK tax purposes, but is simply an amount calculated by taking the arithmetical difference between two interest rates. The essential characteristic of interest is lacking, since the sum of money by reference to which the settlement payment is calculated – the notional amount of principal – does not represent any kind of real debt. They are not 'annual payments' and do not come within the definition of 'management expense' (Section 77 ICTA 1988, previously Section 304), nor of the 'incidental costs of raising capital' (Section 77 ICTA 1988, previously Section 38 Finance Act 1980).

The Inland Revenue does regard FRA transactions by financial institutions as giving rise to Schedule D Case I receipts or expenses for financial institutions. There are no problems for banks as such other than UK trading companies. They *may* find the interest differential paid on the settlement date treated as a Case I receipt or deduction from trading profits. If, however, a counterparty in an FRA is an investment company, then the net *receipt* accruing to such a company will be brought into charge to tax under Case V or Case VI of Schedule D (on the assumption that an FRA is not a 'security'), whereas no deduction whatsoever will be available in respect of a net *payment* made by an investment company.

There is a very serious potential problem, amounting to a tax trap, for *when* is an interest differential payment brought into charge to tax? The basic rule is that a trading receipt can only be assessed when all the contractual conditions that precede its payment have been fulfilled and it can truly be said to have been earned. Similarly, an expense will be deductible in the period in which it has been incurred. One major departure from these rules may arise if a payment and receipt does not have the 'necessary characteristic of finality', this will occur if the sum in question is conditional in the sense that ultimate payment is dependent upon the fulfilment of certain conditions which are precedent to any legal liability.

Caps, collars and cylinders

There are various types of transaction, caps, collars, cylinder options and the like, which are really variants on the option theme. The only way for a treasurer to see whether or not these are a good bargain is to break them down into their components, and to compare the cost of buying each separately.

An interest rate cap gives a borrower a guarantee that the interest he pays on a floating rate facility cannot exceed a specified figure, but he does get the benefit of a *fall* in market rates. In substance, therefore, the transaction is an interest rate option combined with a loan. The 'premium' may either be a single up front payment, or may take the form of slightly higher periodic interest payments.

From a tax point of view any premium paid for an interest rate capping agreement is clearly not interest – see Section 74(f) and *Re Euro Hotel (Belgravia) Ltd*, cited in the representation by the British Banker's Association. This case 'held that the principal sum on which interest is purportedly paid must represent a sum of money due to the person to whom the "interest" is paid. It is not sufficient that this principal amount is merely a figure in an arithmetical calculation.' In practice, it may be treated as an 'annual payment'.

This problem presumably does not arise when the payment for the cap takes the form of higher interest payments. It is conceivable, but in practice unlikely, that the Inland Revenue would seek to unbundle the transaction and disallow part of the interest. This procedure is available only when the immediate counterparty is a bank or actual lender. Corporates would prefer to be free to make a separate payment for a separate service without adverse tax consequences.

There is also a problem for the recipient of a cap premium. He will have an obligation to make payments, in certain circumstances over a period of years. Should the receipt be brought into account in the current year, or amortised?

The British Bankers' Association representation explains that, as the holder of a cap has future rights which can be quantified using an option pricing model, he would seem to be in a position analogous to that of the building companies in the cases of *Utting* v. *Hughes* and *Heather* v. *Redfern*. These companies had to reflect the cost or market value (whichever was the lower) of certain trading assets that they continued to own once the houses they had built were disposed of – namely, their reversionary interest in the freehold land on which the houses stood. The BBA suggest that similar reasoning should apply to the holder of cap agreements. Is this in fact Revenue practice?

The cap *writer* will receive one or more payments of premium in consideration for a contingent obligation under the option. The BBA state:

It is a well established principle [*Southern Railway of Peru* v. *Owen* and *CIR* v. *Titaghur Jute Factory*] that the mere fact a future liability is contingent does not, of itself, prevent a provision being made for this liability if it can be fairly quantified: It is argued the profits of the writer will not be correctly stated unless the contingent liability he has accepted is revalued at the end of each accounting period during the life of the agreement.

Some transactions, such as cylinders, involve a company receiving the benefit of one option, and in effect 'paying' for it by granting the counterparty a rather different option. This could create a timing mismatch. Corporates would again prefer to be free to unbundle the transactions where appropriate.

Conclusion

If the reader is now thoroughly confused, he may take comfort. So is the Inland Revenue. Modern financial instruments, valuable though they are, constitute a minefield of tax traps. There is no substitute for a thorough, case by case, analysis.

Draft statement of practice by Inland Revenue on the tax treatment of transactions in financial futures and options

1. This Statement sets out the Inland Revenue's views on the tax treatment of transactions in financial futures and options carried out by investment trusts, unit trusts, pension funds and companies which either do not trade or whose principal trade is outside the financial area.

2. Section 72, Finance Act 1985, provides broadly that transactions in commodity and financial futures and traded options on recognised exchanges will be treated as capital in nature unless they are regarded as profits or losses of a trade. Section 81, Finance Act 1987, extends this treatment to other transactions in futures and options. If, under normal statutory and case law principles, profits or losses fall to be treated as trading in nature the Sections 72 and 81 have no application to those profits or losses. It is therefore necessary first to determine whether or not a taxpayer is trading in futures or options without reference to the provisions of Sections 72 and 81.

3. Whether or not a taxpayer is trading is a question of fact to be determined by reference to all the facts and circumstances of the particular case. Consideration is given to the 'badges of trade'. Generally a person will not be regarded as trading if the transactions are infrequent or to hedge specific capital investments. An individual is unlikely to be regarded as trading as a result of purely speculative transactions in options or futures.

4. If the taxpayer in question is a company, which would include an investment trust or authorised unit trust, it is necessary to consider not only the normal case law defining trading but also the case of Lewis Emanuel and Son Ltd v. White (42 TC 369). The broad effect of the judgment in this case is that generally a company cannot speculate and that any transactions carried out by a company must either be trading or capital in nature.

5. If a transaction in financial futures or options is clearly related to an underlying asset or transaction, then the tax treatment of the futures or options contract will follow that of the underlying asset or transaction. In general, the Inland Revenue take the view that this relationship exists where a futures or options contract is entered into in order to hedge an underlying transaction, asset or portfolio by reducing the risk relating to it; and the intention of the taxpayer in entering into the transaction is of considerable importance. Where the underlying transaction is itself treated as giving rise to a capital gain or loss, the related futures or options contract will also be treated as a capital matter and not as trading.

6. The basic conditions which have to be met if the transaction is to be treated as hedging in this sense are:

    (a) the transaction must be economically appropriate to the reduction in risk of the underlying transaction, asset or portfolio; and

    (b) the price fluctuations of the options and futures must be directly and demonstrably related to the fluctuations in value or composition of the underlying transaction, asset or portfolio at the time the hedging transaction is initiated.

7. This applies equally to long and short positions, and is not dependent upon the form of the eventual disposition of the position. In other words it will apply whether the futures position is closed out or held to maturity, or in the case of an options position, closed out, exercised or held to final expiry.

Examples

8. Transactions would be treated as giving rise to capital gains or losses in the following circumstances:

    (a) A taxpayer who holds gilts sells gilt futures to protect the value of his capital in the event of a fall in the value of gilt-edged securities generally.

    (b) A taxpayer purchases an asset in two stages by purchasing a foreign currency future in advance of the purchase of an asset denominated in that currency, or by purchasing an option in respect of an underlying asset as a first step towards the acquisition of the asset itself.

    (c) A taxpayer who holds a broadly based portfolio sells index futures or purchases index put options to protect the risk to the value of the portfolio from a fall in the market (provided the fall in the index futures or options is directly and demonstrably correlated to the loss on the portfolio as it was constituted at the date the hedge was initiated).

9. But even if a transaction is not a hedging transaction in the sense of paragraph 6 above, it may, nevertheless, be regarded as capital in nature, depending on all the facts and circumstances. To take two specific examples:

(a) If a taxpayer is committed to making a bond issue in the near future and enters into an interest rate future or option with a view to protecting himself against rises in interest costs before he is able to make the issue, the Revenue will regard the transaction as being of a capital nature.

(b) If a taxpayer sells or buys options or futures as an incidental and temporary part of a change in investment strategy (e.g. changing the ratio of gilts and equities) that transaction is likely to be treated as being of a capital nature, if the transaction in the assets themselves would be a capital matter.

10. A further uncertainty may arise if a transaction is originally undertaken as a capital hedge but the underlying transaction or motive falls away. If the futures or options transaction is closed out within a reasonably short period after the underlying motive falls away then the transaction will continue to be treated as capital in nature in accordance with the principles outlined above. If however the transaction is not closed out at that time it may be arguable that any profit or loss arising subsequently is of a trading nature. In practice the Revenue would not normally take this point in view of the original intentions of the taxpayer and the practical difficulties of making the necessary calculation.

11. Where a company enters into these transactions as incidental to its trading activity, for example a manufacturer entering into transactions to hedge the price of his raw materials, then the profits or losses from these transactions would be taken into account as part of the profits and losses of the trade.

Part Three

The United States

13

The general implications of the US Tax Reform Act of 1986

The United States Tax Reform Act (TRA) of 1986 is probably the most far-reaching change that any country at any time has ever made in a tax system. The stated intention is to provide 'a more level playing field', leaving corporations free to maximise pre-tax profits, expecting the low rate, broad based tax system to look after itself. In practice it is not as simple as that. The implications of TRA will preoccupy general management, as well as tax specialists, for a long time to come.

Because many of the changes, and indeed many of the peculiarities of the US tax system, interact closely with international treasury and tax planning, a rather fuller description is included here. American readers will notice a subtle difference of approach between international tax planners and domestic specialists; this will come out again and again in the two chapters which follow.

On the international side, TRA is not even *intended* to be simple. There was *meant* to be a deliberate bias in favour of investing in the United States. American corporations with international activities now have to rethink, not only their tax computations, but the very way they approach the strategic problems of international taxation.

Practitioners on the international tax circuit have noted a striking contrast between US-based and European-based multinationals in their approach to international tax. The typical European company would have an 'international tax manager' with an extensive knowledge of the tax systems of all the countries in which his group did business, and would understand how these foreign taxes interacted with each other and with the tax regime at parent level. He would often be senior to, or at least more highly paid than, the domestic tax manager and would, on best practice, have direct access both to the vice-president finance and to international line management. In contrast, the US corporation's 'international tax manager' (if he existed at all) would be a subordinate within the tax department. He would have a detailed knowledge, not of foreign taxes, but merely of *how the United States taxes foreign source income.*

In the past this actually made sense. European companies had to take international tax *strategy* seriously; US companies did not. The US corporate tax rate, at 46 per cent plus state taxes, was by no means the highest in the industrialised world, but it was within the normal range. Credit for foreign taxes was calculated on an 'overall limitation' basis. All that was needed was to make the best use of the credit rules (admittedly a full time study) and keep the average foreign source tax charge below this US rate. This is no longer sufficient. First, it is much harder to get the rate below 34 per cent than to get it below 46 per cent and, second, the already complex rules governing the types of income which are excluded from the calculation ('separate limitation') and defining 'source' have become even more restricted. The 'controlled foreign corporation' rules were also tightened up. American companies which pay even a small proportion of their profits as tax to other countries will now have to take a leaf out of the books of their European competitors and start discovering the mysteries of 'Strategy in International Taxation'.

There are some international quirks. Secretary Baker was 'off the record' as saying that a major purpose of the legislation was to influence cash flows – discouraging Americans from investing abroad and encouraging foreigners to invest in the United States. The package certainly did not meet the economist's test of capital import and capital export neutrality, but the anomalies are not all one way. There are some major tax traps and planning opportunities; specifically the net value of a flow of pre-tax US source will depend on the residence and organisational structure of shareholders.

Until 30 June 1987, companies were taxed at 46 per cent. From 1 July 1987 they were taxed at 34 per cent on all income if it exceeded $335,000. State tax is an additional burden. The effective rate is typically a little over 40 per cent. Many, but not all, states impose tax with reference to the Federal computation.

'Minimum tax'

The old 15 per cent add-on minimum tax, imposed on certain tax preference items, has been replaced by an alternative minimum tax (AMT) at 20 per cent which will apply to a broader base (taxable income plus preferences), if in excess of normal tax. There is an exemption of $40,000, reduced by 25 per cent of the amount by which alternative minimum tax exceeds $150,000.

'Minimum tax' is now an essential part of the tax system. Companies pay:

(a) *either* 34 per cent on a tax base broadened to include some items which are arguably proper business deductions;
(b) *or* 20 per cent on an even broader base, which may well substantially exceed economic profits.

There are many important changes in the basis of computation. These go beyond the scope of this book and are mentioned only when they affect international financing.

Capital gains tax

From the end of 1986 capital gains have been taxed at the same rate as income. This all sounds simple and logical, but it is not. American capital gains tax is not indexed, and gains include a totally (although at present small) unreal element of purely paper gains. Another problem is that capital gains are not *actually* treated as income. They are still subject to a separate tax but at the same rate. Capital losses will not be symmetrically treated, but (apart from a $3,000 ration for individuals) will only be available to offset present or future capital gains. A ceiling on capital gains tax is being discussed; future changes are now likely to be in the direction of increasing, rather than reducing, the difference between the treatment of regular income and capital gains. The technical distinctions remain important to the treasury planner.

Generally the tax reform package ignores inflation in its treatment both of capital gains and of depreciation. If the rate of inflation increases significantly, there will be a seriously adverse effect on fixed capital formation and pressure for special reliefs. If these were conceded it would destroy the revenue neutrality of the package. This is one of the two potentially fatal flaws in the TRA concepts.

It was argued by venture capitalists that the TRA package would destroy their industry. Maybe, but it has certainly created a new industry in leveraged buy-outs.

Double taxation of corporate profits

This is the most serious defect of the tax reform package. It has led directly to a predictable boom in leveraged buy-outs and a general movement towards the disincorporation and leveraging of US industry. This aspect received surprisingly little comment in the United States itself (but see Rudnick, 1989). Maybe it needed a European perspective to foresee it.

The United States is one of the few remaining industrial countries (the Netherlands is another) to impose full double taxation on distributed profits, with no imputation credit, 'split rate' or corresponding relief. The combined effect of corporate tax at 34 per cent and personal tax at 28 per cent is an effective charge on distributed profits of 52.48 per cent:

Profits	$100.00
Corporate tax (34%)	34.00
	66.00

Profits distributed	$ 66.00
Personal tax (28%)	18.48
Profit net of taxes	47.52
Total taxes	52.48

Retaining profits merely postpones the problem, as the increase in value generated by the retention will eventually be realised as capital gains taxed at the same rates, with no indexation relief for inflation.

Compare what happens if the same flow of business profits is owned directly by individuals. There is only one level of Federal tax, normally at 28 per cent:

Profits	$100.00
Personal tax (28%)	28.00
Profit net of taxes	72.00
Total taxes	28.00

The value of the net cash flow is increased by over 50 per cent. This does *not* involve a return to sole trading. It can be achieved by a 'sub-chapter S' or 'tax option' corporation which combines the benefits of limited liability and corporate organisation with the right to be taxed as if it were a partnership. A sub-chapter S corporation cannot have more than 35 shareholders; it also cannot have foreign shareholders: a significant planning point.

Even if there is no change of organisation, the benefits of debt over equity have been significantly increased. The present position is as follows:

1. Profits of American business owned by common stockholders suffer immediate tax of 34 per cent, and an eventual Federal tax charge of

52 per cent whether enjoyed as dividends or as capital gain.

2. Profit of American business owned by partners, by domestic shareholders in certain closely controlled corporations, or in the form of debt securities suffer an immediate Federal tax charge of 28 per cent.

Generally, the change in the value of pre-tax cash flows routed in different ways has had dramatic effects on the structure of US industry. There has been a boom in leveraged buy-outs and head-shrinking reconstructions.

Investment into the United States by foreigners

American corporate tax rates are now relatively low, although we must never forget to take state taxes into account. The total tax burden on foreigners will depend on the relevant rate of withholding tax (for subsidiaries) whether the new 'branch profits tax' applies.

Foreigners will have more difficulty than Americans in by-passing the corporate form. They cannot own shares in sub-chapter S corporations which can opt to be taxed as if they were partnerships. There may be scope for a 'look through' limited partnership, but this may have adverse tax consequences in a (high tax) country of residence. It may require a 'tax haven' resident to file a US personal tax return, which may not always be acceptable and may bring 'treaty shopping' rules into operation.

A US subsidiary of a foreign company will pay tax at 34 per cent in the same way as a US company. Where these profits are distributed there is in principle a 30 per cent withholding tax on the dividend and where this applies the effective total tax burden would be 53.8 per cent.

In the past, *branches* simply paid corporation tax but under the new rules branches will pay a 'substitute withholding tax' which in principle will bring the tax rate on branch profits (including effectively connected capital gains) to 53.8 per cent:

Profits	$100.00
Corporate tax (34%)	34.00
	66.00
BPT (30%)	19.80
Net profit	46.20
Total taxes	53.80

This new regime substitutes for the (generally easily avoided) 'secondary withholding tax' on dividends paid *by* a foreign company which derived part of its income from US sources.

On prior law the rate of withholding tax on dividends is, and continues to be, reduced by double tax agreements, typically to 15 per cent but in a few cases to 5 per cent. The 'branch profits tax' (BPT) will be ruled out by the non-discrimination clauses of most treaties, provided that the treaty permits the 'secondary withholding tax' rule to apply. The exemption, in any case, will only apply to 'qualified residents' of the treaty partner.

The branch profits tax is imposed on the 'dividend equivalent amount' which:

is calculated first by determining the amount of current earnings and profits of the foreign corporation (unreduced by any distributions made during the year) which are attributable to income which is effectively connected with the conduct of its US trades or businesses. In calculating such earnings and profits, net operating losses carried forward from prior years may *not* be deducted . . . . In calculating the dividend equivalent amount certain items that would otherwise be included in earnings and profits are eliminated including earnings and profits attributable to the sale of any interest in a US real property holding corporation.

The 'dividend equivalent amount' is further reduced (but not below zero) 'by any increase in the foreign corporation's US net equity during the taxable year'. This amount is equal to the corporation's money and aggregate adjusted bases of property treated as connected with its US trades or businesses reduced (including below zero) by liabilities treated as so connected. If US net equity subsequently decreases, then the dividend equivalent amount is increased by a reduction.

Foreigners will not normally be subject to tax on the disposal of US companies, but may have a liability in their country of residence. 'Exit planning' is essential at the investment stage.

The effective abolition of the Section 337 route (the 'General Utilities' principle) by which a US subsidiary could distribute appreciated (non-real estate) assets in liquidation to a shareholder without incurring a US capital gains tax charge is another factor which will cause many foreign investors to re-think their US acquisition strategy.

Foreign investment by US parents

American companies investing abroad will now often pay tax at more than the US rate. It will still often be possible to 'mix in' low tax income, although changes in the 'separate limitation' and 'source' rules will make it more difficult to keep the foreign tax charge down to 34 per cent. Where there is an excess foreign tax charge the 'overspill' relief cannot flow through to a shareholder. The total burden on profits distributed from a 50 per cent source is:

	50%	35%
Foreign profits	$1,000	$1,000
Foreign tax	500	350
	500	650
Personal tax 28%	140	182
Profit net of taxes	360	458
Total taxes	64%	53.2%

Although this has on the whole swung the balance of advantage against foreign *direct* investment by US corporations, foreign *portfolio* investment is actually now more attractive. For instance, the effective rate of tax on UK corporate profits distributed to a US shareholder is 34.1 per cent, far more favourable than the corresponding treatment of US source corporate profits or to UK source profits earned by a US parent and distributed to US shareholders.

Profit	$1,000
Tax 35%	350
	650
Distribution	650
Imputation credit	265
	915
US tax	256
	659
Effective tax rate (%)	34

This is perhaps the most dramatic example, although there are similar anomalies in several other countries. Correspondingly, it is now relatively unattractive for foreign portfolio investors to invest in US equity securities.

Tax credit relief

The United States, in common with other major countries, taxes foreign source income but allows a tax credit for taxes paid in the country of 1986. Perhaps reflecting the enormous scale of American outward direct investment, the US rules are far more complex and have been subject to many more policy changes than is the case in other countries. The subject is quite central for US parents investing abroad, and is useful background for non-US multinationals with US activities.

History of tax credit relief

The principle of the foreign tax credit (first introduced in 1918) is to prevent US taxpayers from being fully taxed twice on their foreign income – once by the foreign country and then again by the United States. The foreign tax paid may be offset against US tax. However, it is the intention (although not always the practical result of the legislation) that the credit may not reduce the US tax on US income – there is a 'limitation' on the foreign tax credit. The general credit rules may be modified by the terms of tax treaties to which the United States is a party, but the general principles apply unilaterally.

Credit is given both for taxes directly borne (e.g. withholding taxes, and taxes on the trading profits of foreign *branches*) and there is an 'indirect credit' for the corporate taxes on profits underlying a dividend paid by subsidiaries and other companies in which there is at least a 10 per cent shareholding interest.

In contrast to the position in the United Kingdom and in many other countries, the indirect credit can only be traced through to 'great-grandchildren' and not to remoter sub-subsidiaries. (This raises serious tax planning problems, beyond our immediate concern, when a US corporation acquires control of a foreign corporation which already has a substantial international network.)

The concept of '*limitation*' is central to our analysis. One factor affecting the shaping of US tax policy is that there are those in Congress who regard the tax credit, not as a civilised way of making international business possible by bringing world-wide taxation into account, but as a 'tax preference' enabling corporations to avoid *American* taxes. Although this rather narrow view has fortunately never dominated the making of tax policy, it has influenced some of the compromises which are a feature of the American legislative process.

The general principle is that the taxpayer should pay the higher of the domestic or source country rate of tax. Thus, if the US tax rate is 34 per cent and the foreign tax rate (as calculated) is 20 per cent an extra 14 points of tax will be picked up in the United States. If, however, the foreign tax rate is 40 per cent the extra six points have to be borne and cannot (in principle) be 'overspilled' against tax that would otherwise be payable on US source income.

From 1954 to 1960 credit was calculated on a 'per country' limitation.

If the US rate for a particular year was 50 per cent, while the rate in Country A was 30 per cent, an additional 20 percentage points would be levied as tax in the United States. If the rate in Country B was 60 per cent, income from that source would bear this 60 per cent rate and the intention (not always achieved in practice) of public policy was to ensure that this extra 10 percentage points could not be offset against either US source income or income from sources in Country A. This, reasonable enough from the point of view of government, left businesses with the worst of both worlds. They suffered the unrelieved penalty in high tax countries, while any tax benefits in low tax countries were clawed back by Uncle Sam.

Business made various arrangements to by-pass this 'limitation'. One was to extract from Country B, inter-group *interest* deductible against corporate profits and subject either to a nil or low rate of withholding tax. When this was treated as *Country* B source with a low effective rate of tax, it could be averaged in with dividends from the operating subsidiary to give a more favourable overall effect. To counteract this Congress introduced the concept of 'separate limitation' by which certain types of lowly taxed income from a particular country could not be mixed in with the general fund of highly taxed profits. Another technique was to 'mix' sources through an intermediate holding company.

Between 1960 and 1975, taxpayers could choose between 'per country' limitation and 'overall' limitation. Since 1975 *only* overall limitation has been allowed.

Where this basis applies, a US company might have income from two sources:

	Income	Tax rate	Foreign tax
Source A	$100,000	60%	$ 60,000
Source B	200,000	22%	44,000
Total	300,000		104,000

In this case the total foreign tax is just 34 per cent of total income. No US tax would be payable and no credit is wasted on per country limitation; an extra $24,000 would be payable on Source B, and the surplus credit on Source A would be wasted.

From the taxpayer's point of view it is obviously desirable to characterise low tax *income* as having a foreign, rather than a domestic, source and to offset *losses* or deductions, including interest expense, against US rather than foreign income.

The international tax planning strategies of US parent companies will depend on whether they have a surplus or a shortage of foreign tax credits. They will aim to characterise gains on exchange as foreign source (to increase the denominator in the limitation calculation) and losses as domestic. Under prior law (Section 861 and 862) the passage of title rules could be manipulated and characterisation was often at the choice of the taxpayer.

The rules have been changed considerably by TRA. Generally, profits may be treated for this purpose as 'foreign source', even though no foreign country is claiming tax jurisdiction. We need to ask two questions, and the answers to both are changed by TRA.

Is a *gain* domestic or foreign source? Under Section 904 (which limits credit for foreign taxes paid), there used to be a presumption that the gain on the sale or exchange of capital assets outside the United States is domestic source regardless of where title passes. The effect of this can be to restrict the denominator of the 'overall limitation' calculation, and treatment will not be symmetrical.

Similarly, is a *loss* to be allocated against domestic or foreign source income? Regulations under Section 861 also provide that certain expenses have to be allocated to domestic or foreign source income in computing the double tax credit. The Tax Reform Act of 1986, while retaining the concept of 'overall limitation', introduced a number of restrictions and special categories. Separate limitations apply to the following five items:

(a)   financial services income;
(b)   shipping income;
(c)   interest income subject to a foreign withholding tax of at least 5 per cent;
(d)   dividends from non-CFCs for which an indirect credit can be claimed;
(e)   passive income, *including certain foreign currency gains*.

A report, *'Tax Reform Proposals: Taxation of Foreign Income and Foreign Taxpayers'* prepared by the staff of the Joint Committee on Taxation for the use of the Committee on Ways and Means, dated 18 July 1985 gave an excellent overview of the then current law and various proposals on this and a wider range of issues.

Controlled foreign corporations

Where a US parent owns a foreign subsidiary, *in general* no US tax is payable until the profits are distributed as dividends. Since 1962 there has been legislation by which the profits of 'controlled foreign corporations' can, in certain circumstances, be subject to current US taxation, even though they have not been distributed. Subject to these rules there is some scope for timing the payment of subsidiaries to optimise the US tax position. The 'narrow' elements in Congress regard *all* tax deferral, even by the subsidiaries operating in high tax industrialised countries, as being an unjustified tax benefit. This view has, again, influenced the detail of tax policy.

One obvious weakness of the CFC legislation from the point of view of business competing in a free world economy is that the rules cannot be applied in reverse to allow *losses* incurred by such companies to be offset against profits earned elsewhere.

The 1984 Tax Reform Act changed the source rules on income derived from a 'US owned foreign corporation' (a broader concept than a 'controlled foreign corporation'). Certain categories of such income are now treated as 'US source' (Section 121 amending Section 904 IRC). Previously there had been scope for diverting income to a CFC in a way which did not avoid tax as such, but which improved the credit mix calculation. It was also possible to sidestep the 'separate limitation' rules for calculating tax credit on certain types of interest income by routing it through a CFC, and converting into foreign source dividends.

14

The tax treatment of interest

Interest paid by US taxpayers is, in general, deductible. The Internal Revenue Code provision is broad: 'There shall be allowed as a deduction all interest paid or accrued within the taxable year on indebtedness.' (Section 163(a).) There are some anti-avoidance provisions directed more against individual tax shelters than against the corporate borrower. The Tax Reform Act of 1986 tightened these up very considerably.

The structure of TRA has, as already explained, given a dramatic incentive to debt, as opposed to equity, financing of domestic US corporations. The changes affecting international financing are more subtle.

A US company which borrows for the purposes of *investing abroad* will not be denied a deduction for the interest merely because the income generated by the investment of the funds borrowed is not outside the scope of immediate US taxation or is eligible for credit relief. However, Treasury Regulations issued under Section 861 require this interest to be *allocated* between domestic and foreign source for the purpose of calculating source of income, which in turn affects credit relief. This is an important tax planning factor which needs careful mathematical analysis and which has no direct parallel in other countries. The 'source' rules are substantially modified by TRA – see below.

The more general restrictions and anti-avoidance provisions include Section 265 which provides that expenses incurred or interest on money borrowed, for the purpose of earning tax exempt income, is not deductible. This can, in principle, affet corporations, which borrow to invest in tax exempt securities.

Certain types of interest on money borrowed for corporate acquisition is disallowed (Section 279). This is directed as the 'head-shrinking' type of operations and applies only to interest paid in excess of $5 million.

Although the Tax Reform Act of 1986 made no major changes

affecting the general right of business to deduct interest expense (leaving aside the limitations imposed by a general assault on tax shelters) there had already been significant changes in 1984. One effect of these was to broaden the range of transactions characterised as interest for tax purposes. Where real property is sold in exchange for a debt, e.g. $1 million for five annual instalments of $240,000 implying a rate of interest of 10 per cent, the vendor hopes to have the extra $200,000 categorised as an addition to his capital gain rather than as income. Under prior law, some part of the payments would be categorised as interest but the calculation was typically at below market rates, and the interest was deemed imputed only at the time the instalment was received. Under the 1984 Act interest is imputed to the outstanding balance at current market rates and on an accrual basis even if no money has in fact been paid.

Although this legislation was mainly aimed at domestic transactions it has important international repercussions. It can apply, for instance, on exports to the United States on commercially deferred terms, the 'interest cost' of which is reflected in the price. In principle, part of this could be characterised as interest and be subject to withholding tax. Fortunately this will not concern arm's length sales which will normally be covered by the elimination of withholding tax for portfolio debt, but could be an important planning point affecting sales from companies in non-treaty countries to their US affiliates.

Also in 1984, Section 172, adding Code Section 7872, extended the concept of 'disguised loans' on which interest income can be imputed. These can now include 'gift loans' and deemed loans. In certain circumstances, the difference between:

(a) the amount loaned, and
(b) the present value of all payments which are required to be made under the terms of the loan

can be treated as 'original issue discount' and taxed as discussed below.

The United States had for many years taxed bondholders on 'original issue discount', 'market discount' (e.g. zero coupon bonds) and had given a corresponding relief to the borrower. The implications of this are discussed in detail below. However, 'market discount' enjoyed capital gains tax treatment. For instance a bond with a 5 per cent annual coupon might have been issued at par some years ago when that represented a market rate of interest. Assume that, with two years to maturity, it stands at about 89.72 to yield 11 per cent. A buyer could enjoy the profit to maturity (about half the total return) as a capital gain. In the case of obligations *issued* after 18 July 1984 (Section 41, and adding Code Section 1276–8) holders will be taxed (broadly) under the same apportionment principles as original discount bonds. The rules do not apply to preference shares.

The main planning points

Apart from these specialist provisions, the main problem areas for international business are as follows:

(a) thin capitalisation and the arm's length rules (affecting the financing of US subsidiaries of foreign companies;
(b) the 'allocation' rules for interest expense and the 'source' rule for tax credits limitation (affecting US parents with foreign operations);
(c) the 'allocation' rules for branches (mainly affecting US offices of foreign banks).

Thin capitalisation

Section 385 gives the Internal Revenue Service broad powers 'to prescribe such regulations as may be necessary or appropriate to determine whether an interest in the corporation is to be treated for the purposes of this title as stock or indebtedness'. If it is indebtedness, interest will be deductible; if it is characterised as 'stock', the interest will not be deductible or treated as if it were a dividend paid out of tax profits.

Regulations under this Section have been under discussion for fourteen years. A comprehensive draft was published on 24 March 1980 but was never finalised. On 3 May 1983 Assistant Secretary John Chapoton said that if agreement could not be reached 'we would withdraw the regulations and recommend repeal of s 385'. The regulations are now dead but the concept remains in principle.

A finding that a debt claim is an equity interest would apply for all tax purposes, both domestic and international, and would result in interest being treated not as a deductible expense but as a dividend distribution out of taxed profits. This would bring into play the withholding tax rules as applied to 'dividends', not repealed by the 1984 Act.

Arm's length rules

Section 482 of the US Internal Revenue Code empowers the Internal Revenue Service to investigate transactions between 'related parties', broadly defined. Following the publication of a White Paper in late 1988, this whole subject is now under review. However, Carlson, Fagorasi and Gordon 'The Section 482 White Paper: Highlights and Implications' *Tax Notes* October 31 1988 comment that:

the entire area of financial instruments is ignored. The failure to address these issues leaves wide gaps in the guidance . . . . The proper allocation of currency risk is of particular importance.

Most commonly, but not exclusively, these rules will be invoked against transactions between parent and subsidiary, or between fellow subsidiaries. The Internal Revenue Service may allocate income and deductions between them, in order to prevent the evasion of taxes or to clearly reflect income. The purpose of the Section is to place a controlled taxpayer on a tax parity with an uncontrolled taxpayer, by determining, according to the standard of an uncontrolled taxpayer, the true taxable income from the property and business of a controlled taxpayer (Regulation Section 1 482–1(b)(1)).

Originally (as with parallel legislation in other countries) the intention was to prevent artificial transfer prices being used to divert income from the United States to a 'tax haven'. Since the 1960s the provision has been used aggressively by the Internal Revenue Service, even on transactions between associated companies in 'high tax' jurisdictions. In these cases any reallocation to the United States would be mainly at the expense of the foreign tax authority on the other side of the transaction. This attitude has inevitably induced retaliation – with a rise in corporate compliance costs. If there is no compensating adjustment on the international level, double taxation will occur. Many international tax treaties have addressed the problem. Although most provide that when an income or other reallocation is made by one signatory, the other signatory will make an appropriate adjustment to the tax owing to him, there is no binding procedure for settling disputes when the 'competent authorities' disagree.

Section 482 generally applies to intra-corporate interest. The general rule is that 'where one member of a group of controlled entities makes a loan or advance directly to, or otherwise becomes a creditor of, another member of such a group, and charges no interest, or charges interest at a rate which is not equal to an arm's length rate . . . the district director may make appropriate allocations to reflect an arm's length interest rate for the use of such loan or advance'.

In determining an arm's length rate of interest all relevant factors are to be considered, including the amount and duration of the loan, the security involved, the credit standing of the borrower, and the interest rate prevailing at the situs of the lender or creditor for comparable loans. Safe haven rules were provided; in relation to loans made after 1 July 1981 the rate of interest actually charged may be accepted as arm's length if it is between 11 per cent and 13 per cent; otherwise the appropriate rate is 12 per cent unless the taxpayer can establish a more appropriate rate. It is now provided that these 'safe haven' rules apply only to *US dollar* loans; there were previously very valuable planning opportunities to be derived by using a currency with a very different rate structure. None of these rules applied to 'alleged indebtedness' which was in fact a contribution to capital.

Financing of foreign owned US business

There are changes in the rules affecting the financing of US activities by foreigners. Interest paid by the US trade or business of a foreign corporation will be treated as US source interest, subject to 30 per cent withholding tax. It is not clear how interest paid will be allocated to US and non-US activities, or whether and how the rules governing deductibility will tie up with those governing the requirement to withhold.

TRA also imposes a 30 per cent tax on 'excess interest' defined as the excess of 'the amount allowable as a deduction for interest against a foreign corporation's income effectively connected with its US trade or business' over 'the interest paid by the US trade or business during the taxable years'. This appears to be intended to catch interest accrued and deducted but not paid during the taxable year. It is suggested (Roberts and Holland) that:

there is a risk that accrued interest may be taxed twice: once as excess interest when it is deducted and again through withholding when the interest is paid in a subsequent year. There can be no assurance, however, that the Regulations will take this position . . . . care should be taken to ensure that interest obligations of US trades or business are paid currently.

Allocation of interest expense

Where money is borrowed by a US corporation partly or wholly for the purpose of foreign operations, interest will be allowed as a deduction, but will have to be allocated between 'US source' and 'foreign source' income. This may have the effect of restricting the foreign tax credit which can be claimed against the US tax. It is not, as such, a restriction on deductibility (such as operates in principle in the Netherlands) but can affect the 'bottom line' calculation of after-tax profits.

Regulation 1.861.8 (e) (2) goes into some detail on the allocation of interest expense. The Regulations in their present form take the view that money is fungible in that the use of borrowed money for one purpose frees up funds for other purposes. Each operating entity must allocate interest expense to all of its income producing activities on the basis of the US dollar value of the assets generating each type of income.

Revised Regulation 1.861–8 seeks to apportion certain costs (including interest) of doing business between those which are properly allocatable to earning US profits and those which should be allocated to earning foreign source profits. It was estimated that this administrative measure would bring an extra $300 million per annum in revenue, much of it probably at the expense, not of taxpaying companies but of the tax authorities of other countries.

Source

This brings us naturally to the key concept which links tax credit and international financial management – that of '*source*'. To prevent abuse by the type of transactions just described, the United States needs a comprehensive definition of what constitutes 'US source' and what constitutes 'foreign source' income. (Where a 'per country' limitation applies, each item of income must be allocated to a source within a particular country.) The 'source' definitions adopted by the US tax code need not and, in practice, quite frequently will not, coincide with the definition of taxable income adopted by other countries. It is perfectly possible for income to fall within the tax net of another country while being excluded from the US definition of 'foreign source income'.

Another complicating factor is that the statutory provision on expenses (including interest expense) reallocated against different categories of income (sub-Section 861 (8) of the Internal Revenue Code) is relatively short. The Regulations interpreting it are long. Specifically, where a US company borrows extensively (by bond issues or otherwise) at the parent company level, part of the *interest expense* may be allocated against foreign source income, thereby restricting the double tax relief calculation.

Dividends and interest income are treated as having their source in the country of incorporation of the paying entity with the exception of an '80/20' company (a formerly important tax planning concept). In some respects, therefore, the US definition of 'source' is likely to be wider than the host country definition, although the 'expense' rules are less favourable.

Zero coupon and original issue discount bonds

The current fashion for zero coupon or deep discount bonds began in the United States. Under US tax law 'original issue discount' is taxable to the holder as income, but is deductible to the issuer.

The discount is ignored to the extent that it does not exceed ¼ per cent multiplied by the number of years to maturity. If it exceeds this figure it is treated symmetrically, at least at domestic level. What is taxable to the bondholder is deductible to the borrowing corporation. Discount was on prior law divided by the number of *months* to maturity and this amount was taxable to the investor each year (in accordance with the number of months held) as if interest had been paid, even though no cash changes hand (Section 1232(a)(3)). The amount taxed was treated as an adjustment to the 'basis' cost of the bond for capital gains tax purposes.

Thus a ten-year zero coupon bond purchased at 38.55 would yield 10 per cent to maturity. The taxpayer was then liable to tax on 0.51 per cent of the face value for each month during each tax year that the bond was held. If, after two years, it was sold, the acquisition cost would be deemed, for capital gains tax purposes, to have risen by 12.29 (the taxed income) to 50.84. The difference between that figure and actual sales proceeds would be treated as a capital gain or loss.

The straight line apportionment did not give quite the right answer, and what was a trivial error at low interest became significant when rates rose to 12 per cent or more. By exploiting the anomaly, corporate borrowers (or at least those of them who employed and took the advice of someone who understood compound interest) could save about 75 basis points on their borrowing costs.

More precise rules apply to bonds issued after 1 July 1982, other than obligations issued under a binding written contract entered into before 2 July 1982. For these amortisation, for both borrower and lender is on a compound interest basis, the calculation being made annually. The true rate of interest is imputed on the original rate of interest on the theoretical value at the beginning of each year. This also gives a mathematically correct answer from the point of view of borrowers, or of a holder throughout the life of the bond. Computations are on a daily, rather than a monthly, basis.

Section 163(3) gives a corresponding deduction to the corporate borrower. This cross-refers to Section 1232 (and now 1232(a)) in such a way as to ensure symmetry of treatment between borrower and lender. There is also a *deduction* for bond *premiums* given by Section 171. The wording of the Section (and the corresponding Regulations, published in 1957) is directed at a deduction granted to an *investor* who purchases a bond at a *premium* over redemption price. It has been interpreted to grant a deduction to a corporate borrower who issues bonds at a discount.

Market discount bonds

The above rules apply only to 'original issue discount' bonds. What of a bond that was issued at par, but is subsequently bought in the market at a discount? A subsequent profit on redemption used to qualify for capital gains treatment on realisation. Section 1276 changed the rules: where such bonds are purchased after 18 July 1984, subsequent gain is taxed as ordinary income to the extent of the accrual market discount. This provision is less relevant as long as the TRA rule equalising the rate of tax on income and gains continues.

Withholding tax

Before 1984 the gross amount of interest payments made by US persons to foreign creditors was subject to withholding tax of 30 per cent. (If the interest was 'effectively connected' with a US trade or business it would be assimilated to 'branch' income and be subject to tax at corporate or personal rates. Treaty provisions would not apply to such income.) This withholding tax was eliminated by a number of treaties but US borrowers wishing to tap the Eurobond markets were obliged to structure their borrowings through third countries such as the Netherlands Antilles.

The 1984 Provisions

Section 127 of the Deficit Reduction Act of 1984 abolished withholding tax on portfolio interest (including original issue discount) paid to non-residents on obligations issued after 18 July 1984. There are important limitations on this exemption, some of which affect the international planner. Interest is not exempt if:

(a) the payer is a corporation and the recipient owns (directly or indirectly) 10 per cent or more of the voting power of the payer; or

(b) the payer is a partnership and the recipient owns (directly or indirectly) 10 per cent or more of the capital or profit interest in the payer; or

(c) interest received by a bank on an extension of credit made pursuant to a loan agreement entered into in the ordinary course of its business other than with respect to interest paid on an obligation in the United States or the interest received by a controlled foreign corporation from a related person; or

(d) interest is effectively connected with the conduct of the US trade or business.

Exemption on interest paid on registered form securities is given only if the US payer has received a statement that the beneficial owner is not a US person. The Secretary of the Treasury has powers to refuse to accept statements from a particular source, e.g. financial intermediaries in third countries believed to be acting on behalf of US shareholders.

Eurobond issues are normally in bearer form. Bearer securities will be eligible for exemption from withholding tax provided that:

(a) the obligations are sold under procedures reasonably designed to prevent sales to US persons;

(b) interest is payable only outside the United States; and

(c) the obligations and coupons indicate on their face that US holders are subject to limitations under US income tax laws.

The Secretary to the Treasury has power to issue regulations excluding bearer debt from the exemption and therefore to require registration. He is also entitled to remove the exemption for payments to any person within a foreign country if he considers that the exchange of information between the United States and that country is inadequate to prevent evasion of tax by US persons.

15

Foreign exchange taxation

United States – tax treatment of foreign exchange

The Tax Reform Act of 1986 brings, at least in concept, a spirit of rationality and common sense to the whole subject but in practice problems remain. The subject is developing rapidly as Regulations are published, Technical Corrections are discussed in Congress, and Internal Revenue Service attitudes become clearer; this chapter can only give an overview of the issues. Chapter 16 discusses some of the older cases which may still be relevant.

In the past, relevant law in the United States has, overall, been just about as unsatisfactory as in the United Kingdom. To quote from Philip Kaplan (*Journal of Strategy in International Taxation*, vol. 1, No. 5, p. 376):

Present US law on measuring income or loss following from variations in the value of a foreign currency as against the US dollar is, in a word, a mess. Different rules are applied to transactions in related but separate areas, or at times, in the same area. The courts are frequently in disagreement as to the US tax effects of a transaction and at times base their decisions on purely formalistic reasoning, such as the fact that repayment of a loan does not constitute a sale of exchange. As always where chaos prevails, someone profits and someone loses. In this case, the government and taxpayers have been in both camps.

These words were written before the Tax Reform Act of 1986 'simplified' the tax system. How much has changed? To quote a more recent author (Stephen J. McGarry. *International Tax Journal*, Winter, 1988):

Chaotic, unsettled, confused, multidirectional, inconsistent, illogical, complex, uncertain – these are but a few of the terms used in articles describing the taxation of exchange transactions.

To be sure, long-term capital losses (and gains) on liabilities are treated similarly to gains and losses on assets, thus eliminating the more blatant form of tax fragmentation, Type 1, found in the United Kingdom. To compensate (if that is the right word) the border-line between capital gain and ordinary income has been rather less clear cut, particularly with modern hedging instruments. The computation of tax credit relief and its 'limitations' has been complex and confusing, and are seriously distorted by foreign currency risk.

The main criticism of *UK* law was that, although the inadequacy of statute law has been obvious to all concerned since 1976 (and to specialists since 1970) nothing has been done to amend it. In the United States there have, arguably, been too many changes.

The Tax Reform Act enshrines the concept of 'functional currency' along the lines suggested in the classic US Treasury *Discussion Draft on Taxing Foreign Exchange Gains and Losses* (December 1980). The principles in that draft resurfaced, with some deterioration in English style, in the *President's Proposals* (*Treasury 2*) in May 1985. Each entity or 'qualified business unit' (more or less the same concept as a 'self accounting branch') must have a 'functional currency' which may be the US dollar or another currency.

The second important concept is that of a 'Section 988 transaction' where the taxpayer is 'entitled to receive or required to pay a sum denominated in a currency other than the functional currency'. As explained in Chapter 13 we have to consider the 'source', 'character' and timing of any such transaction. Generally this is straightforward, but the more one studies the small print the more one sees possible anomalies, mainly in the definition of source. It is also envisaged that certain foreign exchange gains and losses will be treated as analogous to interest, although in this case (as with so much of the Tax Reform Act) we will have to await Regulations before we know exactly how it works.

In the United States, long-term capital gains were, prior to the TRA, taxed at a lower rate (a maximum of 20 per cent for individuals and 28 per cent, for corporations) than normal income or corporate profits. Short-term gains had been taxed at normal income rates. The holding period of twelve months to qualify for long-term treatment was reduced to six months for assets acquired after 22 June 1984 and before 1 January 1988. It was important to determine whether a foreign currency transaction gave rise to a long-term short-term gain (or loss) or to regular income treatment.

The Tax Reform Act reduced the personal maximum rate to 28 per cent (33 per cent in a 'catch-up' zone), while corporations pay 34 per cent. Capital gains are taxed as regular income, but with limited relief for capital losses. The distinction between income and capital gain may be less important than before, but other problems remain. Indeed, one of the great advantages of this approach is that, generally, it makes it clear that gains or losses on hedging transactions will be characterised as ordinary income; it should remove the ambiguities and uncertainties of the 'Corn Products' doctrine.

Generally each 'qualifying business unit' (QBU) is required to determine the tax effect of 'Section 988 transactions' undertaken in a currency other than the 'functional currency' of that QBU. Where the functional currency is not the US dollar we have to translate to determine the US dollar tax consequences.

One of the many problems remaining is that the apparent logic of the '988' approach may conflict with other provisions, notably the 'straddle' provisions of Sections 1092 and 1256. These were designed to prevent the use of the commodity straddle as a tax postponement or avoidance device and the principle has been stretched beyond endurance by attempts to apply them to modern financial and risk-shifting techniques. This can result in a variant of the 'killer rule'.

Qualifying business units and functional currency

The 'functional currency' in which the initial calculations are made is either the US dollar or 'in the case of a qualifying business unit (QBU), the currency of the economic environment in which a significant part of such unit's activities are conducted and which is used by such unit in keeping its books and records'. The concept is adapted from the accounting standard FASB 52, which replaced the notoriously innumerate FASB 8. Where a QBU is operating in a foreign country, the taxpayer may, in certain circumstances, *elect* to use the US dollar as the functional currency. It must then maintain its accounts in US dollars, and use 'separate transactions' accounting for non-dollar transactions (Section 985(b)). This is intended mainly for higher inflationary economies.

Section 988 transactions

A 'Section 988 transaction' is one in which the taxpayer is entitled to receive, or is required to pay, a sum denominated in a currency or currencies other than the functional currency of the entity (Section 988(c)(1)(A)). This is sometimes referred to as a 'non-functional currency' or NFC.

Section 988 begins with the words

Except as otherwise provided in this section, any foreign currency gain or loss attributable to a section 988 transaction shall be computed separately and treated as ordinary income or loss (as the case may be).

Corporate treasurers should particularly note that the definitions include as Section 988 transactions 'the acquisition of a debt instrument or becoming the obliger under a debt instrument' (Section 988(c)(1) B(i)). US treatment was, and remains, symmetrical with regard to *liabilities*. Significantly, the definition of 'debt instrument' includes the sentence 'to the extent provided in regulations such term shall include preferred stock' (Section 988(c)(4)).

We need to examine the following aspects of a foreign currency transaction or exposure:

(a) the tax treatment of the transaction against the functional currency of the relevant entity (Section 988); and
(b) where the functional currency is not the US dollar, the tax consequences of translation or conversion.

There are, as explained in Chapter 13 the three following 'characterisation' questions:

1. Is the gain or loss capital or regular income?
2. Timing – when is it recognised?
3. Source – US or foreign?

Subsidiaries

Section 986 sets out the procedure for computing the tax liability of a US resident shareholder of a foreign corporation. The profits must be calculated in the functional currency, and 'when distributed, deemed distributed or otherwise taken into account' shall 'be translated into dollars using the appropriate exchange rate'.

Capital or income?

This is now less relevant than it was. However, even if the rates remain the same, the rules for loss offset are different. The general rule is that Section 988 transactions 'shall be computed separately and treated as ordinary income or loss (as the case may be)' (Section 988(1)(a)).

The distinction between short-term and long-term capital gains is still important because a short-term capital loss is deductible from ordinary income. The holding period is now again twelve months.

Timing

When is the gain or loss recognised? This only affects the timing of tax payments but it can be worth quite a few basis points on financing costs. Taxpayers will wish so to arrange matters that year-end losses on currency exposure can be recognised in the current year, while profits can be deferred. The 'straddle' rules specifically limit certain types of postponement transaction.

Generally, a 'closed and completed transaction' doctrine is adopted. Section 988(c)(2) and (3) define 'booking date' and 'payment date' respectively. There must be a 'realisation event'. The 'booking date' is the date that the taxpayer:

(a)   acquires, or becomes an obligor on a debt instrument;
(b)   accrues or otherwise takes into account an item of expense, gross income or receipts; or
(c)   enters into or acquires a forward or futures contract or option.

The 'payment date' is the date that the taxpayer:

(a)   makes or receives payment on a debt instrument or item of expense, gross income or receipts *or* in the case of a forward or futures contract or option the date of completion.

Source

The central importance of the concept of 'source' has been discussed in Chapter 13. Correct planning for tax credit relief requires a thorough understanding of the definitions and can materially affect the global tax burden.

There are some special points affecting currency. The 1976 Tax Act provision (Section 904(3)(c)), which treated what would otherwise be foreign source capital gains as having a US source, is repealed.

The 'source' question is relatively simple where a US operation has a branch with a functional currency other than the US dollar. Section 987 provides for the use of the 'profit and loss method' to calculate branch income. The calculation must be made separately for each QBU, and the profit or loss is then translated into US dollars using the 'weighted average' rate (whatever this means, see below) for the period over which the income or loss accrued.

If the profits are remitted at a time when the exchange rate is different from this average a foreign currency gain or loss will be recognised. This will be characterised as 'ordinary income' having the same 'source' as the income to which it relates (Section 986(c)).

Section 989 defines various terms. The 'appropriate exchange rate' is 'except as provided in regulations . . . the spot rate on the date and the distribution or deemed dividend is included in income'.

For some other purposes the expression 'weighted average exchange rate' for the taxable year is used, but not otherwise defined. What does this mean? Is it simply the arithmetic mean of the closing exchange rates on each business day during the relevant year? This is the basis on which the UK Inland Revenue's official figures are calculated, but if this is what is wanted the term 'weighted' adds nothing to the meaning. Otherwise, do we have to make a more subtle attempt to 'weight' with the actual volume of transaction of the particular taxpayer? The point is not specifically included in the list of matters to which Regulations will apply.

Foreign exchange gains as 'interest'

Section 988(a)(2) provides that 'to the extent provided in regulations any amount treated as ordinary income or loss . . . shall be treated as interest income or expense (as the case may be)'.

The Conference Report (vol. II, p. 665) suggested this may apply for selected purposes only. This raises the question of whether such gains (not being 'fixed determinable annual or periodical income') can be treated as 'interest' when received by non-residents. It seems difficult to apply withholding tax, unless the transaction is (e.g.) associated with a swap. Will the computation be on a realisation or an accrual basis?

Treasury 2, stated

Exchange gain or loss with respect to financial assets or liabilities denominated in a currency other than the functional currency of an entity may properly be thought of as an economic equivalent to interest. In most transactions the parties anticipate that exchange gain or loss with respect to a foreign-currency-denominated financial asset generally will offset the difference between yield in the foreign currency and the yield for a comparable dollar asset over the life of the asset. It is therefore appropriate to treat foreign exchange gain or loss as the equivalent of interest for tax purposes.

In order to prevent the mismatching of income and deductions that can arise if foreign exchange gain or loss is not taken into account until it is realized, 'anticipated exchange gain or loss' would be recognised on an accrual basis with respect to a foreign-currency-denominated financial asset or liability that provides for a fixed or determinable payment in the future (e.g. an accrued item of income or expense, or an obligation). Anticipated exchange gain or loss would be determined under rules comparable to those which apply to impute interest with respect to obligations issued for property. Unanticipated exchange gains and losses would be recognised when realized.

A US borrower might have borrowed Deutschmarks at 6 per cent when he could have borrowed dollars at 12 per cent. Assuming a five-year fixed rate loan and an initial exchange rate of $1 = DM3, the borrower 'breaks even' on his decision if in five years $1 = DM2.28.

Treasury 2 would amortise this expected foreign exchange cost over the period, presumably adapting formula applying to deep discount bonds. After a year, the anticipated rate would be 2.84, a theoretical exchange loss (on a DM3 million borrowing) of $56,000. This would be allowed as if it were interest, even if (apparently) the dollar had actually *risen* in value. Correspondingly, the taxpayer with a Deutschmark deposit would be assessed on national income.

Over the five years the borrowing taxpayer will have received deductions (and the depositor will have received notional assessments) of $317,000 in addition to actual income paid or received). If the rate is now $1 = DM1.5, the actual loss to the borrower (gain to the lender) will be $1 million, and the balance of $683,000 would be relieved or assessed. If the rate is $1 = DM4, the borrower would actually make a profit and the lender a loss of $250,000:

The Administration will consider whether it is possible to establish safe harbors for circumstances where the mismatching of income and expense would not be material.

The proposal, although at first sight rational and internally consistent, has not been universally welcomed.

The 'interest equivalency' rule, in effect introduces the concept of a synthetic dollar loan – *as if* the borrower had swapped his foreign borrowing into a dollar loan of the same maturity at then market terms, even though such a transaction was inappropriate on the facts. It would often create, rather than remove, fragmentation.

Fragmentation or integration?

The United States has treated, and in principle continues to treat, foreign currency as 'personal property'. One conclusion from this is obvious enough: gains and losses from buying and selling foreign currency are taxable (or deductible) according to normal tests; they may be characterised as 'capital' or 'ordinary income'.

Another conclusion has more serious consequences. The sale of an asset for foreign currency, and the subsequent sale of the currency for dollars, may be treated as two separate transactions: 'sub-fragments'. The 'separate transaction' principle was adopted in KVP Sutherland versus Commissioner, but was not followed in others. It appears to be codified by Section 988(a)(1)(A). Generally, there will be a separate basis in the US dollar value of the foreign currency, and in the value of the asset acquired with the foreign currency.

Another conceptual approach is 'fungibility' which would treat the repayment of a foreign currency as the mere return of property.

The Conference Report (vol. II, pp.663–4) stated that 'foreign currency gain or loss is recognised only to the extent of the total gain or loss, taking into account gain or loss on the underlying transactions'. This appears to suggest an integrated approach.

Straddles and swaps

The general principles for dealing with straddles are to be found in Section 1256. This section was first enacted in 1981 and was directed to trading in commodity futures. 'Commodity straddles' had been used aggressively as a tax planning device. A trader would buy, for instance, contracts in 'March soya beans' while selling contracts in 'January beans'. These are treated as separate assets. Provided that soya moves in price (it does not matter whether up or down) there will be a substantial profit on one leg of the straddle, and a more or less identical loss on the other. Towards the end of his tax year, the trader will 'lift a leg', realising the contract showing a loss, but will run the profitable contract on into the following year. (The risk could meanwhile be hedged, perhaps by a May contract.) Straddles could thus be used to postpone profits for a year, to transmute regular income into capital gain, or (in a more aggressive variant which does not always work) to transfer profits from a taxpayer to an associated tax free entity.

Section 1256 countered these arrangements by requiring certain contracts to be 'marked to market' for tax purposes, i.e. by treating *unrealised* gains (and losses) at the year end as coming into the tax computation. This procedure is a notable exception to the general principle of taxing gains when realised, and the rule obviously raises serious problems of definition. It was introduced in 1981 (and substantially amended in 1984) at about the time that the financial futures markets were expanding. The rule has been grossly over-stretched. A 'Section 1256 contract' means:

(1)   any regulated futures contract
(2)   any foreign currency contract
(3)   any non-equity option and
(4)   any dealer equity option.

Where the Section applies, 'each Section 1256 contract shall be treated as sold for its fair market value on the last business day of each taxable year'.

Under TRA 'Section 1256 transactions' are *excluded* from the definition of 'Section 988 transactions'. Section 988(c)(1)(B)(iii) defines the latter to include:

Entering into or acquiring any forward contract, futures contract, option or similar financial instrument if such instrument is *not* marked to market at the close of the taxable year under Section 1256.

Correspondingly, the definition of a straddle in the Section 1092(c) contains a proviso 'entering into or acquiring any forward contract, futures contract, option or similar financial instrument *if such instrument is not marked to market* at the close of the taxable year under Section 1256.

One problem is the definition of a 'foreign currency contract'. A simplistic view is that Section 1256(8) applies to any currencies where 'regulated futures contracts' are traded. There are active markets in Canadian dollars, yen, Deutschmarks and Swiss francs. French francs, Dutch guilders, Australian dollars and Mexican pesos have been traded at various times. It *appears* that only US markets are relevant. Edward Kelinbard (page 68) states that:

(1)   the contract must require delivery of a foreign currency (or have a cash settlement feature);
(2)   the foreign currency in question must be one in which positions are traded through regulated futures contracts;
(3)   the contract (*not*, as some would read it, the foreign currency) must be 'traded in the interbank market'; and
(4)   the contract must be entered into at arm's length at a price determined by reference to the price in the interbank market.

Does Section 1256(g) favour foreign markets which are a 'national securities exchange' which is registered with the Securities and Exchange Commission (SEC)? (At one time the only two exchanges covered were the International Futures Exchange (Bermuda) Limited and the Mercantile Division of the Montreal Stock Exchange.)

Another query is the effect of the mark to the market rule on foreign currency contracts which are traded on the inter-bank market. Treasury has expressed the view that this requirement is satisfied if the bank with which the contract is entered into trades on the inter-bank market. Does this limit Section 1256 to bank forward contracts? What is the characterisation of a swap?

Section 988(a)(i)(B) permits a taxpayer to elect to treat as capital gain or loss 'any foreign currency gain or loss attributable to a forward contract, a futures contract, or option . . . described in sub-Section (c)(1)(B)(iii) which is a capital asset in the hands of the taxpayer and which is not part of a straddle (within the meaning of Section 1092(c))'. This is presumably favourable to the taxpayer where he can offset the gains against otherwise unusable capital losses.

Kelinbard, referring to Fuller, states that 'most practitioners, have concluded, I believe, that currency swaps are not "foreign currency contracts" within the meaning of Section 1256(g)'.

A key provision used to be Section 1233(a) (anti-straddle) which provides that 'gain or loss from the short sale of property shall be considered as gain or loss from the sale or exchange of a capital asset to the extent that the property, including a commodity future, used to close the short sale constitutes a capital asset in the hands of the taxpayer'. Section 1233(b) goes on to deal with the 'holding period' rules. Section 1234(a) (introduced in 1981) brought into account as capital gains the profit or loss on the cancellation, settlement or lapses of obligations, even though there is no sale or exchange.

The definition of a straddle in Section 1092(c) contains an important proviso 'entering into or acquiring any forward contract, futures contract, option or similar financial instrument *if such instrument is not marked to market* at the close of the taxable year under Section 1256'. The Conference Report vol. 11, p.665 refers to the authority to bring in regulations 'to provide certainty of tax treatment for . . . hedging transactions . . . and to ensure that such a transaction is taxed in accordance with its economic substance'.

A change in the functional currency is treated as a change in the accounting method for the purpose of Section 481. (This Section provides for 'Adjustments required by changes in methods of Accounting' and was not, as such, amended by TRA) (Section 985(b)(4).) Regulations are expected. These will probably require consistent accounting treatment even if several different functional currencies are used by an enterprise.

Section 988(a)(3)(c) gives a special rule for certain related party loans:

Except to the extent provided in regulations, in the case of a loan by a United

States person or a related person to a 10% owned foreign corporation which is denominated in a currency other than the dollar and bears interest at a rate of at least 10 percentage points higher than the Federal mid-term rate (determined under Section 1274(d)) at the time such loan is entered into the following rules shall apply:

(i) for the purposes of Section 904 only such loans shall be marked to market on an annual basis

(ii) any interest income earned with respect to such loan for the taxable year shall be treated as income from sources within the United States to the extent of any loss attributable to clause (i).

The effect of this is to reduce the amount of the interest recipient's foreign source income and bring the 'excess' interest in as US source income.

16

US case law on foreign exchange taxation

The cases discussed in this chapter were decided on the law as it was before TRA 1986. They may or may not still be relevant. See Chown, 1982, for a fuller account of prior law from a 'foreign' viewpoint.

Two of the cases (*B. F. Goodrich Co.* v. *Commissioner* TC 1098 (1943) and *Gillin* v. *United States* 423 F 2d 309, 311 (Ct Cl 1970)) affect foreign currency *liabilities*, but there is less distinction between the two sides of the balance sheet than in the United Kingdom.

Other cases involve hedging transactions. Foreign exchange exposure can be hedged (or speculative transactions opened) by *forward* transactions (usually with a bank) or by buying or selling *futures* contracts on an organised exchange. Such transactions may be afforded capital treatment. The taxpayer would like to set up his transactions so as to claim any *losses* as ordinary income (or short-term capital) losses, while arranging that any *profits* are long-term capital gains. Case law suggests that this may be a feat that is difficult to achieve. Such scope as there is *may* be found in future markets, although this too is dangerous territory.

The *Corn Products* case (*Corn Products Refining Co.* v. *Commissioner* 350 US 46 (1955)) threw some light (or not as the case may be) on the hedging principle. Certain transactions in corn futures were characterised as a 'loose hedge' and treated as giving rise to ordinary income.

International Flavors & Fragrances v. *Commissioner* 62 TC 232 (1974) followed this principle. A forward sale of foreign *currencies* was a 'loose hedge' against potential currency losses in foreign subsidiaries. The *gain* on the sale of the contract right was taxed as regular income. A similar conclusion was reached in *Wool Distribution Corp* v. *Commissioner* 34 TC 323 (1960) where the company, a dealer in foreign wool, sold foreign currency forward to protect the (currency-related) value of the inventory.

The Hoover case

The *Hoover* case (*Hoover Co. Ltd* v. *Commissioner*) 72 TC 206 (1979)) is probably no longer relevant, but as the classic US horror story on tax fragmentation, is of considerable historical interest. It concerned forward sales of foreign exchange to hedge *translation* exposures but this time the taxpayer made a loss and *sought* ordinary income treatment. At all relevant times Hoover owned about 55 per cent of its UK subsidiary Hoover Ltd. The parent, due to receive a dividend of £300,000 on 6 September 1967 sold this amount of currency forward. The pound was not in fact devalued during the period of that hedge. The effect of the transaction was (presumably) to fix the amount of the dividend – the *1967* tax liability was not at issue in the case. Subsequently, Hoover 'decided not to engage in such hedging transactions for the balance of 1967 as it did not believe devaluation of the pound sterling was imminent'. The pound was in fact devalued on 18 November 1967.

Translation produced an exchange loss of $3.6 million which was treated in accordance with 'generally accepted accounting principles' (a phrase which seems to strike irrational dread in the hearts of American corporate treasurers) as an extraordinary charge against consolidated earnings. This produced a fall in earnings per share from $2.09 to $1.54. There was of course no actual recognised or realised loss for Federal tax purposes. (Finnish and Danish subsidiaries made a contribution to this total loss.)

The horse having bolted, Hoover began a policy of hedging its translation exposure. The transactions are set out in detail in the judgment and make fascinating reading for a financial adviser. For instance at the end of 1968 the company calculated the attributable interest in 'net assets subject to risk' in Hoover UK at £7.5 million and sold sterling forward in the amount of £7.25 million at an average price of $2.3136. The various contracts were closed (in various ways) at a loss. No attempt appears to have been made to calculate the hedge in after tax terms, as prudent modern practice would dictate.

Hoover sought to characterise these losses as regular income losses. The Inland Revenue Service contended, and the Court upheld, that 'the forward sale agreements did not constitute *bona fide* hedging trans-actions and that the outcome had to be treated not as ordinary gains and losses but as capital gains and losses'.

Many arguments were put forward on behalf of Hoover. From our point of view the most interesting was an attempt to assimilate the transactions to a *bona fide* hedging transaction qualifying under Section 1233. The Court said:

although financial reporting rules require a parent corporation to reproduce consolidated earnings by exchange losses . . . on its consolidated income statement, the exchange losses are neither recognised nor realised for tax purposes. These losses merely represent the worst possible financial picture if the parent corporation were to liquidate . . . the reporting of these losses for accounting purposes does not reflect corporate reality. The subsidiaries here, and in the usual case, continue to operate with the same assets, and an earning potential perhaps greater, perhaps reduced. Dividend payments may or may not decline. The value of the subsidiaries stock does not necessarily go up or down because of currency fluctuations. In the final analysis we are not convinced that a real risk of economic loss, either ordinary or capital in nature, is present under these circumstances.

The finding in Hoover seems generally in accordance with economic reality but the mere fact that the case had to go to court at all suggests that there was a violation of symmetry. Had these transactions been entered into in 1967 instead of the following year there would have been a substantial profit on foreign exchange transactions against an unrealised capital translation loss. Hoover would no longer have had to show a loss of $3.6 million on the income statement. It would have collected the equivalent sum in hard cash and would have had to pay tax on this. Would the Internal Revenue Service have accepted this gain as a capital gain or would it have contended for revenue treatment? Clearly, in retrospect, Hoover should have concentrated on setting up its hedge in a tax neutral way, doubling up where necessary. A comparison between Hoover and International Flavors and Fragrances (IFF) suggests to many taxpayers that the Internal Revenue Service are playing on 'head I win tails you lose' rules. A *profit* is evidence of *trading* intent while a loss is capital.

Goodrich

The courts have treated foreign currency, not as a medium of exchange, but as a commodity. A central problem (the borrowing and return of fungible property) was brought out in the Goodrich case *(B. F. Goodrich Co 1 TC 1098 (1943))*.

B. F. Goodrich Company borrowed F Fr 11 million in 1933. These francs were *not* converted into US dollars (an important point) but were immediately re-lent to a French subsidiary. At that time the rate of exchange was F Fr 16.9 to the dollar and the dollar equivalent of the transaction was $651,133. Three years later, the franc, having depreciated to F Fr 21.4 to the dollar, the company purchased F Fr 11 million in the spot market for $514,163 and used the francs so purchased to repay its indebtedness. The Internal Revenue Service sought to assess the company on a gain of $136,970.

The Tax Court found for the company arguing: 'Suppose the petitioner had borrowed eleven bars of metal with an obligation to return their equivalent rather than their money value, and, after using that particular metal the petitioner had spent some of its United States funds to obtain eleven new bars which it turned over to the lender in satisfaction of its obligation.'

It was argued that no real gain or loss could result from the mere borrowing and return of fungible property. Economically, though, there *was* a gain, and later decisions have brought the law more into line with financial reality.

At first sight, therefore, it would appear that Goodrich benefited from asymmetrical treatment, and that, applying the same principle, a US company which had borrowed Swiss francs in 1971 would today find itself with an enormous unrelieved loss. Most reports of the case (which concentrate on the *legal* issues) suggest that this would have been the consequence. The economic reality – in this case – seems rather different if we look a little further ahead into time.

The debt from the subsidiary was still outstanding. The book value of that debt was $651,133, and if it had been repaid at a lower rate the company would have been able to claim the loss as a deductible loss for tax purposes. The sting in the tail of the Tax Court's ruling was that the asset was henceforth to be treated as having a basis for tax purposes of $514,163, which is the actual cost of the dollars used to purchase the equivalent francs. Although the profit on the repayment fell out of account, the potential unrealised loss was correspondingly reduced. The treatment was therefore symmetrical in the long run, but perhaps only on its facts.

More recent cases have modified this doctrine. *KVP Sutherland Paper Co* v. *United States* 344 F 2d 377 Ct Cl (1965) goes closer to recognising the economic reality directly. KVP purchased spot Canadian dollars and lent these to its Canadian subsidiary, the loan being denominated in Canadian currency. Five years later the Canadian dollars were repaid and subsequently (not immediately) converted by the parent into US dollars. The Court held that these transactions had to be treated separately and that there was a gain (or loss) on the repayment of the Canadian dollars even though conversion back into US dollars was not at that stage complete. There would be further gain or loss on the final conversion but this was (presumably) treated as a short-term gain or loss.

A similar conclusion was reached in *Gillin* v. *United States* 423 F 2d

309 Ct Cl (1970). Mr Gillin had borrowed a total of $260,269 in Canadian dollars in Canada, but had immediately converted these into US dollars for use in the United States. (He had no business in Canada, and simply found Canadian borrowing terms more favourable.) He eventually repaid the Canadian dollars for $US19,510.76 less than the US dollar proceeds of converting the loans. This was held to be an ordinary gain. Judge Skelton argued that the gain should be a short-term capital gain. His reasoning was different but the conclusion would have been the same.

Fragmentation or integration?

A number of cases, have held that it may be appropriate to adopt an integrated approach. In *Seaboard Finance Company* v. *Commission* 55–2 USTC 9644 (9th Cir. 1955), the taxpayer, in order to increase the Internal Revenue Code Section 904 limitation on the foreign tax credit, claimed capital gains treatment on the gain on a foreign currency bank deposit made with another contracting party to guarantee the performance of a contract for the purchase of stock. The Court upholding the Commissioner held that the gain arising from the obligation had to be matched against the loss from the foreign currency deposit which was purchased to secure its performance.

Other cases which have held for an integrated approach include: *Wool Distributing Corporation* 34 TC 323 (1960); *Columbia Sand and Gravel Co.* 11 TC 794 (1952); and *William H. Coverdale* 4 TCM 713 (1945).

Part Four

Canada

17

The general tax system

Introduction

There is never an easy time to write about Canadian taxation. Finance ministers have a habit of announcing tax changes, which are then left unimplemented and undebated in Parliament until after an election. The effective date of the legislation is then the date of the announcement and between that date and the subsequent bill becoming law the unfortunate taxpayer must guide his actions by a ministerial statement not expressed in precise legal language and which has not been subject to parliamentary scrutiny. For instance, changes affecting two matters vital to the corporate treasurer (withholding tax on Eurobond borrowings, and net financing) were announced in the Budgets of 12 November 1981 and 28 June 1982. These were only incorporated in due legislation by a 1983 Act which completed its parliamentary stages on 30 March 1983. The text of the Bill was published in December 1982 as what was described as 'an early' end to tax uncertainty! In spite of this long delay, some of the provisions were retrospective to the earlier dates. This is not a unique example: measures announced on, and retrospective to, 16 November 1978 were enacted only in 1980. Recent developments suggest a further aspect for discussion and possible litigation. Will measures be retrospective to the date of the official budget, or that of the unofficial leak?

We are again in one of these limbo periods, following the election in November 1988. In Party terms, this was 'no change' and tax reform will doubtless be picked up on the previously announced path.

Tax reform

Canada has been moving (although more reluctantly) to the lower rate,

The author is indebted to Mr J. Scott Wilkie of Stikeman Elliot, Toronto for helpful comments on the Canadian chapters.

broader base type of corporation tax pioneered by the United Kingdom in 1984 and subsequently adopted and extended by the United States in 1986. Michael Wilson's budget on 26 February 1986 proposed to phase down Federal tax rates on different categories of Canadian companies, the full reductions only coming into effect on 1 July 1989. The White Paper of 18 June 1987 abandoned these proposals and substituted some rather simpler ones. The basic Federal rate of corporation tax was to be reduced in one step from 36 per cent to 28 per cent on 1 July 1988. The Federal rate on manufacturing income was to be reduced from 30 per cent to 23 per cent in stages ending 1 July 1991. The companies eligible for both the active business income rate and for the small business deduction were, from 1 July 1988, simply subject to a 12 per cent tax rate.

Canadian federal tax

	%	Proposed
General business	35%	28%
Manufacturing business	28%	23%
Small Canadian-controlled companies		
general	14%	12%
manufacturing	8%	12%

(Note the 'manufacturing business' category will phase down from 26 per cent to 23 per cent.)

All these rates are subject to a 3 per cent temporary surtax on the otherwise taxable amount which came into effect on 1 January 1987 and which will continue until the sales tax reforms are implemented. Other more recent proposals include a Federal tax on capital, in some cases creditable against corporate surtax.

Companies are also subject to provincial taxes. The effective combined rates for certain provinces are shown below. These figures assume no change in the provincial tax rates. If the base broadening measures are effective, these rates will bring in an enhanced provincial revenue and there may be pressure to lower provincial as well as federal rates.

	Manitoba	Ontario	Quebec
General	45%	43.5%	33.9%
Manufacturing	40%	37.5%	28.9%
Small C.c.			
general	22%	22 %	15.2%
manufacturing	22%	22 %	15.2%

Canada operates a modified imputation system. Domestic shareholders are eligible for imputation credit (the rates of which have been reduced) on Canadian dividends paid. Inter-company dividends are effectively tax-free subject to complex and changing rules for preferred shares.

Companies pay tax on their profits whether distributed or not. Dividends are distributions of after-tax profits, but double taxation of distributed profits is mitigated by giving a tax credit or inter-company deduction. A dividend of $100 is treated in the hands of an individual Canadian resident shareholder as if it represented gross taxable income of $125 on which $25 tax is deemed to have been paid taking into account provincial effects.

The Canadian imputation system differs from that of the United Kingdom and France in being 'imputation without clawback'. There has been no 'precompte' or 'ACT' procedure designed to claw back from the company credit where dividends are paid out of profits which have not borne tax. (One is now in effect for certain categories of preference share - see below.) There is also no refund of credit to non-resident shareholders.

Dividends paid to non-residents are not eligible for imputation credit and are indeed subject to an additional withholding tax: see below. Double tax agreements generally reduce the rate of withholding tax on dividends but none of them extend to the concept of imputation credit to residents of the treaty partner country or reduce the tax to a zero rate. Furthermore, there is a 'branch tax' which in effect acts as a substitute withholding tax when the foreign corporation organises its Canadian operations via a branch. There are provisions in double tax agreements exempting a slice of profits from this branch tax. This can be useful to the smaller companies setting up operations in Canada.

An unusual feature of the Canadian tax system is the way in which it allocates various reserves and funds for separate treatment - what has been referred to as 'the pot theory of taxation'. One effect of this is that a private company can generally repay the whole of its share capital free of individual tax on dividends.

The concept of 'Canadian paid up capital' (PUC) is an important one. It may be desirable to structure an acquisition to maximise PUC and there are anti-avoidance provisions designed to prevent artificial transactions to step-up and revalue PUC. Because the concept is different from that adopted in other countries it is often possible to structure a return of capital between Canada and another country in a way that is deemed to be dividend in one country but not in the other.

Canada is also in the course of introducing a general anti-avoidance provision (GAAR) which is a major preoccupation to Canadian practitioners. It is too early to offer guidance about how this provision might be applied to the financing transactions discussed in these chapters although it seems to reflect jurisprudence relating to tax avoidance. Suffice it to say that care may be necessary.

Preferred shares as a tax efficient financing tool

Interest is in general deductible to the payer but taxable to the recipient. Where the borrower is a taxable corporation and the recipient is tax exempt or taxed at lower rates (a pension fund or a foreigner) it is better to use loans. In other cases, a 'net loan' may be better.

A fiscally starved company might want to borrow $10 million from a bank and, assuming the appropriate interest rate to be 10 per cent, a straightforward loan would cost $1 million per annum. The company would have no otherwise taxable income against which to offset this interest, and should have been recommended to use a different, and more tax-efficient, structure. It would issue a preferred share redeemable at the end of an agreed period of, say, five years, with a coupon of 6 per cent. This would cost the company only $600,000 per annum in cash flow. The payments, being dividends rather than interest, would not be tax deductible, but no matter. The dividend received by the bank would be treated as aftertax income.

The rate of dividend could be, and often was, a 'floating rate', typically expressed as *half* the prime rate plus (say) 1 per cent. One way of looking at these transactions was to regard them as a method by which the fiscally starved company could 'sell' the benefit of its tax loss or surplus tax allowances to a taxpayer company for a 'price' of lower financing charges.

It was no surprise to the business and professional community when, in November 1978, the Canadian government took its first steps to change the rules. The device of the 'term preferred share' was then said to be costing the Canadian Revenue some $500 million per annum. The first measures did not fully succeed: the latest measures, announced in 1987, were enacted on 13 September 1988.

The first attempt at closing the loophole were directed specifically at 'bank' arrangements, Section 112(2.1) denied a deduction for dividends received by a 'specified financial institution' on a 'term preferred share', defined in Section 248(1). Such dividends were then fully subject to tax as if they were payments of interest: the paying company was *not* allowed to treat the payments as tax-deductible interest. The legislation therefore had a substantial 'overkill' element.

More stringent rules applied to preferred shares owned by a financial institution which had control of the company issuing the shares. There were certain exemptions for companies in financial difficulties (rigorously defined) and for shares quoted on a Stock Exchange. These exceptions were sufficient to ensure that preferred shares remained available, attractive and widely used.

Further changes were made by Budget Resolutions on 12 November 1981 (enacted, after the usual delays, on 31 March 1983). These provided the following:

1. Dividends on *prescribed* shares received, not issued after *23 October 1979,* were excluded from the application of subsection 112(2.2) of the Act.
2. With respect to dividends received after 12 November 1981, the provisions of sub-Section 112(2.2) of the Act relating to guarantee agreements were extended to guarantees with respect to an interest in a trust or a partnership.
3. Dividends received on a share (other than a prescribed share or a share issued under the 'financial difficulty' provisions) acquired after 12 November 1981, would not longer qualify for a deduction under Sections 112 or 138 of the Act in any case where, within five years from the date on which the share was issued, the holder of the share *may require* the redemption, cancellation or reduction of the paid-up capital of the share or the acquisition of the share by the issuer, a person related thereto or a partnership or trust of which the issuer or a person related thereto is a member or beneficiary.
4. The definition 'term preferred share' was amended to remove the ten-year exception for shares issued after 12 November 1981.
5. Provisions, similar to those in sub-Paragraph (h)(ii), (iii) and (iv) of the definition 'term preferred share' be introduced for shares (except shares referred to in paragraph (e) of the definition) issued after 15 November 1978, and before 12 November 1981.
6. The exception in sub-Paragraph (h)(iv) of the definition 'term preferred share' with respect to shares issued to a specified financial institution or acquired from such an institution do not apply to any share acquired after 12 November, 1981, unless the acquisition is pursuant to an agreement in writing made before 24 October 1979, and the comparable exception with respect to income bonds and income debentures be similarly restricted.
7. The use of the funds received on the issue of a share or an income bond or income debenture issued after 12 November, 1981, in circumstances of financial difficulty be restricted to the financing of a business carried on in Canada,
8. Effective after 12 November 1981, for the purposes of Section 112 of the Act and the definition 'term preferred share', a person who has an interest in a trust, either directly or indirectly or through an interest in any other trust, be deemed to be a beneficiary of the trust.

9. The definition 'term preferred share' be amended to clarify that sub-Paragraph (b)(iii) thereof applies to a corporation that acquired a share after 11 December 1979, and is associated with any corporation described in Paragraph 112(2)(2.0)(a) of the Act.

10. With respect to a share issued after 12 November 1981, pursuant to the financial difficulty provision in the definition 'term preferred share', the maximum term of any such share be limited to five years.

11. With respect to a share or an income bond or income debenture issued after 12 November 1981, pursuant to the financial difficulty provisions in the definitions 'term preferred share', 'income bond' or 'income debenture', only those payments of dividends or interest in excess of 6 per cent per annum be treated as taxable dividends except where the share or obligation was issued before 1982 pursuant to an agreement in writing to do so entered before 12 November 1981.

Further proposals were announced on 16 June 1987, and draft legislation based on this were published on 16 December 1987. Further relevant announcements were made in the Tax Reform package on 13 April 1988, and the legislation was enacted on 13 September 1988.

The approach is to substitute new legislation for Section 82(2) of the Income Tax Act, which deals with the tax treatment of dividends received from corporations resident in Canada. It affects Section 112 (inter-corporate dividend deduction) and Section 121 (dividend tax credit). There are also provisions relating to deemed dividends (Section 84). (Section 258(1) is effectively replaced and repealed.)

In effect, in most cases an 'ACT' approach is adopted. Everything seems to work at 40 per cent tax rate (250 per cent of tax paid is allowed as a deduction) which in turn implies a 12 per cent provincial rate. This is not always the case.

There are now six kinds of preferred shares, as follow, which are differently treated.

(a)   guaranteed preferred share;
(b)   secured preferred share;
(c)   term preferred share;
(d)   short term preferred share;
(e)   taxable preferred share;
(f)   taxable restricted financial institution (RFI) share.

These imposed 'refundable tax' of 25 per cent, 40 per cent or 66.6 per cent, which gave a rough justice effect. The rules are to be tightened up following the 1989 Budget.

18

The tax treatment of interest

Deductibility – general rule

The rules governing the deduction of interest from Canadian profits are more precise and exacting than the very general rule found in the United States, Section 163. Although in practice and in the majority of cases the rules governing what is and what is not deductible in the two countries come to much the same; in the United States interest is presumed to be deductible unless there is a specific provision that it is not. Revenue Canada rulings and court decisions confirm that interest is *not* to be regarded as deductible unless the circumstances are such that it can be brought within the strict test of the statute. This narrow construction has recently been upheld in the Bronfman case (1987) and the whole subject, in common with so much of Canadian tax law, is in mild turmoil. There is some hope that statute law will be rationalised – but not before 1990. Meanwhile, proposed legislation addresses aspects of interest deduction in the case of borrowings to make distributions.

Section 18 restricts what is allowed as a deduction. It is a long list but includes:

18(1) General limitations. In computing the income of a taxpayer from a business or property no deduction shall be made in respect of

18(1)(a) General limitation: an outlay or expense except to the extent that it was made or incurred by the taxpayer for the purpose of gaining or producing income from the business or property;

18(1)(b) Capital outlay or loss: an outlay, loss or replacement of capital, a payment on account of capital or an allowance in respect of depreciation, obsolescence or depletion except as expressly permitted by this Part;

18(1)(c) Limitation re exempt income: an outlay or expense to the extent that it may reasonably be regarded as having been made or incurred for the purpose of gaining or producing exempt income or in connection with property the income from which would be exempt.

The basic rule on interest is Section 20(1)(c) of the Canadian Income

Tax Act which sets out the conditions under which interest paid by a Canadian taxpayer is deductible in computing profits:

Notwithstanding paragraphs 18(1)(a), (b) and (h), in computing a taxpayer's income for a taxation year from a business or property, there may be deducted such of the following amounts as are wholly applicable to that source or such part of the following amounts as may reasonably be regarded as applicable thereto:

(c) Interest. An amount paid in the year or payable in respect of the year (depending upon the method regularly followed by the taxpayer in computing his income), pursuant to a legal obligation to pay interest on:

 (i) borrowed money used for the purpose of earning income from a business or property (other than borrowed money used to acquire property the income from which would be exempt or to acquire a life insurance policy),

 (ii) an amount payable for property acquired for the purpose of gaining or producing income therefrom or for the purpose of gaining or producing income from a business other than property the income from which would be exempt or property that is an interest in a life insurance policy).

(Sub-Paragraph (iii) deals with specified government aid measures: (iv) with money borrowed to purchase an annuity.)

(d) Compound Interest. An amount paid in the year pursuant to a legal obligation to pay interest on an amount that would be deductible under paragraph (c) if it were paid in the year or payable in the year.

Apart from the general 'use' test there are several grey areas.

In the present climate of tax reform, these issues need to be addressed from the point of view of trends as well as of the present interpretation of present law.

1. What happens when interest is incurred on investments which may not yield income for many years? The 12 November, 1981, Budget contains restrictive interest rules: these were later withdrawn.

2. What happens when a Canadian company borrows to capitalise a foreign subsidiary? *Prima facie* the interest is deductible: the resulting income will be taxed in the host country and will return to Canada as an exempt dividend.

3. Can payments in some manner relating to interest (e.g. swap fees) be made under protection of the general deduction rules of Section 9(1) even if they are not within the letter of Section 20?

The use test

Where money is *borrowed* we have a 'use' test. Where money is due on a purchase in instalments there is a *slightly* different 'purpose' test. The question discussed in the *Trans Prairie* case is what happens when the taxpayer applies some capital to the operation of the business and some to a non-qualifying use. (Non-qualifying use under the law as it then was included borrowing to earn intercorporate dividends or to operate a mine in respect of which a tax holiday applied.) The effect of the *Trans Prairie* decision appears to be that the test is the use of the 'mass of capital dedicated to that business through all the different forms through which it passes, while it remains in the business' rather than 'using money to make a particular payment as a result of which the payer no longer has that money'. Unless it can be established that the money was borrowed for a specific non-qualifying purpose, the tests will be satisfied with reference to the employment of the general funds of the company.

This last point appears to be in issue (although not directly) in the *Lakeview Gardens* case. The corporation borrowed money to buy a business asset and some years later acquired shares of a foreign subsidiary, income from which would be exempt (under the law as it then was). Although there were no further borrowings at the time of the share acquisition and the internally generated cash flow would have been sufficient to buy the shares, none the less a portion of the interest on outstanding indebtedness was disallowed. The Court concluded that not the entire payment for the shares could be regarded as having been made out of borrowed money, but only such portion as exceeded the company's available surplus . . . perhaps this case illustrates that *Trans Prairie* is, after all, a two-edged sword; just as one cannot trace borrowed money to a non-business, one cannot trace it to a business use.

In *Canada Safeway Limited* v. *MCR* (57 DTC 1239) the company borrowed money to purchase the share capital of MacDonalds Consolidated from their mutual US parent. Was money 'used' simply to earn dividends from MacDonalds? As those were then exempt the interest was not deductible. The unsuccessful (but economically sounder) view was that Canada Safeway borrowed to acquire control of a wholesaler, thereby procuring goods at keener prices and enhancing consolidated profits. This doubt could not have arisen under the US or UK approaches which look to 'group' profits. The Supreme Court found for form over substance, and disallowed the deduction. Canada Safeway had to regard the transaction as an investment in a separate dividend paying company and not as a means of producing a favourable business relationship through the exercise of voting control. This confirms that in Canada it does matter how a transaction is carried out: an asset acquisition would have had different consequences.

Following Trans-Prairie, Revenue Canada issued Interpretation Bulletin IT 80 (27 November 1972) *Interest on Money Borrowed to Redeem Shares or to Pay Dividends*.

This put a reasonably civilised gloss on the case. Interest would be allowed on money borrowed to replace capital used to earn profits; or to pay dividends in cases where accumulated profits are used to earn taxable income. This remained practice until 1987 when, following the Bronfman decision handed down on 29 January 1987, it was cancelled with effect from the date of the decision (Press Release, 12 February 1987).

The Bronfman case

The key case is now *The Queen* v. *Phyllis Barbara Bronfman Trust* (87 DTC 5059). In 1969 and 1970 the Trust made capital allocations to a beneficiary, and funded these by borrowing instead of realising income producing investments. The minister disallowed the deduction on the grounds that the interest expense was not incurred for the purpose of earning income as required by the strict wording of Paragraph 20(1)(c). The decision of the six Supreme Court judges was unanimous.

The interest was disallowed. Although the case concerned the non-business use of trust funds, Revenue Canada is seeking to apply it to corporate transactions. The implications so far appear to be that the 'use' test will be strictly applied and that interest relief cannot be claimed by the back door of Section 9(1). A strict legislistic approach to motives and to 'tracking' will be applied (see Lawlor 1987).

Accrual

Interest is generally deductible on an accrual basis. However, Section 78(1) dealing with 'unpaid amounts' restricts this where the loan is from a non-arm's length party. Deductible payments, including interest, remaining unpaid at the end of the year following the year in which the expense was accrued will be added back. The parties can avoid the application of this rule by filing an agreement with the Revenue by which unpaid interest is deemed to be paid and reloaned on the first day of the third taxation year. The detailed provisions are complex and should be checked carefully.

Withholding tax

Interest paid by Canadian entities to non-residents is in general subject to a withholding tax of 25 per cent of the gross amount (Section 212(1)(b)). Most double tax agreements reduce the rate to 10 or 15 per cent, but there are no treaty routes for eliminating withholding tax altogether. Because of this, where funds were to be used in Canada there was never any real scope for structuring public bond issues using offshore financing companies. The normal approach has been to bring such issues within the scope of one of the specific exemptions.

Canadian 'interest' provisions being more precise than those of many countries, there has been scope for structuring inter-company loans so that the payments do not constitute 'interest'.

Certain government provincial and municipal bonds are exempt: the detailed provisions vary with the date of issue (Section 212(1)(b)(ii)(A) (B) and (C)). The exemption extends to certain corporations that are 90 per cent owned by a province or municipality. In practical terms, the investor simply needs to select bonds which are in fact exempt.

There is also an exemption for foreign pension funds or charities which receive Canadian source income which would normally be subject to withholding tax. Section 212(1)(b)(iv) provides for exemption on interest payable on any bond, debenture or similar obligation issued after 13 June 1963 to a person to whom a certificate of exemption has been issued. These certificates are issued where the recipient pension fund or charity is exempt from tax in its own country and would also qualify as exempt in Canada.

Canadian borrowers on the Eurobond market

From the point of view of the corporate borrower, the most important exemption from withholding tax was that granted to certain types of medium-term corporate indebtedness. This measure was introduced specifically to enable Canadian borrowers to have access to the Eurobond market. The history is characteristically complicated. The concessions were restricted by the 1983 Finance Act which completed its Parliamentary stages on 30 March *1983*. It incorporated provisions announced in the two Budgets of 12 November *1981* and 28 June *1982* and some of the provisions were retrospective to the earlier dates.

The key provision, Section 212(1)(b)(vii), provides an exemption for interest payable by a corporation resident in Canada to a person with whom that corporation is dealing at arm's length: 'on any obligation . . .

under the terms of the obligation or any agreement relating thereto the corporation may not be obliged to pay more than 25 per cent of *the principal amount of the obligation within five years of the date of issue, except in the event of a failure or default'*.

The Finance Act 1983 replaced the words in italics and, following a further amendment in 1986 the provision now concludes:

and for the purpose of this paragraph, where interest is payable on an obligation other than a prescribed obligation, and all or any portion of the interest is *contingent or dependent upon the use of or production from property in Canada*, or is computed by reference to revenue, profit, cash flow commodity price or any other similar criterion or by reference to dividends paid or payable to shareholders of any class of shares in the capital stock of a corporation, the interest shall be deemed not to be interest described in sub paragraphs (ii) to (vii) and (ix).

This was intended to prevent 'hybrid' securities taking advantage of the concession. Amendments effective from 19 December 1986, while tightening up this provision, extended the exemptions to convertible securities by adding Section 212(1)(vii)(E): 'If the person exercises a right under the terms of the obligation or any agreement relating thereto to convert the obligation into, or exchange the obligation for, a prescribed security.' Relief was also extended to deposits with 'prescribed financial institutions'. Draft Regulations defining what was meant by 'prescribed' in both cases were issued on 6 April 1988; a not untoward delay by Canadian standards.

Thin capitalisation

There are restrictions on the deductibility of interest by a Canadian company to 'a specified non-resident', i.e. a non-resident shareholder or related person (or Canadian non-resident-owned investment corporation) which in association with others not dealing at arm's length, owns 25 per cent or more of *any* class of issued shares of the corporation (Sections 18(4)–18(6)).

In such cases, interest is deductible only on an amount equal to three times the 'equity' (as defined) of the corporation. The basis of computation is the *maximum* debt outstanding during the year. If this were, for example, six times the equity, half of the actual interest paid would be disallowed on an apportionment basis – even though the *average* debt on which the interest had been paid was less than three times capital.

Section 18(4) defines the terms as follows:

1. the amount, if any, by which
    (a) the greatest amount that the corporation's outstanding debts
         to specified non-residents was at any time in the year
    exceeds
    (b) three times the aggregate of
         (i)   the retained earnings of the corporation at the com-
               mencement of the year, except to the extent that those
               earnings include retained earnings of any other corpor-
               ation.
         (ii) the corporation's contributed surplus at the commence-
               ment of the year, to the extent that it was contributed by
               a specified non-resident shareholder of the corporation,
               and
         (iii) the greater of the corporation's paid-up capital at the
               commencement of the year and the corporation's paid-
               up capital at the end of the year, excluding the paid-up
               capital in respect of shares of any class of the capital
               stock of the corporation owned by a person other than a
               specified non-resident of the corporation.

Section 18(6) contains provisions intended to prevent avoidance of the
rules by the device of a loan made through a third party. A *specific* loan
to the third party subject to the *specific* condition that money be relent
to the Canadian corporation would clearly be caught. Interest paid to a
Canadian bank in the normal course of the bank's business, with the
guarantee of the parent appears to create no problems. On which side of
the line would a 'back to back' loan fall? A detailed examination of the
statutory rules in any particular case might be rewarding, but the
provisions of the GAAP now also need to be considered.

Deep discount bonds

Where discount bonds are issued after 19 June 1971, the tax position on
redemption is set out by Section 20(1)(f). If the obligation was issued
for an amount of not less than 97 per cent of the principal amount, *and*
the actual yield to maturity does not exceed four-thirds of the coupon
rate of interest, the *whole* of the premium on redemption is deductible –
in effect as if it were interest.

In other cases 75 per cent of the premium on redemption is deductible
in the year in which the bonds were redeemed. The sub-section refers to
an obligation 'on which interest was stipulated to be payable' which
appears to rule out a zero coupon bond in the absence of a legal

presumption that the discount or premium is 'legal interest'. There are no provisions (cf. the United States, France) for amortising the original discount; the taxable event is redemption at a price other than subscription price.

Canadian investors in Canadian securities are symmetrically treated in that 75 per cent of capital gains are added to, and 75 per cent of capital losses are deducted from, taxable income subject to transitional rule to 1990.

Section 16(3) imposes a charge to tax on the first Canadian taxpaying owner of a discount bond issued after 18 June 1971 by an exempt organisation or a non-Canadian issuer. The rule does not apply unless the redemption yield exceeds four-thirds of the coupon – see Section 20(1)(f) but without the 97 per cent proviso complex rules require domestic accrual of a variety of 'prescribed debt obligations' and 'investment contracts'.

Prior law (Section 16(2)) still applies to current transactions in bonds issued at a discount after 20 December 1960 but before 19 June 1971. This had similar provisions but with a '5 per cent' safe haven coupon.

Canadian tax law thus distinguishes three situations.
1. Original issue discount by Canadian taxable issuers – 75 per cent gain taxable on *redemption* but only 75 per cent deductible to corporation.
2. Original issue discount by foreign, or non-taxable Canadian, issuers – discount taxed on *purchase*.
3. 'Non-original' discount – 75 per cent tax on redemption or other disposal.

Section 39(3) deals with the case where (after 1971) bonds were re-purchased by the issuer rather than redeemed. The difference between the purchase price and the amount for which the obligation was issued is treated as a capital gain or loss. In calculating a *loss* the basis is 'the greater of the principal amount thereof and the amount for which it was issued' (Section 39(2)).

Section 214(7) deems the discount on certain bonds issued or sold to a non-resident to be interest for the purpose of withholding tax.

Warrant issues

Debt securities are sometimes issued with various extra rights as well as interest. These features will generally reduce the cost of borrowing but raise a tax question. How will the value of the extra inducement be taxed to the investor or relieved to the issuer?

Interpretation Bulletin IT–96R4 *Options Granted by Corporations to Acquire Shares, Bonds or Debentures* (current version 21 February

1985) now requires the value of the securities issued to be allocated between the 'bond' and the 'warrant' element. This may result in the bond being treated as issued at a 'deep discount', as discussed above.

In other cases, bonds have been issued where the amount of the interest is linked to the price of a commodity such as oil (Home Oil) nickel (Inco Limited) or gold. More recently, Royal Trust has followed US precedents in issuing securities carrying 4 per cent minimum interest, extra interest being paid on a formula varying with the level of the Standard and Poors Index. Are these extra payments 'interest' within the strict Canadian definitions? These issues are discussed by Richardson (1988) pp. 43–69.

19

Taxation of forex gains and losses

Prior to 1972, Canada had no capital gains tax; the gain or loss whether on an asset or a liability had, as in the United Kingdom, to be within the concept of 'trading' to be taxable or deductible.

The 1971 tax reform introduced a tax on capital gains, generally treating *half* the gain as if it were regular income to the individual or corporate taxpayer. Liabilities are in general symmetrically treated with assets, and there is a little risk (or scope) for tax fragmentation type 1. Type 2 certainly exists (and is important), and there are the usual 'timing' anomalies.

Capital or revenue?

As with the other countries so far considered we have to ask, *first*, whether or not a gain or loss is on capital account and, *second*, whether it is to be brought into account on an 'accruals' or a 'realisation' basis. The Canadian Revenue's view of general principles are set out in notice IT95, extracts from which are appended. There was an important change in late 1984 reflected in cases in that a loan to a thinly capitalised affiliate is no longer presumed to be on capital account.

A look at the cases suggests that the courts have had slightly more bias towards the 'revenue' interpretation than in the United Kingdom or the United States. Fifteen cases cited in either or both of two tax services can be analysed as follows:

	Tax payer Won (No. cases)	Lost (No. cases)
Gain held to be capital (not taxable)	2	
Loss held to be capital (not deductible)		2
Gain held to be revenue (taxable)		8
Loss held to be revenue (deductible)	3	

These figures appear to show not only a bias in favour of 'revenue' treatment, but against the taxpayer. He was in a 'heads you win, tails I lose' situation where Revenue Canada was likely to succeed in taxing him on a forex gain, and in denying him relief if he made a loss. This conclusion could be misleading, as we do not have details of cases settled without reaching the courts. It may well be that a 'defeat' for one taxpayer subsequently proved to be a favourable precedent for others!

Timing

Where foreign exchange gains or losses are on revenue account, taxpayers have a choice between using a cash or an accrual method of accounting. Both have been blessed by decided cases and the rules are set out in Paragraph 7 of IT95. Treatment must be consistent and tax treatment must accord with accounting treatment. This is broadly in line with what one would expect on other assets and liabilities. It does not seem possible to get the best of both worlds by using a 'lower of cost or market' approach. Rather there is, as elsewhere, some scope for using the 'cash' basis and carefully timing the realisation of transactions.

As in the United Kingdom, more precise rules apply to transactions on *capital* account. A gain is only taxed, a loss can only be claimed on actual realisation. If the statute had made no specific mention of foreign exchange gains and losses the general rules for capital gains and losses would presumably have applied. Many decided cases concerned liabilities and it seems never to have been suggested that gains and losses on foreign currency liabilities would be other than symmetrically treated.

Although foreign exchange gains and losses would normally be included in the computation of capital gains (Section 39(1)), they are in fact specifically and separately dealt with by Section 39(2). At first sight this does not appear to add anything material to the general law other than the exclusion of the first $200 of gain, *de minimis* provision intended for individuals. It does seem that some forex gains and losses (e.g. on liabilities) may be brought within this charge, while others, perhaps the forex element in the gains and losses on the corresponding asset, may be included in the normal assessment. This may result in tax fragmentation.

There are some restrictions on the application of capital gains tax rules on a disposal between connected parties (Section 40(2)(e)) and on the disposal of a debt (Section 40(2)(8)(ii)). 'Valuation day' transitional provisions may still occasionally be relevant.

The cases

In *Eli Lilly and Company (Canada) Ltd* v. *MNR* (Supreme Court 55 DTC 1139) goods were purchased on open credit account (denominated in US dollars) from the parent company over a period of years. This debt was settled in full in 1946 by the issue of common shares to the parent. This resulted in a foreign exchange gain, which was held (by a majority of the Supreme Court) to have arisen, in the course of trade, and to be taxable as income.

Similarly in *Tip Top Tailors Limited* v. *MNR* (Supreme Court 57 CTC 309), the taxpayer had incurred sterling bank overdrafts to purchase cloth in the United Kingdom. The Canadian dollar profit arising from the repayment following the 1967 devaluation of sterling was held to be earned in the course of the trade and to be taxable.

The taxpayer in *DWS Corporation* v. *MNR* (Exchequer Court 68 DTC 5045) succeeded in claiming an income loss in respect of funds borrowed in 1961 from parent corporation to repay affiliates and for commercial purchases. In this case it was specifically held that the length of time the debt was outstanding did not determine its nature as income or capital. However, in *Canadian SKF Company Ltd* v. *MNR* (Tax Appeal Board 66 DTC 140) the company incurred Swiss bank loans over the period 1952–61 to repay inventory purchased from the Swedish parent corporation. The repayment date of the loans was extended, and the taxpayer claimed part of the unrealized foreign exchange loss in his 1961 tax return. The loans were, in this case, held not to represent circulating capital but long-term capital financing. The losses were capital and not deductible.

A similar principle was followed in *Columbia Records of Canada Ltd* (Federal Court – Trial Division 71 CTC 839) where the taxpayer made foreign exchange losses on repaying US dollars from its parent. The taxpayer argued that as capital and reserves exceed the book value of fixed assets the loans were used to finance current assets. This argument did not succeed; as the taxpayer was not a dealer in foreign exchange, the loan was *prima facie* on capital account.

In a more recent case (*Ethicon Sutures* 2 CTC 6 (FCTD)) the Canadian subsidiary kept funds on short-term deposit in US dollars for the purpose of paying dividends to the US parent. During 1978 it paid dividends totalling $Can1,297,000 of which just over half was actually paid in US currency. It also spent $Can1,400,000 acquiring capital property. It appears that if these had been its only purposes, the forex gains of some $Can120,000 during the year would have been capital but the Court held that the funds were not earmarked, and there was a 'secondary' purpose of holding the funds to purchase inventory. The transactions were therefore treated as 'trading'. The company's balance sheet had classified the short-term deposits as 'current assets' and the profit and loss account referred to the gains as 'gains on foreign currency transactions'. Neither description can have helped. This case is subject to appeal. The conclusion seems perverse, although the detailed facts were against the taxpayer.

IT–95R – Foreign exchange gains and losses

The Canadian Revenue view is summarised in Interpretation Bulletin IT–95R, *Foreign Exchange Gains and Losses* issued 16 Decemer 1980 to cancel and replace an earlier bulletin dated 15 March 1973. Key passages read (our sub-headings and note):

General principles

1. There are no provisions in the Act which specify whether a foreign exchange gain or loss is on account of income or capital. Thus the major problem in determining the income tax status of foreign exchange gains or losses is the identification of transactions from which they result, or *in the case of funds borrowed in a foreign currency*, the use of the funds.

Capital versus income

2. Where it can be determined that a gain or loss on foreign exchange arose as a direct consequence of the purchase or sale of goods abroad, or the rendering of services abroad, and such goods or services are used in the business operations of the taxpayer, such gain or loss is brought into income account. If, on the other hand, it can be determined that a gain or a loss on foreign exchange arose as a direct consequence of the purchase or sale of *capital assets*, this gain or loss is either a capital gain or capital loss, as the case may be. Generally, the nature of a foreign exchange gain or loss is *not affected by the length of time between the date the property is acquired (or disposed of) and the date which payment (or receipt) is effected.*

3. Generally, where borrowed funds are used in the ordinary course of a taxpayer's business operation, any foreign exchange gain realized on the repayment of the loan is considered to be an income gain and any foreign exchange loss incurred on repayment of the loan is considered to be an income loss. *The fact that a company which borrowed in a foreign currency*

was adequately capitalized does not automatically result in capital treatment of any foreign exchange gains or losses arising on repayment. Capital treatment will result where it can be shown that the borrowed funds form part of the permanent or fixed capital of the company, regardless of the use of the funds. In other cases on inadequate capitalization, the use made of the borrowed funds will determine whether such gains or losses should be income account or on capital account).

(*Note*: The italic words in Paragraph 3 reflect an important change in policy, effected by Correction Sheet No. 11, 19 October 1984. Previously, the passage read: 'However, where it is obvious that the capitalization of a company is insufficient, to the extent that funds can be shown to have been borrowed in a foreign currency to offset this deficiency, any gain or loss as a result of repayment of such funds will be on account of capital, regardless of the use of the funds.').

4.   Where current foreign funds, i.e., funds obtained as a result of transaction on income account, are used to make a capital payment, such as a payment to purchase a capital property or a payment on a capital debt obligation, the exchange gain or loss on those current funds is reflected on income account at the time of the capital payment as though the funds had been converted to Canadian dollars and the same amount of Canadian funds had been used to make the capital payment. In such circumstances, there could subsequently be a capital gain or loss on the discharge of the capital debt obligation.

Timing of income transactions

7.   The Department will accept any method used to determine foreign exchange gains or losses on income transaction provided that method is, under the circumstances, in accordance with generally accepted accounting principles. Further the method used should be the same for both financial statement and income tax purposes.

Part Five

Continental Europe

20

Continental Europe

The European Community is ambitious to create a single market by the end of 1992. It is argued that this will require the harmonisation of company tax systems. To this end there is a long list of unimplemented proposed Directives, two of them dating as far back as 1969. For some time, it had seemed that little progress was being made, and that in any case the proposals so far tabled by the Commission would not achieve their objectives. There are signs that this issue is now regarded as more urgent.

This book cannot attempt a comprehensive overview of the law in every country; these proposals for harmonisation form a useful framework for a glance at the situation in continental Europe. This chapter also explains the important and continuing role of Luxembourg and Dutch holding companies.

It is proposed that European Community company taxation be based on a imputation system of the type pioneered by France and adopted in the United Kingdom in 1972. Some features of this system have been discussed in Chapter 9. The West German system is a variant of this, and could be brought into line with a few changes, more of form than of substance. Meanwhile, the peculiarities of the West German system are causing difficulties. The Netherlands and Luxembourg are the last two member states to persist with a 'classical' system, with double taxation of distributed profits. Companies in both these countries retain an important role in tax efficient international planning.

Continental European countries typically use a 'comparison of net worth' approach to taxing companies and their shareholders. The extreme forms of tax fragmentation are thus avoided. Foreign exchange gains and losses come into the general tax computation in a fairly rational way: the main problems are on timing and on the computation of double tax relief. Generally, too, interest on money borrowed for business purposes is deductible; some exceptions to both general principles are noted below.

Harmonisation – early history

The first document to address itself to the issue of tax harmonisation in the EEC was the Neumark Report *Tax Harmonisation in the European Economic Community* (1962). This recommended a split rate system in the form then in use in West Germany. The report also commented that the (pre-1965) UK system was then, in substance though not in form, substantially similar. France contemplated making such a change, but discovered that this would reduce the French Revenue's share of the total tax taken from the profits of American investments in France (the 'shadow effect') and in 1965 actually adopted an imputation system. In the same year the United Kingdom took a temporary backward step to full double taxation of companies and their shareholders.

The next initiative was by Van den Tempel. *Company Tax and Income Tax in the European Communities* (1971), which made the last serious case for this so-called 'classical' system. At about this time, a UK Conservative government adopted an imputation system in 1972, and most of the subsequent discussion on general systems has accepted the principle of the imputation system.

Meanwhile, three draft Directives, which are today still on the table unimplemented, addressed specific aspects of harmonisation. There are some indications that, after many years of delay, there may be action on all these in time for '1992'. Two, published in January 1969 addressed parents and subsidiaries and mergers respectively. Another, in 1976, proposed an arbitration procedure for dealing with transfer pricing disputes. These three are collectively referred to as the 'three Directives tax package' in the Company Law White Paper, published in July 1988, and it is the Commission's stated intention to continue to pursue adoption of all three as a package.

The 'mergers' draft would extend roll-over relief, loss carry-forwards and other benefits into cross-frontier mergers within the EEC. (The 'capital duty' exemptions proposed have been implemented.) The 'parent-subsidiary' draft proposes exemption from withholding tax in the member country of source and from corporate tax at parent level.

Four final sticking points were identified in 1984 which have continued to prevent agreement, namely:

(a) the problem raised in the framework of the 'mergers' directive by the West German system of co-determination;

(b) the inclusion, in the scope of the same directive, of exchanges of shares;

(c) the authorisation for West Germany to continue to levy a withholding tax on dividends distributed to parent companies in other member states;

(d) the jurisdiction of the Court of Justice if the arbitration procedure for the elimination of double taxation is enacted by means of a convention between member states, on the basis of Article 220 of the EEC Treaty.

There has been little change until recently. It was hoped that the new West German government in 1987 would have signalled a change in attitude and given an opportunity to reach a compromise solution. In the meantime, the new member states – Spain, Portugal and also Greece – have been given more time to comment on the implication of the directives.

The European Commission's central harmonisation proposal *Concerning Systems of Company Tax and of Withholding Tax on Dividends* was published on 1 August 1975, and also came out in favour of an imputation system. It gave a range of rates for both corporation tax and the proportion of this to be granted as an imputation credit to shareholders.

Both the Budgets Committee and the Economic and Monetary Affairs Committee of the European Parliament presented favourable reports on the draft Directive. However, in the plenary session of December 1977, Parliament rejected both reports. Some members thought the proposals had gone too far, others not far enough.

Mr Nyborg (Danish DEP) was appointed the new rapporteur for the Economic and Monetary Affairs Committee and produced an 'Interim' Report on 2 May 1979. The Report made the following three main suggestions:

1. The Commission should abandon altogether its proposals for common rates for corporation tax and for tax credits on dividends and should restrict itself to laying down guidelines for the operation of the present systems. (Netherlands and Luxembourg could continue with no relief while West Germany would continue with its 100 per cent relief.)
2. The European Parliament should invite the Commission to produce a new set of proposals for a Council Decision for harmonising the tax base before considering the harmonisation of tax rates.
3. While the Commission were drawing up new proposals the European Parliament would continue its examination of the Commission's present proposals.

The European Parliament passed a Resolution on 8 May 1979, on the basis of the Nyborg report. Effectively their Resolution refused to give a final opinion on the Commission's proposals until the Commission produced its proposals to harmonise the tax base; Parliament insisted that harmonisation of the rates of corporation tax and tax credits must take place in parallel with the gradual harmonisation of the systems for assessing companies' taxable profits.

This not unreasonable request was met nine years later when, in early ` 1988, the Commission published its Preliminary Draft of a proposal to harmonise the tax base. This is discussed below.

Meanwhile the theme of its Convergence Report (1980), that tax neutrality is essential to ensure that investment decisions are not determined by the tax environment 'but are made, in response to economic considerations and guarantee the optimum utilization of financial resources and production factors in the Community', has been repeated frequently in connection with the 1992 Programme for completing the internal market.

The Single European Act, passed in 1986 to introduce changes to the legislative procedure including qualified majority voting in the Council, is unlikely to have any positive effect on the decision-making process in taxation matters. Tax harmonisation Directives are expressly excluded from the qualified majority procedure and unanimity is still required. Moreover, nothing in the Single European Act negates the power of individual member states to veto any decision affecting a vital national interest – the so-called Luxembourg 'agreement'.

Carry-over of losses

Another proposal in 1984 constituted the Commission's first step towards harmonising the tax *base* and set out a basis for resolving disparities in the tax treatment of the carry-over of losses. This, the Commission believed, could be agreed without waiting for the broader proposals to be published. It proposed to give companies the option to carry forward losses without a time limit but it imposed a limit of two years (subsequently amended at the request of the Parliament to three years) for the carry-back of losses for budgetary reasons, and only against non-distributed profits. Despite the Commission's high hopes, both these proposals remain unadopted.

Tax base preliminary draft

The publication of the tax base Preliminary Draft Directive in 1988 has revived the company tax harmonisation debate within the Community.

It did at first seem that this would share the fate of drafts going back for nearly twenty years. Recently, though, it has become clear that there is now to be a determined attempt to push through some, if not all, of these measures. In the explanatory memorandum to the tax base Draft the Commission outlines its guiding objectives behind the proposals:

(a)   to achieve a greater degree of tax neutrality in the investment decision-making process of commercial operations;

(b)   to prepare the way for a closer alignment of companies' tax burdens across the Community by establishing a more transparent and simpler tax environment as 'an indispensable first step towards harmonising tax rates' and therefore allowing future tax legislation to be placed on more stable foundations. 'In this way, it will be much easier for firms, especially small and medium-sized ones, to set up in other Member States';

(c)   to improve the competitive position of European Community firms against non-member firms;

(d)   to prevent member states giving away incentives by way of the tax base, except in the form of tax credits and grants, etc., as permitted under the existing state aids measures.

The proposals cover rules of depreciation, capital gains and capital losses realised in the course of business on items forming part of fixed assets; provisions for liabilities and charges, stocks and deductible charges and expenditure, and provisions governing certain items forming part of fixed or current assets. The intention is to allow maximum business flexibility, and, as far as the United Kingdom is concerned, would, with exceptions, do much to improve the tax system.

Trans-European mergers

Even if these problems are solved, there would remain the key question of cross-border mergers. After a flurry of excitement in the early 1970s there have been few *genuine* mergers between EEC companies, although there have been many joint ventures and other compromise arrangements. These are not altogether satisfactory, particularly where the effective controllers of the underlying international ventures are not directly responsible to shareholders. Within a common market, genuine mergers should be as common across frontiers as other countries. It should be commonplace for a UK and a West German company of equal size to merge, resulting in a single parent with activities and shareholders spread between both countries.

There are no comparable obstacles to mergers between, for instance,

New York- and California-based companies. One diffence, of course, is that the California resident shareholder in a California company would not lose any sleep over the prospect of exchanging his holding for shares in a New York company; many West German shareholders, however, would still regard UK shares as 'foreign' and unfamiliar.

Even if the EEC 'mergers' directive were implemented, it would remain impossible, without serious tax penalties, to create a company with its activities, and its shareholders, spread across the whole of the enlarged Common Market. Only the Americans, and increasingly the Japanese can take a 'European' view of expansion. Nestlé, in Switzerland can build up a Europe-wide network of subsidiaries. There are tax resons (apart from others) why Rowntree could not. These can be stated simply as follows:

1. Mature publicly quoted companies will typically distribute about half of their profits to their shareholders as dividends.
2. Under the tax systems of many EEC countries, including the United Kingdom and West Germany and certainly under the imputation system recommended as the base for harmonisation within the EEC, the total tax burden at company and shareholder level increases dramatically when the company passes the 'prejudice point' – beyond which it cannot entirely service its dividends out of profits which have borne tax in its home country.
3. It follows that, on present arrangements, such a company cannot really afford to diversify to the extent that its 'foreign profits' are materially in excess of its domestic profits. So long as 'domestic' in this context means 'British' or 'Dutch' rather than 'community wide' we cannot really have true European companies. The domestic markets of even the larger members do not exceed 20 per cent of the whole Community market.

France

France has an imputation system, and at present taxes companies at 42 per cent. Dividends paid to a French resident are eligible for an *avoir fiscal* or imputation credit of 50 per cent of the dividend. The arithmetic of full distribution is

Profits	Fr. 100
Corporation tax	42
Net profit = dividend	58
Avoir fiscal	29
Grossed up dividend	87

The shareholder receives 58 net, but is taxed at his personal rate as if he had received a dividend of 87. He is then deemed, for credit purposes, to have paid tax of 29, i.e. at a rate of 33.3 per cent. If his tax rate is higher, there is more to pay; if it is lower (or zero) he can reclaim.

Where a dividend is paid out of profits which have not been subject to French tax, including profits which have enjoyed a credit for foreign taxes, the company must pay a *precompte mobilier* effectively neutralising the *avoir fiscal*. The effect is similar to the UK ACT procedure. There is one difference: in certain (rare) circumstances a group of companies can opt for *bénéfice consolidé* on world-wide profits.

Interest on money borrowed for the purpose of a French company's trade or business is normally deductible on taxable profits. This general principle applies even though France operates a (heavily modified) 'source' basis of taxation. Generally, 95 per cent of dividends received from French companies or from foreign companies resident in a country with which France has a double tax agreement are exempt from tax provided the recipient has at least a 10 per cent holding in the company. Even where money is borrowed specifically to make such participations (and therefore for the purpose of earning income which is virtually tax free in France) interest will be allowable.

Profits from foreign branches are also exempt from tax. A proportion of Head Office expenses will be attributed to the branch and therefore effectively disallowed in the French computation. It does not appear to be the practice to apportion interest costs in this way. It does seem that such an allocation could be made and that the French authorities could disallow interest on money borrowed for the purpose of financing a foreign branch. On the same general principle it normally follows that a foreign loss cannot be deductible.

Interest paid to shareholders is deductible only if the capital is fully paid up. This rule can apparently be relaxed in certain circumstances, provided that the capital becomes fully paid within three years. Where interest is paid at a rate of more than two percentage points above the Banque de France discount rate (*taux d'avances*) any surplus will be disallowed and treated as a distribution *but without the benefit of the avoir fiscal*. These rules apply in principle to all loans from shareholders.

Excessive interest paid to a non-resident may also be disallowed under the transfer pricing rules of Article 57. It appears not to be the practice to impute interest to interest-free loans or waivers of loans made for good commercial reasons.

It may be possible to by-pass the restrictions by loans via a sister company or a back to back. The Conseil d'Etat decision of 11 December 1974, stated that the limits on deductibility contained in Article 212 of the Code Générale d'Impôts (CGI) must be interpreted strictly and do not in any case apply to any company (including a sister company) which is not itself a shareholder.

Where bonds are issued at a *discount* after 1 January 1972, the borrower may elect deduction in the year of redemption or may amortise the discount on a straight-line basis over the term of the issue.

Foreign exchange gains and losses

The proceeds of sale of current assets denominated in foreign currency are normally treated as converted into domestic currency at the date of the sale. When payment is made in a later fiscal year, the taxpayer has an option between adjusting the domestic currency proceeds, or recognising an 'exceptional' profit or loss.

Generally, France does not suffer from the extreme forms of tax fragmentation. Tax treatment broadly follows accounting treatment, but this does not produce entirely consistent results. French tax law and practice has moved in the direction of a 'mark to market' approach for taxing, or relieving, unrealised gains, but in some cases realisation is the test. Where fixed assets are bought in one year and paid for (in foreign currency) in another, exchange differences must be added to, or subtracted from, the cost for the purposes of calculating depreciation. Where foreign currency debt is incurred to buy foreign currency assets, gains or losses may be applied to adjust the original cost for calculating gain on disposal.

West Germany

West German companies pay Federal tax at 56 per cent on undistributed and 36 per cent on distributed profits. There is also a net worth of 0.7 per cent. Municipal trade tax is payable on trading profits, but deductible in computing Federal tax. As in the United States, the effective burden is therefore materially higher than the Federal figures alone would indicate. A major tax reform is promised for 1990; it would not, in its proposed form, solve the harmonisation problems.

The 36 per cent tax on distributed profits is creditable against the personal tax liability of a West German resident dividend recipient. Dividends paid to foreigners suffer withholding tax at 25 per cent reduced by most treaties to 15 per cent. This puts up the total burden to 52 per cent (about 59 per cent including municipal tax) or 45.6 per cent (about 53.8 per cent).

These rates are now high by international standards: the expected reforms are unlikely to bring rates into line with the United States and United Kingdom. Although the West German system (derived from the previous split rate system) is, at the domestic level, similar in substance to the imputation systems of France and the United Kingdom the international implications are very different. A high rate of withholding tax is needed to preserve the integrity of the system. This fits in badly with EEC preoccupation with tidy, mirror image withholding tax rates, and is a major obstacle to harmonisation.

The present corporation tax structure, introduced by the tax reform of 1977, increased the effective tax charge imposed on West German subsidiaries of foreign companies, and correspondingly increased the advantages of successfully extracting profits as interest. West Germany has the usual 'arm's length transfer pricing' rules, supplemented by the rather fiercer provisions on 'hidden profit distributions'.

This concept is very important in West Germany. A reallocation of profits is defined as any benefit transferred from a corporation to a shareholder which would not have been granted to a third party. This would include any transfer price adjustment, including any interest adjustment on inter-company loans. If a company is too aggressive in its attempt to extract profits as interest, or otherwise than as a distribution of taxed profits, there is a double penalty. The payment will be disallowed and added back to taxable profits but will *not* be treated as a 'distribution' for the purpose of the reduced rate of tax.

There has in the past been considerable scope for 'head-shrinking' companies by merging an existing company into a thinly capitalised company with substantial debt. Interest on this debt can then be deducted using the *Organschaft* rules. This question of thin capitalisation was addressed by the decree of 16 March 1987, issued by the West German Ministry of Finance. The legal status of this has been disputed. Debt can be recharacterised as equity if the structure is considered abusive within the meaning of Section 42 AO.

There would be a *prima facie* assumption of abuse if liabilities had to be guaranteed by the parent or if

absent any satisfactory business reasons, a shareholder not entitled to the imputation tax credit or another related person has made loans or other funds that do not constitute equity capital available to the corporation in connection with the reduction of capital that was designed to pay the capital back to the shareholder or the foreign shareholder or a related person has made loans or other funds that do not constitute equity capital available to or has left them with the corporation although the equity capital was obviously disproportionate in relation to the assets of the corporation.

There is now a 10 per cent (i.e. 9:1 debt–equity ratio) guideline but it is not clear that this is a safe haven. There is also a requirement that the ratio must not be significantly lower than is typical for the particular industry. The rule is being interpreted to mean that equity must not be less than 10 per cent of the book value of the assets (as defined) in the balance sheet for the preceding year. Thus all debt, and not just debt reverted directly or indirectly by the parent, is taken into the calculation.

If the test is not met the recharacterisation penalty applies only to sufficient debt to bring up the equity to the 10 per cent requirement. Adjustments are said to be more aggressive for the purpose of local income tax.

West Germany, in common with most continental European countries, uses a comparison of net worth approach to the computation of taxable profits. The Anglo-Saxon distinctions between 'income' and 'capital' do not arise, and neither, consequently, do the more extreme forms of tax fragmentation on foreign exchange gains and losses. Unlike France, gains and losses are not normally recognised until realised. Like the United States, the concept of 'source' is important for tax credit calculations.

Luxembourg

Luxembourg taxes companies at 36.72 per cent (1988). Tax is imposed on a classical system, and a withholding tax of 15 per cent is payable on dividends. Luxembourg, although the smallest of the EEC countries, is very important as a location for holding companies.

Under the Law of 31 July 1929, a properly qualified holding company is not subject to any Luxembourg tax on income, either when it is received or when it is distributed as dividends or interest. In this respect the law is more favourable than the *Deelneming* privilege in the Netherlands discussed below.

The Luxembourg holding company must undertake no activities and receive no income, other than those coming within the definition of the 1929 Law. It may otherwise lose its status and become subject to Luxembourg corporate tax. Over the years the interpretation of the law has become somewhat more liberal.

Luxembourg holding companies are specifically excluded from the benefits of double tax agreements to which Luxembourg is a party. It follows that full non-treaty rates of withholding tax at source would apply to any interest or dividends flowing *into* Luxembourg.

The Law of 31 July 1929 defines a holding company as 'any

Luxembourg company with the exclusive purpose of taking interests in any form whatsoever in other Luxembourg or foreign establishments and of managing and developing such interests in such a manner that it does not carry out its own industrial activities or maintain a public commercial establishment'. What constitutes a material interest is not defined. A 25 per cent interest is certainly acceptable, but less may be appropriate with supporting evidence of a general commercial interest. It is *not* sufficient for this purpose for a holding company to acquire a nominal holding in a publicly quoted company.

The decision of 1965 authorised a new variant: *the financial holding company*. Such a company could make loans to other companies within its own group even though it was not itself a direct investor in the companies to which it was making loans. To qualify, a financial holding company must be organised as a *Société Anonyme*; its shares must be in registered form and the parent (or other members) of the group must be shown as founders in the articles of incorporation. The shareholders must agree not to sell their interest in the holding company outside the group so long as any relevant loans are outstanding. The portfolio of the financial holding company must include shares of group companies to the extent of at least 25 per cent of its corporate capital – in most cases this is a formality which is easily complied with.

A financial holding company can make loans only to other companies within its group. The main benefit of this arrangement is to permit the setting up of 'money box' companies which can make loans either by the public issue of bonds or by private syndication.

Although Luxembourg holding companies do not pay tax on their income, there are material levies on capital and these should be fully taken into account in any tax planning calculation. There are provisions limiting 'thin capital' structures, intended mainly to limit the scope for avoiding the capital and annual subscription duty. For instance, deposits and other loans (usually from the shareholders) may not exceed three times the subscribed capital. This limitation does not apply to public bond issues which are taken into account in calculating the annual subscription tax. However, the value of public bond issues is not permitted to exceed ten times the paid-in capital.

The Netherlands

The Netherlands has a classical corporation tax system, not an imputation system. As from 1 January 1988, the corporate tax rate is 35 per cent. Dividends received from Dutch corporations are subject to 25 per cent Dutch dividend tax. Generally, there is no recoupment by individuals or corporations of the underlying corporate tax paid on the profits from which the dividends are paid and the Dutch system effectively taxes distributed profits at both the corporate and personal levels.

The Netherlands disallows interest paid on money borrowed, whether from domestic or foreign sources, *specifically* to make foreign acquisitions. The Dutch argue, logically enough, that since income from overseas subsidiaries is in general exempt from Dutch tax (although it may be taxable elsewhere), it is unreasonable for interest on the money borrowed to be charged against the Dutch profits of the parent. The problem for the Dutch Revenue, and the opportunity for the taxpayer, is in establishing the purpose for which a specific borrowing was undertaken.

The primary incentive for the establishment of holding companies in the Netherlands is that the Dutch tax code provides for relief to those corporate shareholders who can claim a qualifying participation exemption (*Deelemingsjuristelling*) in the dividend paying companies. The conditions that must exist for a corporate shareholder to claim such a qualifying participation and therefore relief from corporate tax on dividends are that:

1. The Dutch resident company must own at least 5 per cent of the share capital of the payor company.
2. The shares must have been held since the beginning of the fiscal year of the parent company in which the dividends are received.
3. If the payor of the dividends is non-resident, it must be subject to local taxation on its income. This does not mean that the foreign company's profits out of which dividends have been paid must have incurred foreign taxation and in many cases a very low rate of foreign taxation on profits is sufficient to comply with the requirement. The exemption will not only apply if the foreign company has been subject only to a flat rate tax.
4. If the payee is non-resident, the holding must not be considered to be a portfolio holding.

If the above conditions are met, dividends received by a Dutch holding company are exempt from Dutch corporate taxation and may be paid on to the company's shareholders subject only to the Dutch dividend withholding tax, which may be substantially reduced under double tax agreements.

The Dutch holding company must perform a group function such as management or the provision of finance. The mere payment of dividends may constitute such an essential function, but some greater degree of involvement is generally advised.

In contrast with Luxembourg, the *company* does not have to qualify as a finance company or holding company. It is the source of *income* which is relevant. The Dutch Tax Administration is normally prepared to give a ruling as to the terms and conditions on which it would agree not to impose tax on the income of a Dutch resident company.

The Netherlands can also be used as an interest conduit. Interest paid from West Germany (for instance) direct to Bermuda would be subject to a 25 per cent withholding tax. Interest paid to the Netherlands, and interest from the Netherlands to Bermuda, are both exempt from withholding tax.

Finance companies set up in the Netherlands are subject to Dutch tax on the profits representing the difference between interest receivable and interest payable less administration expenses. Where the Dutch company is used to raise money from non-related debtors, e.g. in the Eurobond Market. The spread of interest must be 0.25 per cent with decreasing spreads for loans above 1 and 3 million guilders.

21

Interest withholding tax in the European Economic Community – a current dispute

Some member states of the European Community impose withholding tax on interest payments to non-residents. The Netherlands is a notable exception. Typically, withholding tax is waived altogether by double tax agreements when the interest is paid to a resident of a treaty country. The French want to bring pressure on the Community to impose a common minimum rate of withholding tax. They claim that this would prevent tax evasion.

In January 1989 the European Commission proposed a Directive which would require all member states to impose withholding tax on interest payments at a minimum of 15 per cent. The EEC is committed to abolishing exchange control, at least between member states. This is equivalent to total abolition, given that some members no longer impose exchange control. The French (who, one suspects, would prefer to impose ring fence controls around Fortress Europe) are pressing for a uniform withholding tax to be imposed.

Denmark, Luxembourg and the Netherlands impose no withholding tax, but residents are in principle fully liable to tax on interest income. Belgium and France have withholding taxes on certain types of income which can be treated as a 'final' tax. Other member impose withholding taxes, often with exceptions for certain types of security.

The preamble to the Directive states: 'The Commission believes that the most effective measure for combating fraud is a common system of withholding tax at source on payments of interest income.' If they believe that, they will believe anything. Someone with 'black' money tucked away, whether in Luxembourg or the Bahamas has no need to invest it back into the Community. Further background is given in an information note (XV/233/88–EN Rev) dated 8 February 1989. This states that:

1. Article 6(5) of the Council Directive of 24 June 1988 on the liberalization of capital movements states that 'the Commission shall submit to the Council, by 31 December 1988, proposals aimed at eliminating or reducing risks of distortion, tax evasion and tax avoidance linked to the diversity of national systems for the taxation of savings and for controlling the application of these systems'. It also provides as follows: 'The Council shall take a position on these proposals by 30 June 1989.'

There is then some discussion (Paragraphs 3–6) of the broader implications for tax harmonisation. Paragraph 7 states:

7. The two proposals are not intended to bring about complete harmonization of the taxation of savings, something which is neither necessary nor desirable at the moment. They are designed primarily to deal with the increased risks of distortion, avoidance and evasion which will be a direct result of the final phase of the liberalization of capital movements, agreed on 24 June 1988. Community residents will be free to transfer their savings into bank accounts in any other Member State. There is thus a risk that, once investors are free to open bank accounts in other Member States, they will not declare their interest income to their national tax authorities and will thus illegally evade payment of tax. The consequences might be a substantial loss of budgetary revenue in many Member States and an unjustifiably favourable treatment of income from capital.

The arguments for the measures taken can be summarised from Paragraphs 11–18:

11.   In its communication of 4 November 1987 on the creation of a European financial area, the Commission indicated that there were three ways (not mutually exclusive) of reducing the risks of avoidance and evasion:

- an obligation on banks to disclose automatically to the tax authorities the interest payments they make;
- the introduction of a general withholding tax;
- the strengthening of cooperation between tax authorities in Member States.

13.   A withholding tax system, however, has a number of advantages. It is administratively effective in that it ensures immediate collection of the tax before the saver receives the income. It thus reduces the risk of evasion. It would also fit into the tax systems of most Member States, nine of which already apply withholding tax to interest paid to their own nationals. However, most Member States do not apply withholding tax to non-residents. The main innovation provided for in our proposal is the introduction of a minimum withholding tax on interest paid to all Community residents. This new tax concept of 'Community resident' is entirely appropriate in the context of the creation of a European financial area.

16. Member States need not levy withholding tax where the recipient is a resident of a third country. The aim here is to safeguard the competitive position of financial centres in the Community. The Commission also envisages the Community entering into negotiations with certain third countries on the principle of withholding taxes of the type introduced by this proposal.

18. None of the measures described above, nor any other possible measure, will provide a watertight solution to the problem of tax evasion, given the risk that savings may be transferred to third countries to escape tax. It is for this reason that the Community should enter into negotiations, either bilaterally or within a multilateral framework such as the OECD, with a view to improving international cooperation in tackling this problem, and extending the withholding tax.

These arguments are flawed. The incidence of withholding tax falls not on the foreign investor but on the domestic borrower, who has to compensate the foreign investor. The economic well-being of the Community, rather than the administrative convenience of tax gatherers, surely requires a unified, rather than fragmented capital market. This can best be achieved by abolishing withholding tax at source, but collecting tax at bondholder level.

A West German attempt to impose withholding tax on interest reveals some of the problems, and provides a warning on a broader EEC initiative.

It was originally announced in 1988 that West Germany was to impose a withholding tax of 10 per cent on interest payments made by West German issuers after 31 December 1988. There were to be no 'grandfathering' provisions for bonds already in existence, and the tax would apply regardless of the currency in which securities are denominated, and not only to bonds, but also to debt securities such as certificates of deposit.

On 9 November it was announced that part at least of the measures would be postponed for three years, i.e. to the beginning of 1992. The tax, as such, was in fact introduced for a time, but the complex rules designed to catch accrued interest were postponed and, it was widely expected that they would never be introduced. Meanwhile some DM200 billion of funds had been switched out of the West German domestic market. In April 1989, after a political battle, the tax was abolished: excellent news for the opponents of the French stance.

The main technical problem arose from the proposed treatment of accrued interest. This was intended to enforce the structure and to ensure that the economic burden of the tax falls in what was (from the tax-gatherers viewpoint) the right place. Tax would have been imposed on the payment of a coupon or, in the case of original discount bonds, on maturity. It would thus fall in the first instance on the current holder at that time. However, that holder would be eligible for a credit against his German tax liability (or in the case of a foreign holder in a treaty country a refund of tax withheld) *only in respect of that part of the interest that relates to the actual period of ownership.* Those who have sold with the benefit of accrued interest would be entitled to the corresponding credit for the proportional period even though they have not directly borne any tax.

If this procedure were to be effective, market settlement of 'ordinary coupon' bonds would have to be made at the 'clean' price plus nine-tenths of the accrued interest.

Withholding was also to apply to original issue discount including 'zero coupon' bonds. This would be collected at the time of redemption. Such a bond may be issued at 40 and ultimately be redeemed at 100. The final recipient would then be paid 94, i.e. 10 per cent of the rolled-up interest would be deducted and paid over to the West German Revenue. This was apparently intended to apply even to existing bonds.

This raised several queries on how zero coupon bonds are actually classified. They had in the past come within the 'discount' rules rather than the definition of 'interest and other receivables'.

The announcement also raised intriguing questions on the impact of double tax agreements, and was not clear on the transitional rules. It may well be that it was an attempt to draft these which uncovered the unsoundness of the proposals.

There were also to be consequential changes in the rules governing bank borrowings and *Schuldschein* securities. The latter are non-negotiable evidence of debt transferable by assignment rather than delivery. They would remain exempt from withholding tax unless they had 'a similar designated purpose to debt securities' and were assignable more than three times. Unless these conditions were met they would be treated in the same way as debt securities.

Withholding tax would, it seems, have applied to interest paid by a German domestic 'credit institution' (a term rather broader than that of bank) unless the lender was another German bank (including a branch of a foreign bank) or from certain types of *bona fide* foreign banks. An individual or corporate deposit would be caught. Non-bond borrowings by a German business enterprise would attract withholding tax, the main exception proposed being that (in this case unlike bonds) administrative exemption from withholding tax would continue to be available where the lender or depositor was resident in a treaty country.

Part Six

Australasia

22

Australia

General tax system

A major reform of the Australian tax system was announced on 19 September 1985. Proposals for the final part of the package, on *Controlled Foreign Companies*, were published in early 1989. This will bring within the Australian tax charge profits accumulated in certain foreign subsidiaries, and will require a major re-think of strategy for the growing breed of Australian based multinationals. Australia had no general capital gains tax. The new package included a capital gains tax, and replaced the previous 'classical' system of corporation tax with a full imputation system. Foreign source income, much of which had previously been exempted, was subject to tax with a credit for foreign tax paid. In 1988, in line with international trends, the company tax rate was reduced from 49 per cent to 39 per cent. The top rate of personal tax remains at 49 per cent, but rate reductions are foreshadowed for 1989–90.

The capital gains tax applies only to assets *acquired* after 19 September 1985 (D-Day). The problem of death is solved by treating death neither as a realisation nor as 'wiping the slate clean', but by giving the heirs a new starting base. Heirs are treated as acquiring pre-D-Day assets at valuation, and post D-Day assets at the testator's adjusted cost basis.

The tax is indexed, but applies at full personal rates. However, as in the UK 1982 version, indexation is not symmetrical as it cannot be applied to increase a loss. Another asymmetrical feature of the tax is that, although capital gains are added to income gains (and can be offset *by* income losses), capital losses can only be carried forward (at a declining real value after inflation for which no adjustment is proposed) against future capital gains.

These last provisions create the equivalent of the UK 'Case VI' trap

which discriminates against risky investments and has adverse consequences for markets in modern financial instruments. Imperfect
indexation will also penalise those active investors who realise a
combination of gains and losses. Those who can arrange to be taxed as
dealers in securities will not suffer these disadvantages and will be taxed
symmetrically, but will not enjoy the benefits of indexation.

There is a problem of double taxation of gains realised by corporations. Distribution of such gains *may* eliminate this, but could favour
shareholders who bought their shares after D-Day as against those who
bought before.

Imputation system

The imputation system first applied to profits earned in the year
commencing 1 July 1986, and to distributions made after 30 June 1987.
By international standards, it includes some odd features. Imputation
applies at full corporate rates, a principle that had been explored and
rejected in the United Kingdom, France, Germany and Canada.
However, unlike the rules in those countries, imputation credit is never
refundable. ('Individuals facing lower marginal rates will be able to
apply their tax credit to reduce their tax liability on non dividend
income. The credit will not give rise to cash refunds where it exceeds tax
otherwise payable.') The rate of corporation tax was raised from 46 per
cent to 49 per cent, but has since been reduced to 39 per cent.

It was not intended to grant imputation credit to non-residents
although it is said that double tax agreements will need to be
renegotiated. In the end, after some uncertainty, Australia did not
follow the Canadian precedent of imposing withholding tax as well as
denying imputation.

Individual shareholders receiving a franked dividend are assessed to
tax on the total of the net dividend plus the imputation credit, but can
offset the credit against their tax liability from that or other sources.
Optimum strategy is to pay full dividends; some companies are paying
full dividends associated with opportunities to the shareholders to
invest. The attitude of the tax authorities to requests for rulings on sub-
transactions has been broadly favourable but a little ambivalent.

A franked dividend is one paid out of a 'franking account', which is
credited whenever the company pays Australian tax, and debited when
it pays a dividend. The basis of credit is (at a 39 per cent tax rate) $^{61}/_{39}$
times the Australian tax paid. Franked dividends can flow through a
succession of Australian companies.

Australian subsidiaries of foreign parents

The 'franking account' is of no value to the company, nor to its non-Australian shareholders. The interaction of foreign tax credit with imputation credit is vitally important and can as in the United Kingdom, create a 'prejudice problem' for Australian companies unable to cover their dividend out of *Australian* taxed profits. The 'franking account balance' is based on *Australian* tax after credit relief. The maximum unprejudiced dividend is (at a 39 per cent tax rate) $^{61}/_{39}$ times the Australian tax paid. Consider an Australian company which earns $1000 profits taxable in Australia, and a further $1000 which has borne 39 per cent (average) foreign tax. Ignoring dividends paid, the overall tax charge would be:

Source	Australia	Foreign	Total
Profits	$1,000	$1,000	$2,000
Foreign tax	—	390	390
Australian tax	390	390	
Less FTC	—	390	
Net Australian tax	390	—	390
Net profits	610	610	1,220

The company can pay up to $610 as dividend, leaving $610 retained, without penalty. Such a dividend would attract imputation credit of $390 and be worth $1,000 gross to shareholders.

Within this ceiling figure (the 'prejudice point') $100 of gross dividend costs $61 of net retentions forgone, the same relationship as an all-Australian company. If it earns an extra $100 of profits, either in Australia or abroad, it can retain $61. There is no discrimination against foreign-source income. If the company wishes to pay an *extra* $100 of gross dividends, beyond the 'prejudice point', the dividend will be unfranked. It will cost the company $100 in retentions to pay $100 *gross* ($61 net) to the shareholders. The marginal rate of tax on foreign-source distributed income is 68.9 per cent, compared with 49 per cent on Australian source distributed income – or foreign source income paid direct to an Australian individual.

Taxation of non-Australian source income

The tax reform has changed the previous 'exemption' approach to foreign source income. The changes have been in two stages. From 1 July 1987, Section 23(q) was abolished and the Section 46 relief from tax on inter-corporate dividends was withdrawn in respect of foreign dividends. Foreign source income is now taxed, with a credit for foreign taxes paid, a system long familiar in the United Kingdom, the United States and elsewhere. From 1 July 1989, an accruals basis is to apply to tax the undistributed profits of certain foreign companies in which Australians have an interest. The credit system will be modified.

The foreign tax credit

Credit extends to underlying tax where the Australian company has at least a 10 per cent shareholding 'in a foreign subsidiary or sub-subsidiary'. (Section 160 AFB). This will extend to third-tier and remoter companies, provided that the Australian parent has an aggregate direct and indirect interest of at least 5 per cent in each relevant company. The formula for computing underlying tax seems (at first sight) to be rational. (Section 160 AFC (4)). For multitier companies the formula is:

$$\frac{A\,(B + C)}{D}$$

> where A is the dividend paid
>
> B is the underlying tax paid by the paying company
>
> C is the underlying tax paid by lower-tier companies, using the same formula at each stage.
>
> D is the excess of available profits out of which the dividend is paid, over B.

Relief is limited to the foreign tax rate or to the Australian rate whichever is lower. Overall limitation will apply, but Section 160 AFA (1) limits the credit to:

(c)   the amount of that foreign tax; or
(d)   the amount of Australian tax payable in respect of that foreign income, whichever is the less

Separate limitation for interest incomes applies (Section 160 AF (7)). *Section 160 AFA treats as deemed interest, part of dividends received from foreign companies where 10 per cent of the income of the foreign company arises as interest.* The tax authorities have issued a ruling, IT 2498, setting out in detail the way in which foreign currency translation affects the tax credit computation.

No credit is available (Section 6 AB(6)) for foreign taxes calculated on a 'unitary tax' basis (a retaliatory measure) nor for 'credit absorbtion' taxes. The latter are defined as taxes which would not have been payable but for the shareholder's entitlement to a credit in Australia. This is to prevent capital importing countries trying to claw back pioneer relief where the beneficiary is not the investor but a foreign government. However 'pioneer relief' for tax spared by incentive legislation in developing countries will continue to be available under the terms of existing or renegotiated double tax agreements, or may be granted unilaterally by Regulation (Section 160 AFF).

Branch losses are quarantined and are not available for offset against Australian profits. Accumulated foreign losses incurred in the period seven years before July 1987 can be carried forward and set off against later income from the same branch or activity in the same country (Section 160 AFD).

Credit is calculated at the *average* rate of tax borne on profits earned from 1 July 1987. Dividends in excess of such profits will be treated as derived from earlier profits on a LIFO basis (Section 160 AFC).

Excess foreign tax credits cannot be carried forward or backwards, but can be surrendered within *wholly owned* groups (Section 160 AFF). This can create problems for companies with minority interests.

The accruals basis ('controlled foreign corporations')

The 25 May 1988 Economic Statement announced further changes in the taxation of foreign-source income. These were to come into effect from 1 July 1989. In principle, Australian shareholders will be subject to tax on their attributable share of the undistributed profits of non-Australian companies operating in a 'designated low tax country', broadly, those with a tax rate of less than 25 per cent. The accruals basis will apply if the Australian corporate or individual shareholder has a 10 per cent or greater voting interest; in contrast with US and UK 'controlled foreign corporation' provisions, there will be no requirement that Australians *control* the company. There will be 'tracing' provisions to deal with cases where ownership is indirect, and via non-designated countries.

In the case of high tax countries there is to be a reversion to the exemption system of taxing dividends: this will give much the same final answer as a tax credit. (These principles are set out in more detail in an *Information Paper* published in April 1989.)

Interest

Interest is generally deductible (Section 51) under a 'use' or 'purpose' test. Private mortgage interest is not deductible. Interest on convertible bonds is deductible provided that strict conditions laid down in Section

82SA are observed. Interest on discount bonds is deductible on an accruals basis; it is similarly taxable to the resident investor where the security is issued after 16 December 1984 (Section 159GP–GZ). Debt defeasance arrangements are caught as discounts. Interest may be disallowed on debt created by 'head-shrinking' sales of assets between non-resident controlled associated companies (Sections 159GZY–GZZF). Incidental expenses of raising loan capital are not allowed as interest. Section 67 gives specific relief for many of these. The initiated will recognise from the number of suffix letters that this part of Australian tax law has been subject to heavy and frequent amendments.

Tax treatment of foreign exchange gains and losses

Until 1985, Australia has had no general capital gains tax, but Sections 25A on 26AAA brought into charge 'speculative' and 'under twelve months' gains.

As in the United Kingdom (but with less violation of symmetry) a gain or loss on the repayment of a foreign currency *liability* on capital account had no tax consequences. If the borrowing was on revenue account, gain or loss would be brought into the tax computations. It was therefore important to know which side of the line the transaction was drawn. Again as in the United Kingdom, some cases on foreign exchange fluctuations have dealt with foreign currency borrowings. There were the problems and opportunities of tax fragmentation, but with an even greater degree of uncertainty as to the law itself; the cases cited below illustrate this. Under the new regime these will be of declining relevance; it will be many years before they can be ignored.

Coupled with growing volatility of the major currencies these measures in fact followed a sharp decline during 1985 in the Australian dollar.

Shown below is the total cost (interest and foreign exchange loss) in Australian dollars from borrowing various foreign currencies over the calendar year (January–December) 1985.

	Average interest rate	Currency movement	Total cost to Australian borrower
Australia	16.0	—	16.0
Sterling	9.9	34.1	70.8
US dollar	12.3	17.7	33.6
Deutschmark	9.5	35.7	70.3
Swiss franc	5.4	33.9	60.0
Yen	6.5	34.3	62.1

The increase in costs to Australian companies which have borrowed foreign currencies was far more dramatic than the relatively modest consequential increase in Australian dollar interest rates, about which there was so much whinging at the time.

It has sometimes been possible for Australians to borrow more cheaply abroad. There were, in retrospect, bargains in each of the four previous years. In 1986 it was cheaper to borrow US dollars or sterling but not the traditional 'hard' currencies. In 1987 the US dollar was the only bargain, but without serious disasters elsewhere. 1988 was again a 'cheap' year. The historical record suggests this is not an operation for the faint of heart. On the same basis the cost to the Australian borrower over the year of borrowing, in percentage per annum is as follows:

Year	Australia	United States	United Kingdom	West Germany	Switzerland	Japan
81	12.9	24.4	−5.2	4.3	8.4	4.2
82	14.6	32.1	8.8	23.9	9.9	15.4
83	14.0	20.4	7.2	4.4	4.9	17.8
84	14.5	22.1	−4.7	3.5	−3.1	7.5
85	16.0	33.6	70.6	70.3	59.6	62.2
86	19.9	11.0	15.8	41.3	38.2	36.7
87	19.8	−0.4	28.0	22.4	23.0	24.6
88	18.5	−9.1	−10.9	−19.3	−25.4	−18.7

Capital v. revenue

The 'capital–revenue' dispute will decline in importance over the years. On the basis of the decisions cited below the key test would appear to be the purpose of the borrowing, and the principle in *CAGA* no longer necessarily holds. If funds were borrowed to on lend or (subject to the views of the Federal Court in *Hunter Douglas*) to finance trading assets, any gains or losses would be revenue account and assimilated to interest. If the borrowing were to strengthen the business, profits and losses would not be assessed or allowed. It was by no means clear whether an assessment could be made on unrealised profit, or the circumstances on which a roll-over constitutes, a realisation or a variation in terms of debt. In principle, though, the Commissioner's practice was to assimilate the tax treatment of hedging transactions to the treatment which would apply to the underlying transactions. Speculators would normally have been assessed under Section 25A or 26AAA.

The Campbell Report (Paragraph 16.102) had recommended that all realised foreign exchange gains and losses borrowing should be treated as revenue items and that all hedging and forward contracts should be similarly treated.

On 18 February 1986, the Treasurer announced how the principles of tax reform would be applied to foreign exchange gains and losses. The text of his statement reads:

In the 19 September 1985 Statement on Tax Reform, under the proposed arrangements for the capital gains tax (CGT), it was noted that the taxation treatment of foreign exchange gains and losses was an outstanding issue yet to be decided.

The Government has now decided that all future foreign exchange gains and losses which are in the nature of interest are to be treated on revenue account, i.e. gains would be assessable and losses deductible for income tax purposes.

Specifically, foreign exchange gains and losses realised after today (18 February 1986) in respect of:
- borrowings or loans contracted for after today,
- all delayed payments for acquisition of assets and delayed receipts for sales of assets entered into after today, i.e. exchange rate effects between the contract dates and the dates of actual payment or receipt of purchase moneys, or
- instalment purchase arrangements contracted for after today,

are to be assessable and deductible respectively for income tax purposes.

Consistent with this treatment, premiums and discounts associated with forward cover and other hedging contracts entered into after today in respect of overseas borrowings or lendings contracted for after today, or in respect of sales or purchases or assets contracted for after today, are also to be treated on revenue account.

For these purposes, the contract date of each borrowing under a drawdown facility will be taken to be the date on which the borrowing is actually drawn down.

As an anti-avoidance measure, a deduction is to be denied foreign exchange losses covered by a hedging contract or similar arrangement, where the hedging contract produces a gain which is not assessable income of the Australian resident taxpayer. It will apply whether the arrangement is entered into directly by that taxpayer, through an associate or by an arm's length party under a reimbursement agreement.

Where an asset such as plant or shares is sold overseas by an Australian taxpayer, exchange rate gains or losses between the purchase and sale contract dates will be taken into account under the CGT arrangements. That is, the indexed CGT cost bases of these assets and the prices of their foreign sales will take into account relevant exchange rate movements.

The cases

Thiess Toyota Pty Ltd v. *FC of T 78 ATC 4463*

The taxpayer held the Australian franchise for Toyota. Imports were financed by sterling drafts. As a result of the 1967 sterling devaluation, the Australian dollar cost of meeting the then outstanding sterling liabilities was reduced. The consequent gain was held to be an assessable profit.

The facts were simple; the gain arose from the reduction in the local currency cost of imports. The other cases discussed below were more complex.

AVCO Financial Services Ltd. v. *FC of T 82 ATC 4246*

AVCO was a wholly owned subsidiary of AVCO Financial Services Inc. (USA) carrying on a consumer finance business in Australia. As in Marine Midland, the company had borrowed substantial sums for the purpose of its business but, unlike Marine Midland its trading assets were mainly denominated in the local currency, Australian dollars. The company borrowed both locally and in the United States. At the first relevant date in November 1972 there was US dollar denominated debt of $23 million and Australian dollar denominated debt of $10 million. Thereafter the emphasis switched to Australian denominated borrowings and in November 1977 debt was $A111 million and $US17 million. However in 1975 and 1976 it proved impossible to raise funds for planned expansion in the Australian market and there was a sharp but temporary increase in US dollar borrowings.

For the first four years of this period the Australian dollar was stronger than the US dollar and the company made gains on repaying its US dollar debt of $6 million in 1973. In 1975 and 1976 there were both gains and losses on different transactions, but in 1977 the company incurred a substantial loss on the 1976 Australian dollar devaluation. The figures were:

Year to 30 November		$A'000s
1972	Gain	175
1973	Gain	1,579
1974	Gain	298
1975	Net gain	243
1976	Net loss	(126)
1977	Loss	(2,800)

The company claimed that this loss should be on revenue account and accepted that this treatment should apply over the six-year period. The Commissioner (showing even more presumption even than his UK opposite number!) actually assessed the company on gains in the years 1972–5 and disallowed the deduction for losses incurred in the years 1976–7.

The Supreme Court of New South Wales found for the taxpayer. Judge Kearney held that the borrowings were essential steps in the performance of its day-to-day activities, and therefore not related to capital account. The gains were income, the losses deductible. The Commissioner appealed to the Federal Court, which found that the transactions were (consistently) of a capital nature.

During the period none of the borrowings was from the parent company. The US dollar borrowings were of two kinds. Commercial paper was issued in the US money market for ninety- or one-hundred-and-eighty-day periods. Formal term loans were arranged for periods of between one and five years with an average of about two-and-a-half years. In many cases the proceeds of borrowings were rolled-over; the proceeds of the new borrowings were applied in repaying foreign borrowings, the entire transaction being carried on within the United States. The taxpayer did not treat any foreign exchange difference as a realisation of foreign exchange gain or loss until there was a final repayment.

The Commissioner had based his submissions on *Commercial and General Acceptance Ltd (CAGA)* v. *F. C. of T* 75 ATC 4201; 77 ATC 4375, previously regarded as the authority on this point. It was held in *CAGA* that an exchange gain or loss on the repayment of moneys lent will always be a capital gain or loss and can never be taken into account in the assessment of income.

In the *AVCO* case one of the three federal judges accepted this principle. Another found for the taxpayer. The third, while finding for the Commissioner on the facts (that the borrowings were undertaken with a view to establishing or setting up the business of the company) reserved his position on the more general questions.

The final appeal was to the High Court, where the Chief Justice (Gibbs CJ) expressed disapproval of his own dictum in *CAGA*. He quoted *Texas Co. (Australasia) Ltd* as authority for the proposition that expenditure may be deductible in some cases even if it be designed to secure an advantage of a capital nature. The Court found (it seems with some difficulty) that 'money' might be included in the definition of 'trading stock'. The High Court restored the decision of Judge Kearney in favour of the taxpayer.

Exchange gains and losses, even on long-term borrowings by a bank or finance company, are now established as being taxable or deductible. However, borrowing to strengthen a business entity are not so treated and are still covered by *CAGA*. The term of the borrowing is no longer relevant.

(Hunter Douglas Ltd v. *FC of 1982) ATC 4450 (1983) 83 ATC 4562*

Hunter Douglas Ltd was an Australian subsidiary of a Dutch company. (How and why the parent became Dutch is an interesting story for the international tax specialist, but irrelevant to the Australian case.) It has multicurrency standby facilities for working capital with three major banks, BEC (Belgium), AMRO (Netherlands) and Orion Term Bank (London). Most of the actual borrowings were in US dollars, although there were some transactions in Swiss francs and Dutch guilders. The company consistently incurred exchange losses on repaying these loans.

In this case (in contrast to the UK *Marine Midland*) the lower courts opted for a commonsense economic answer, which the Federal Court reversed on a strict legal interpretation.

The Supreme Court of New South Wales (14 September 1982) ruled that:

> The drawdowns were of a recurring nature and were required to be made so that proceeds could be and were devoted in the satisfaction . . . . of outgoings of the taxpayer's business of a clearly revenue nature.

The losses should, in current economic circumstances, be perceived to be in the essence and nature of interest. In circumstances such as the present where the borrower enjoys the privilege of nominating the currency in which a loan is to be extended, he takes into account, in determining the appropriateness of interest and the appropriateness of the currency to be chosen, what his expectation is of currency movements. In other words, the compensation of a lower rate of interest may well be in a currency in which fluctuation must in a very real commercial sense be perceived to be nothing more or less than the equivalent of the payment of interest in any guise.

The Commissioner's appeal against this decision was upheld by a majority of the Federal Court (83 ATC 4562–23 September 1983) Judge Franki dissenting. The Court held:

1. The exchange losses were on capital account and therefore not deductible.
2. Whether exchange losses (or gains) made in repaying loans are

capital or revenue items must be determined by reference to the purpose of the borrowing.

In general, loans and repayments of loans are on capital account. Borrowings made by trading companies to purchase trading stock are exceptions to this general rule.

3. Here the taxpayer had borrowed funds to strengthen his profit earning structure. The borrowings and repayments were on capital account. The exchange losses took on the same character.

23

New Zealand

New Zealand, like Australia, is in the throes of a major tax reform. The political disputes over it have already cost the former Finance Minister, Roger Douglas, his job. From our specialist point of view, New Zealand is unusual having a long-standing and clearly drafted provision (Section 71) specifically providing that exchange gains or losses on the repayment of foreign currency debt are assessable or deductible. New Zealand has also recently introduced an accruals basis of taxing financial transactions. This goes further than equivalent legislation in other countries. Its progress should be watched closely.

Features of the tax reform

One controversial feature of the package was the original announcement that a flat rate of personal tax was to be introduced on 1 October 1988. After some political in-fighting, the flat tax was modified in favour of two rates: 24 per cent of $NZ30,875 and 33 per cent thereafter.

An imputation system was introduced in New Zealand from 1 April 1988, applying at the *full corporate rate*, a principle explored and rejected in the United Kingdom, France, Germany and Canada, but already adopted by Australia. (It was originally announced that from 1 October 1988, companies would pay tax at what has been described as an 'internationally competitive rate comparable to but no less than the personal tax rate'.) It is an account based, rather than an ACT-type system. A company will have to keep an 'Imputation Credit Account' (ICA) comparable to the Australian franking account. This will enable tax preferences to be flowed through to shareholders, but will mainly affect capital gains.

Imputation credit will never be refundable. The full benefits of imputation will be enjoyed *only by individual taxpayers*. Reclaims will be possible only by those whose taxable income, including dividends, exceeds GMFI. Will this adversely affect the retired with small investment incomes – or will they simply have to switch into debt securities? Exempt taxpayers will not be able to make a reclaim. *This will discriminate against equity investments by pension funds.*

Bonds issues will be taxed as dividends. This is intended to provide a method for flowing tax credits through without the company disbursing cash. It could have implications for foreign shareholders. Bonus issues will be taxable on distributions but not if they are paid out of share premium reserve. Are there any advantages in making rights and other issues at a premium? Share splits are not regarded as bonus issues (Paragraph 2.7).

It is not intended to grant *imputation credit to non-residents.* Will double tax agreements need to be renegotiated? Is withholding tax to be abolished? It has been imposed at 30 per cent and reduced to 15 per cent by treaty branch profits tax. Australia did not, in the event, follow the Canadian precedent of imposing withholding as well as denying imputation.

The rules differ quite significantly from those introduced in Australia last year, and indeed from international practice generally.

In principle, dividends received by New Zealand residents will be taxable, with a credit for foreign withholding tax, but apparently in no circumstances will relief for underlying tax be granted.

In contrast to most other countries, the withholding tax credit attaching to a dividend received by a New Zealand company will effectively flow through. Indeed, for non-portfolio dividends tax will be postponed until the recipient distributes.

Several countries, including the United Kingdom and Australia, tax the undistributed income of 'controlled foreign companies'. There are 50 per cent plus owned companies in low tax areas. New Zealand proposes to go farther, and tax the due proportion of profits even of minority or portfolio interests.

It does seem to mean that the New Zealand investor will get the worst of both words: New Zealand rate if the underlying tax is lower; no 'sidespill' relief if it is higher.

In New Zealand, all profits will suffer underlying foreign tax, but withholding tax will be allowed as a credit. This gives quite a different answer. The total burden of tax, to a New Zealand shareholder will be the underlying foreign tax, plus the New Zealand tax rate on the balance.

The gross profits required to fund an incremental gross dividend of 100 will be as follows:

Average foreign tax rate	Profits to fund 100 gross dividend
0	100
30	142.9
35	153.8
40	166.7
45	181.8
49	196.1

Interest and the accruals basis

In New Zealand the accruals basis of taxing financial transactions now applies generally. The key legislation is Section 74 introduced by the ITAA 1987. There would appear to be a history of attempts to by-pass the legislation. Some provisions apply from 23 October 1986, those on debt defeasances on 20 December 1986, on variable debt from April 1987 and for shares and options from 18 June 1987.

The general principle is that calculations were made on a yield to maturity basis. The appropriate income (or charge against income) will be calculated in respect of each year of assessment. When the instrument is disposed of or redeemed there will be a base price adjustment designed to ensure that the full economic gain is taxed but that it is not doubly taxed.

There is a difference of treatment when a variation in price arises from a change in the credit status of the debtor.

There are exceptions for annuities and life policies. We also have to watch the inter-relation with the 'specified preference share' rules of Section 194. There is an exemption for cash basis holders (presumably in practice this means individual investors) if their investments do not exceed $400,000, or if their income from such investments does not exceed $50,000 per annum, or if the difference between cash basis and accrual basis does not exceed $15,000.

The notional interest on deep discount bonds, calculated semi-annually on a compound interest basis, is imputed to holders. Dividends paid on redeemable preference shares issued after 7 April 1986, and which may reasonably expect to be redeemable within two years of issue, will be treated as debt instruments. The issuer will be entitled to a deduction, but the holder will be taxed without the benefit of the Section 46 exclusion for inter-company dividends.

Withholding tax

Withholding tax on interest paid by New Zealand companies to residents of non-treaty countries is 15 per cent of the interest paid. This rate is reduced under the terms of some of New Zealand's double taxation agreements, but never to a rate less than 10 per cent.

An exception to this rule is made in certain cases, the only one of any real interest in these circumstances being interest derived 'by a non-resident investment company from any development investments' (Section 310(2)(f) of the New Zealand Income Tax Act 1976).

A 'non-resident investment company' is a company which neither is incorporated in New Zealand nor has its Head Office ('the centre of its administrative management') in New Zealand (Section 241(2) and (3)). In addition, the company must either (i) derive no income from New Zealand except interest and have no investments or other assets in New Zealand except the principal money from which the interest is derived or (ii) be a company more than 50 per cent of whose total assets in New Zealand consists of 'development investment'.

'Development investments' are those which consist solely of interest-producing loans or of a mixture of loans and shares (with the loans accounting for more than 50 per cent in value of the investments) and which are used wholly for the purposes of a 'development project' (Section 5(2)).

A 'development project' must be declared as such by Order in Council (Section 5(2) and (3)) and, in the past, Orders in Council (which are still in force) have declared as development projects such undertakings as cement works, steel works, pulp and paper production, the smelting and processing of aluminium, the sawing of timber, the processing of sawdust and logs, the manufacture of fibre board and the planting of forests in conjunction with the establishment and operation of plywood mills, wallboard mills, paper board factories and bark extraction plants.

Foreign exchange gains and losses

In contrast to Australia, New Zealand tax law (Section 71 Government Tax Act 1976) specifically provides that the exchange gains and losses realised in the repayment of foreign currency debt are assessable and deductible respectively. The legislation is worth quoting in full.

SEC. 71 Gains and losses due to exchange variation in respect of repayment of loans.

(1) For the purposes of this section

'Exchange variation', in relation to the repayment in whole or in part of any loan, excluding interest, means the difference between –

(a) The amount of the repayment expressed in New Zealand currency at the official exchange rate in New Zealand at the date on which the repayment was made: and

(b) The amount expressed in New Zealand currency at the official exchange rate in New Zealand which would have been required to make that repayment on the date on which the loan was first made or on the 8th day of August 1975, whichever is the later:

'Loan' means –

(a) In relation to money lent to any taxpayer, money which –

(i) Is lent on or after the 1st day of January 1974: and

(ii) Is lent with the consent of the Minister under the Capital Issues (Overseas) Regulations 1965 or the Overseas Investment Regulations 1965 or the Overseas Investment Regulations 1974 or with the consent of the Reserve Bank under the Exchange Control Regulations 1978, as the case may require; and

(iii) Is lent in a currency other than New Zealand currency: and

(iv) Is expressed to be repayable in a currency other than New Zealand currency.

(2) (Loan instalments) For the purposes of this section where a loan is received in 2 or more instalments, each instalment shall be deemed to be a separate loan, and repayments made shall, except as otherwise expressly provided by the terms of the loan, be deemed to be applied so that the separate loans are repaid in the order in which they were so received.

(3) (Exchange variation) Nothwithstanding anything in this Act, where in any income year an exchange variation in respect of the repayment, in whole or in part, of any loan made to any taxpayer carrying on business in New Zealand for the purposes of his business in New Zealand being an exchange variation arising in respect of a repayment made after the 8th day of August 1975, and the Commissioner is satisfied that any profit is derived or loss is incurred by that taxpayer in respect of the repayment of that exchange variation, the amount of that profit or, as the case may be, that loss shall be taken into account in calculating the assessable income derived by that taxpayer from that business in that income year.

(4) (Arrangements) Where the Commissioner is satisfied that arrangements have been made between a taxpayer and another person with a view to the affairs of the taxpayer and of that other person being so arranged or conducted that this section would, but for this subsection, have effect more favourably in relation to that taxpayer than would otherwise have been the case –

(a) The amount of any profit which the taxpayer has derived shall not be less than the amount of the profit which that taxpayer would, in the opinion of the Commissioner, have derived – if those arrangements had not been made.

Part Seven

The Far East

24

Japan

General company tax structure

The Japanese tax reform was finally approved on 24 December 1988, after a long political battle; just as the Recruit/Cosmos scandal was moving from specialist financial columns to the front pages of the world's Press. The main dispute was over the introduction of a general sales tax. It was based in the *Report on the Overall Review of the Tax System* published in October 1986.

Japanese companies (and foreign companies operating in Japan) are subject to three taxes, the (national) *corporation tax*, and two local taxes, the *inhabitants' tax* levied by prefectures and municipalities, and the *enterprise tax* levied by prefectures alone. The interaction of the three taxes is analysed.

The two local taxes are collected by the local authorities, but the rates are fairly uniform throughout Japan.

The double taxation of dividend distributions has up to now been dealt with in Japan by a combination of 'split rate' and 'imputation' systems:

(a) by allowing a credit to the (*individual*) shareholder of 10 per cent on the first ¥10 million and 5% on the excess; *and*

(b) by reducing the rate of corporation tax on distributed income from 42 per cent to 32 per cent. The interaction of this 'split rate' with other taxes was complex, but will in future be less relevant.

Under the tax reform proposals of 1990 this will be replaced by a single 37.5 per cent rate (with a 28 per cent rate for small companies). During the fiscal year 1989, the rate is 40 per cent on retained profits and 35 per cent on distributed profits.

Income distributed by a domestic company to another domestic company had qualified for the reduced rate, and the recipient company did not *normally* suffer any further tax on the receipt. Under tax reform, only 90 per cent will be exempted in 1989, and 80 per cent for 1990 and after. However, this is subject to an 'interest' limitation and to a claw-back of 25 per cent when dividends received exceed dividends paid.

The three taxes on companies

The summary treatment assumes a large company and ignores small company reduced rates.

Corporation tax (CT) was, until end 1988, levied at 42 per cent on retained profits, or 32 per cent on profits earmarked for dividends. From 1990 there will be a single 37.5 per cent rate.

Inhabitants' tax (IT) is levied in two parts. The *'per capita* levy' does not concern us. The 'corporation tax levy' is imposed as a percentage *of the national corporation tax burden.* The rate is normally 5 per cent at prefectural level but can be increased to 6 per cent. The rate at municipal level can be between 12.3 per cent and 14.7 per cent, making an overall burden in the range 17.3 per cent–20.7 per cent of the national corporation tax burden.

Enterprise tax (ET) is levied by the prefectures on *income* (not tax burden) as computed for national corporation tax purposes with certain adjustments which are discussed below. Enterprise tax is imposed at a minimum rate of 12 per cent, but this can be increased up to 13.2 per cent. It is allowed as a deduction from taxable income for the purpose of all taxes, including enterprise tax itself, in a subsequent period.

Interaction of taxes

Assuming 'constant' profits (i.e. enterprise tax deduction carried from the previous year = burden on the profits for the current year) and assuming maximum rates of ET and IT, the 'standard' calculation of tax rates (pre-reform) was normally shown as in the first two columns displayed below. The last column shows the presumed effect when the reform is fully operational in 1990.

This formulation was perfectly adequate as a rule of thumb, but needed adjustment for more precise tax planning calculations.

	DIST.	UNDIST.	POST–1990
Profits	100	100	100
Less enterprise tax credit	11.66	11.66	11.66
	88.34	88.34	88.34
Corporation tax 32%	28.27		
42%		37.10	
35%			30.92
Inhabitants' tax (20.7% of tax)	5.85	7.68	6.40
Enterprise tax (13.2% of 88.34)	11.66	11.66	11.66
Total tax	45.78	56.66	48.98
Net profit	54.22	43.45	51.02

Outward direct investment by Japanese companies

Japanese companies are in principle subject to tax on world-wide income, but domestic tax law provides for direct tax credit to be taken in respect of all foreign taxes paid directly by the Japanese company through its branch operations or otherwise, and also for a deemed paid 'indirect' credit for taxes on profits underlying dividends received from an overseas company, provided that the Japanese company owns at least 25 per cent of the voting equity in that company. *No credit is available for second-tier subsidiaries.*

If foreign tax credits can be claimed, both of the following qualifications must be met by the overseas company:

1. Not less than 25 per cent of the shares issued or the paid-in capital of the foreign subsidiary or, where more than one class of shares must have been issued, not less than 25 per cent of its voting shares, must be owned by the Japanese corporation for at least six months.
2. The foreign subsidiary must be a corporation established for the purposes of carrying on business in that foreign country and has not been established for any tax considerations.

The amount of credit is, however, limited to the proportion of Japanese Corporation tax liability attributable to foreign-source income expressed as follows:

$$\text{Limitation} = \text{Corporation tax liability} \times \frac{\text{Total foreign income}}{\text{Total worldwide income}}$$

This limit is calculated on an over-all rather than per-country basis. The amount of foreign source income has to be determined in accordance with Japanese tax laws and regulations but *can exclude net operating losses from foreign projects, even though such losses are taken into account to reduce the tax liability before credit in computing total world-wide income in the above formula*.

If the phrase 'net operating losses from foreign projects' refers to operating losses from operations in foreign countries, the exclusion of such losses is no longer permissible by virtue of amendments to the relevant Cabinet Order effective from 1 April 1983.

If dividends declared by a foreign subsidiary exceed the current year's profit, the excess will be regarded as declared out of profits for preceding years on a 'last-in, first out' basis without limitation. This extends even to pre-acquisition profits.

Under tax reform tax credit is limited to 90 per cent of income; the carry-forward period is reduced from five years to three years. No credit is available for foreign tax credit. Half of any untaxed foreign source income is excluded from the denominator in calculating the credit.

Interaction with enterprise tax

We may need to consider how the enterprise tax deduction interacts with credit relief for foreign taxes. Assume a Japanese company receives gross dividend (or interest) income of 100 which has borne 40 foreign tax. In this case the credit relief equals the whole of the 40, leaving 16.44 to pay on undistributed profits. (It is not necessary to limit credit relief to 40 per cent of *taxable* profits (88.34), i.e. 35.34, leaving 21.10 to pay.)

Credit relief is not actually available against enterprise tax, and any foreign tax in excess of 44.78 per cent or 34.12 per cent would only be available to carry forward for five years (three years under the tax reform proposals). It follows that if profits are distributed out of profits which were eligible for credit at 40 per cent, relief on distributed profits would be restricted. The Japanese charge would be 11.66 (enterprise tax) but there would be a 5.88 per cent carry-forward.

Distribution would improve the position but only slightly. The lower rate of corporate tax would mostly be cancelled out by the 10 per cent withholding tax (typically treaty rate). Pre-reform, and taking account of credit relief, shadow effect and enterprise tax offset, and withholding tax on dividends, optimum distribution was given by the equation:

$$T = 100 - D = Rd \times D + Ru(100 - D)$$

where

T = total tax;
D = dividend;
Rd = tax rate on distributed profits;
Ru = tax rate on retained profits.

Tax haven subsidiaries

When a Japanese corporation owns 10 per cent or more of the capital of a foreign subsidiary in a 'tax haven', it may be assessed on its due proportion of the undistributed profits of the foreign corporation. This provision only applies where 50 per cent of the total capital of the company is owned by Japanese residents and non-resident 'connected persons'.

There are exceptions applying 'business', 'substance' and 'management and control' criteria. Where the main business of the foreign subsidiary is wholesale, banking, trust, security of business, insurance, shipping or air transport it can meet the criteria only if it is conducting its business daily with non-related persons and is not a 'captive' of its Japanese parent. There is a 'black list' of tax haven territorities.

Inward investment by foreign companies into Japan

Dividends paid by a Japanese company to a non-resident are in general subject to 20 per cent withholding tax. Typical treaty provisions reduce the rate of withholding tax to 14 per cent generally added to 10 per cent if there is 25 per cent or more interest in the Japanese company.

Gains on the disposal of a 25 per cent or more interest in a Japanese corporation by a non-resident are generally taxed at corporate rates on the gain. This liability is excluded under the treaties with the United States and Germany, but not on that with the United Kingdom. *This is an important planning point.*

Interest

Interest paid by Japanese corporations is tax-deductible and charged to the profit and loss account as a non-operating expense before recurring income. Except when attributable to the holding of shares (see below), there are few restrictions on the admissibility of interest in computing taxable income, and a deduction will normally be given when the obligation to pay accrues. There appears to be some scope in practice for paying interest in advance and claiming the deduction rather earlier than would be permitted in other countries.

Interest paid to affiliates, either domestic or foreign is in principle, deductible, but is closely scrutinised. It is paid at an excessive rate. The tax authorities may treat the excess portion as either a 'donation of economic benefit', or as a deemed dividend if paid to shareholders.

No deduction is permitted for interest 'paid' by a branch to Head Office. Where the facts warrant, third-party interest paid by Head Office on funds used by a Japanese branch may be deductible. There are no formal 'thin capitalisation' rules.

Interest expense attributable to the acquisition and holding of shares must be set against dividends received from these shares. This rule is applied to all interest, except that due on long-term debt of not less than three years' maturity, corporate debentures and trade notes receivable discounted at banks. The attributable interest is calculated as the proportion of interest expense which the book value of the total stock investment bears to the book value of gross assets. The former must include all stocks owned regardless of the receipt of dividends and the latter must exclude the debts mentioned above. Dividends paid by a foreign company to a domestic company are included in taxable income and may qualify for tax credit. *There is no disallowance of the interest expense attributable to the holding of these shares.*

Withholding tax

Interest is generally subjected to a 20 per cent withholding tax reduced to 10 per cent or 15 per cent under a number of treaties: see Appendix to Chapter 7. There are special measures applying to domestic investors in certain types of public bonds. For interest payable between 1 January 1978 and 31 December 1986, the investor had the choice of accepting special withholding tax of 35 per cent as a final tax with no further assessment. Alternatively he could accept the normal 20 per cent withholding tax, which was then a pre-payment of ultimate tax.

Exemption from withholding tax on interest paid abroad is given unilaterally in certain circumstances.

1. Interest on Japanese bonds or debentures issued on or before 1 July 1931 on the foreign capital markets.
2. Article 7 of the Special Tax Measures Law provides that, interest payable to non-residents of Japan on foreign currency bonds (bonds denominated in foreign currency, or denominated in yen but payable in foreign currency at a fixed exchange rate) issued between 1 April 1974 and 31 March 1985 by Japanese companies whose final maturity is not less than five years are exempt from withholding tax.

This law is renewed every year. It is usual to provide in the bond deed that the issuer would become obliged to pay any taxes imposed in the future. This article is expected to be amended so as to include such Euroyen bonds.

3. Discount on debentures coming within (b).
4. Interest on foreign currency loans or deposits extended or made during the period 1 April 1979 to 31 March 1986 by a foreign government or financial institution to the Japanese government, Bank of Japan or an authorised foreign exchange bank which is a domestic corporation.

These concessions are subject to the usual exclusion for interest attributable to a permanent establishment. In such cases normal withholding at 20 per cent (pre-payment of final tax on the branch) or 35 per cent (final tax, where this option is available to domestic shareholders) will apply.

Withholding tax is not charged on interest received by banks having a place of business in Japan or an interest paid by such a bank in the ordinary course of its business. In addition, interest on most medium-term foreign currency debt securities issued by domestic companies has been exempted from tax, or charged at only 10 per cent, as has interest on the majority of foreign currency loans with maturities of over three years made by non-resident financial institutions unrelated to the Japanese borrower.

Deep discount bonds

Deep discount bonds *issued* in Japan from 1 April 1980 to 31 December 1986 are subject to tax at 16 per cent on the difference between the issue and redemption amount. Tax is collected from the issuer but imposed on the first purchaser as a withholding tax. This is a final tax for an individual and need not be aggregated with other income. The individual holder at maturity is not liable to further tax.

If this special measure did not apply the redemption difference would have been treated as 'miscellaneous income' (not interest). The taxable amount of miscellaneous income is receipts net of expenses, including cost. This tax would not apply to a sale in the market. Investment dealers can buy bonds in the market close to redemption and 'wash out' the final profit.

An individual (not a company) who buys and sells deep discount bonds in the market has otherwise been exempt from tax on the gain, unless he is engaged in 'continuous' transactions. A yardstick of more than 50 transactions involving 200,000 shares per annum applies to shares, but not to bonds. On this regime it appears that a company might issue ten-year zero coupon bonds at 55.84 to yield 6 per cent. Tax of 7.07 per cent would be paid at issue making the cost to the first purchaser 62.91. At this price the tax free yield would be 4.74 per cent.

Where deep discount bonds are issued outside Japan and transferred into Japan before maturity, gains are now taxable as regular income to a Japanese resident. This amendment to the Special Tax Measures Law is effective for disposals from 1 January 1986.

Deep discount bonds are defined as follows:

- Bonds (other than convertible or warrant bonds) with a fixed interest rate of less than 3 per cent.
- Bonds where the issue price is less than 80 per cent of face.
- STRIPS, where the coupon is traded separately from the principal.

Foreign exchange gains and losses

Capital gains realised by Japanese corporations are generally treated as ordinary income. Provided that capital losses can be deducted for income there should be symmetry on the asset, and presumably on the liabilities, side. There appears to be no tax fragmentation of the first two types.

There are some 'timing' angles, broadly based on the accounting treatment. There is a distinction between debits and credits: outstanding credits and debits denominated in foreign currencies at the end of each accounting period according to whether or not they fall due within one year of the end of the accounting period.

In the case of short-term balances there is a choice between two methods, which must be used consistently. The amounts can be translated at the exchange rate ruling at the date of accrual, or at the end period rate. Where there are forward contracts, these are in principle treated as matched.

Long-term financial assets and liabilities must normally be accounted for, and taxed, on an accruals basis. These rules permit a company to bring into account unrealised losses only on short-term assets and liabilities. They would not appear to permit unrealised losses (or require unrealised gains) on longer-term assets or liabilities to be brought into account.

25

Hong Kong and Singapore

Hong Kong and Singapore are rival Far Eastern financial centres. Hong Kong has generally low tax rates and a 'source' basis, but few specific concessions. It is threatened with the end of its independence in 1997.

Singapore has what are now about average tax rates (33 per cent on companies) but a wide range of concessions both for industry and for financial services. For all its political stability and soundly based legislation, it has never generated quite the excitement of Hong Kong.

Hong Kong

Profits tax is levied for each year of assessment at the standard rate (now 16.5 per cent) on every person carrying on a trade, profession or business in Hong Kong in respect of the profits arising in or derived from Hong Kong from such trade, profession or business. The word 'person' includes an individual, a corporation, a partnership or a body or persons. The year of assessment comprises twelve months to 31 March.

'Residence' is not, normally, a basis for determining whether a person is within the scope of profits tax.

Interest tax, the rate of which follows the rate of profits tax, is applied to interest having a Hong Kong source. It has many of the characteristics of withholding tax.

In spite of the generally low rates of tax, tax avoidance is widely practised or at least attempted. A country with a generally low rate of tax needs to protect its tax base. Interest affords considerable scope for the tax planner and problems for the tax administrator.

One device, obvious to anyone whose wits have been sharpened by residence in a high tax country, is for the business enterprise to 'borrow' money in such a way that the interest paid is a deduction from otherwise taxable income in Hong Kong while the corresponding receipt accrues for the benefit of the proprietors in a tax free non-Hong Kong source. It is also easy to arrange for a resident company to arrange for its surplus assets to be invested outside Hong Kong to produce tax free interest.

There would be particular scope for avoidance by financial institutions which could so arrange matters that interest received in Hong Kong only matched deductible interest paid. Investing a relatively small proportion of their assets for the interest abroad could ensure that their net profit was tax free.

The definition of 'source' was therefore amended from 1 April 1978 to catch such interest earned by Hong Kong financial institutions. Another anti-avoidance provision effective from 1 April 1981 brought bill discounts within the scope of interest tax.

There are a number of statutory exemptions from interest tax (Section 28(1) proviso) extending to interest paid by the government by a Hong Kong licensed bank on a tax reserve certificate to a pawn-broker on a government bond or on a loan made by a registered credit union. In 1982, further exemption was made:

(g)   any interest paid or payable after 24th February 1982 on a deposit made in a currency other than Hong Kong currency with a financial institution carrying on business in the colony

This had the worthy purpose of encouraging the intermediation business of such financial institutions. It was in part a response to competition from Singapore. Subsequently, the Hong Kong dollar came under pressure and to avert this pressure the exemption was extended:

(h)   any interest paid or payable after 16th October 1983 on a deposit made in Hong Kong currency with a financial institution carrying on business in the colony

This measure widened (although it did not create) avoidance opportunities. Two further anti-avoidance measures were therefore introduced in 1984. First, with effect from 1 April 1984, all interest income received by or accruing to business enterprises carried on in Hong Kong brought into charge the profits tax notwithstanding that the funds may have been made available to the borrower offshore and irrespective of the currency in respect of which the transactions are nominated. This has brought into focus the question of whether or not a particular company or unincorporated business is 'carrying on business within' Hong Kong. This question, which has long been important in other countries, has been less relevant in Hong Kong to the extent to which the pure doctrine of the 'source' concept applied.

Second, the right to *deduct* interest was to some extent linked with the question of whether the corresponding interest receipt was within the charge to Hong Kong taxation. For interest to be deductible one of five conditions has to be met. Conditions (a) and (b) refer to borrowings by financial institutions and public utility companies respectively. In the case of public utilities the interest must not exceed a 'specified rate'.

Condition (c) requires it to be shown that the interest on which the deduction is claimed will fall to be a taxable receipt of a Hong Kong taxpayer. Where this condition is claimed it will be necessary to disclose the identity of the lender. It applies only to borrowings from persons other than financial institutions.

Condition (d) refers to borrowing from financial institutions and is directed at the practice of 'back to back' loans. The borrower must establish that *either* of the following applies:

1. The loan is not secured or guaranteed by any deposit with a financial institution.
2. The loan is secured or guaranteed by a deposit with a financial institution the owner of which deposit is (a) the borrower or (b) a person who is closely connected to the borrower in any of the various relationships set out in Section 16(3) but the interest payable on such deposit is chargeable to tax in Hong Kong.

A security in the form of back to back deposit with an institution outside Hong Kong (or an institution within Hong Kong in circumstances in which the associated 'lender' escapes Hong Kong tax) would not qualify.

Condition (e) is effectively a let-out. It applies where the money has been borrowed wholly and exclusively to finance capital expenditure on plant and machinery or the purchase of trading stock, and the lender is not associated with the borrower.

The payer is required by law to deduct and account to the authorities for, interest tax on payment of any interest arising in or derived from Hong Kong on any debenture, mortgage, bill of sale, deposit, loan, advance or other indebtedness whether evidenced in writing or not:

(a) any interest paid or payable by the government, or by a bank licensed under the Banking Ordinance, or a public utility specified in the Third Schedule which accrues at a rate not exceeding 13.5 per cent per annum or as otherwise prescribed from time to time;
(b) any interest paid or payable to a bank licensed under the Banking Ordinance, or to a corporation carrying on trade or business in the Colony, or to the government;

(c)   any interest paid or payable on a Tax Reserve Certificate issued by the Commissioner of Inland Revenue;

(d)   any interest paid or payable to any person carrying on business in the Colony as a pawn-broker;

(e)   interest paid to Credit Unions by members in receipt of loans.

The interpretation of the words 'arising in or derived from' has caused some confusion as to the extent to which offshore deposits and loans fall within the scope of the charge. The Commissioner of Inland Revenue in general treats the source or originating cause of the interest as the provision of the credit, but the place where the agreement of the loan or deposit is made also has a material bearing on the determination of the source of interest. With effect from 1 April 1978 the Revenue Ordinance has been amended:

sums received by or accrued to a bank or other financial institution by way of interest which arises through or from the carrying on by the bank/institution of its business in the colony, notwithstanding that the money in respect of which the interest is received or accrued is made available outside the colony.

The amendments have been changed substantially since the original, in order to narrow the offshore activities which are liable to profits tax. It has been promised that when profits are found to be wholly attributable to an overseas branch no tax will be charged and in other cases a 'reasonable apportionment' of the profits will be made. Other amendments provide relief from double taxation where offshore interest earned by Hong Kong banks has already been taxed abroad and also define term 'financial institution' to which the tax provision will apply.

Singapore

Singapore taxes companies at a rate of 33 per cent. (This was reduced from 40 per cent in 1987.) Dividends paid are treated as having borne tax at this rate so that there is no effective corporation tax on distributed profits. The top rate of tax on resident individuals was also reduced, to 33 per cent in 1987. One consequence of this system (essentially the pre-1947 UK system of which this is a rare surviving example) is that the 33 per cent tax at source is a final tax on undistributed profits, on profits distributed to non-residents, and on the profits of Singapore branches of foreign companies.

Another unusual feature (again a survival) is that Singapore resident companies are taxed on profits arising outside Singapore only to the extent to which these are remitted to Singapore. In keeping with the logic of this system interest paid by a company is in general deductible, but subject to 33 per cent withholding tax. There are a number of treaty and non-treaty exceptions to this rule.

Withholding tax at 33 per cent is in principle levied on interest paid or payable including interest reinvested, accumulated, capitalised, put to reserve, or credited to the account of a designated person, or otherwise dealt with on behalf of that person. There are a number of exemptions.

Interest on deposits by non-resident individuals, by non-resident companies not carrying on business within Singapore, and deposits with approved banks are exempt from withholding tax. Interest on approved foreign loans for the purchase of productive equipment is exempt. One of the conditions for approval is that the controller must be satisfied that the exemption does not result in an increase in a liability to tax by the foreign lender in his country of residence – tax sparing provisions.

In 1968, Singapore took steps to become an international financial centre, the chosen instrument being an Asian Currency Unit (or ACU). Interest on deposits with ACUs is exempt from withholding tax. The net profits of ACUs themselves are subject to Singapore tax at a special rate of 10 per cent. (This 10 per cent concession has at various times been extended to other international financial activities – see below.)

An ACU is normally an unincorporated division rather than a separately incorporated subsidiary. The ACU would not then have a separate capital but would maintain a balanced book. As a division of a Singapore bank which guarantees its liabilities and is responsible to the Monetary Authority of Singapore (MAS) for its operation, it relies on the credit standing of its principal bank. Its borrowings and lendings, which can be in any currency other than the Singapore dollar, must in principle balance. The principal bank cannot, without specific consent, transfer Singapore dollars to the ACU for onward lending in another currency, nor can it switch the foreign currency deposits it accepts into Singapore dollars.

If an ACU makes a loss, the parent bank would have to transfer Singapore dollars to make up the deficiency. No margin or liquidity requirements apply to the ACUs. The ACUs may deal in the inter-bank market. They must render separate statements of assets and liabilities, can accept time and demand deposits (but not savings and current accounts) and can borrow in specific currencies from non-residents or from residents subject to the approval of the MAS. The ACU of one bank can accept deposits or borrow from, and extend loans to, other ACUs.

No withholding taxes are levied on interest paid to non-residents' deposits in ACUs, while interest borrowed by a Singapore resident and used within Singapore is subject to a withholding tax of 33 per cent. Commissions or interest received on confirming, refinancing or advising on ACU offshore letters of credit are taxed at the 10 per cent rate.

The government has initiated various tax measures to boost the ACU market. According to the Income Tax (Rate of Tax for Offshore Income) Regulations (Law 26) 1973, income arising outside Singapore is taxable only to the extent to which it is remitted. Section 43(a) provides, however, that the offshore income of a financial institution is subject to tax at 10 per cent whether remitted or not. These have been further expanded in the Income Tax (Amendment) Act 1977 to cover all types of offshore banking operations, and in 1978 to the dividends paid out of such offshore profits.

This concessionary rate is also applicable to all offshore income derived from the issuing, advising or confirming of letters of credit. Asian Dollar Bond related profits are also exempted, irrespective of the place where they are issued. This latter, however, is subject to approval by the Minister of Finance, who may grant full or partial exemption dependent upon whether or not the payments are made for purposes which will promote or enhance the economic or technical development of Singapore. All other offshore income under Section 12(7) of the Income Tax Act, such as royalties, rents, management fees and commissions are liable to the reduced rate of 10 per cent.

Investment managers based in Singapore are also eligible for tax relief. The original concessions provided that foreign investors (not having a permanent establishment in Singapore) were exempt from tax, and that fees derived by ACUs from managing their assets are subject to the 10 per cent rate. More recent changes extend the exemption to investment in local Singapore stocks, offer the 10 per cent treatment to non-bank fund managers who do not have an ACU licence, but are approved by the MAS, and simplify the formalities for establishing the client's non-Singapore status.

The Singapore International Monetary Exchange (SIMEX) as an exchange, enjoys a five-year tax holiday. The Income Tax (Concessionary Rate of Tax for Income from Gold Bullion, Gold Futures and Financial Futures) Regulations, 1985, extend the 10 per cent rate to profits derived by SIMEX *members* on transactions with non-residents, ACUs and other SIMEX members.

Bibliography

Aliber, R. Z. (1978) *Exchange Risk and Corporate International Finance*, Macmillan: London.

Alworth, J. S. (1988) *The Finance, Investment and Taxation Decisions of Multinationals*, Basil Blackwell: New York and Oxford.

Belmore, F. M. (US), Briffell, R. K. N. (UK), Richardson, E. J. (Canada), Green, P. C. (Australia), Guillerm-Kerk, C. (France), Caspary, C. (Germany), Miyatake, T. (Japan), Buit, J. (Netherlands), and Gilling, P. (Switzerland) (1986) *Withholding Tax on Swaps*, Euromoney: London.

Bergsten, F. C., Horst, T. and Moran, T. H. (US) (1978) *American Multinationals and American Interests*, Brookings: Washington DC.

Bracewell-Milnes, Dr. B. (1979) *The Economics of International Tax Avoidance*, Deventer-Kluver: Deventer, the Netherlands.

Brealey, R. A., and Myers S. C. (1981, 1984) *Principles of Corporate Finance*, McGraw-Hill: London.

Briggs, P. W. (1987) *Foreign Currency Exposure Management*, Butterworths: London.

Brooke, M. Z. and Remmer, M. L. (1970) *The Strategy of Multinational Enterprise* (particularly Part II), Longman: London.

Chown, J. F. (1974) *Taxation and Multinational Enterprise*, (Chapters 16–18) Longman.

Chown, J. F. (1982) 'The taxation of foreign exchange fluctuations in the United States and the United Kingdom', *Journal of International Law and Economics*, **16** (2), George Washington University.

Chown, J. F. (1986) *Tax Efficient Forex Management*, Professional Publishing: London.

Chown, J. F. (1986) 'To hedge or not to hedge?', *International Correspondent Banker*, May, pp. 44–5.

Chown, J. F. (1987) 'UK taxation of treasury transactions', *The Treasurer*, January, pp. 11–14.

Chown, J. F. (1988) 'Taxation of foreign exchange gains and losses', *The Treasurer*, January, pp. 17–19.

Chown, J. F. and Bracewell-Milnes, Dr B. (1980) *The Tax Treatment of Overseas Income*, Institute of Directors: London.

Chown, J. F. and Evans, K. (1987) 'Taxation of foreign currency gains and losses: the UK Revenue Statement of Practice', *Journal of Strategy in International Taxation*, **3** (2).

Chown, J. F. and Pagan, J. (1985) 'Swaps: opportunity or tax trap', *The Treasurer,* May, pp. 41–4.

Chown, J. F. and Valentine, R. (1968) *The International Bond Market in the 1960s*, Praeger: New York.

'Claus, S.' (believed to be a pseudonym) (1962) 'Expense is my object', *British Tax Review*, pp. 300–2.

Cooper, D. F. and Watson, I. R. (1987) 'How to assess credit risk in swaps', *The Banker*, February, pp. 28–31.

Cooper, I. and Franks, J. (1988) 'Treasury performance management', Part I, *The Treasurer*, February, pp. 53–9; Part II, *The Treasurer*, March, pp. 59–60.

Corey, W. S. *et al.* (1987) 'Tax Treatment of Foreign Currency, under ss 985–9', Part I, *TMI*, 13 March, pp. 75–99; Part II, *TMI*, 10 April, pp. 127–45.

Couzin, R. and Dart, R. J. (1987) 'The new preferred share rules', conference paper, Chap. 18, pp. 1–37, Canadian Tax Foundation: Toronto.

Cragle, D. R. (1989) 'Interest in the rate swap: will Old Colony die hard?' *TMI* February 10, pp. 65–78.

Ewens, D. S. (1988) 'The new preferred share dividend tax regime', conference paper, Canadian Tax Foundation: Toronto.

Feeny, M. and Verrier, M. (1988) 'Foreign currency hedging opportunities within the *EMS*', *The Treasurer*, February, pp. 35–9.

Flight, H. and Lee-Swan, B. (1988) *All You Need to Know About Exchange Rates*, Sidgwick & Jackson: London.

Fuller, J. (1983) 'Futures–contracts v. forward–contracts', *Taxes International*, September, pp. 50–1.

Granwell, A. (1984) 'Repeal of the US withholding tax on interest', *Journal of Strategy in International Taxation*, **1** (1), pp. 35–53.

Greenwell, W. *et al.* (1984) 'Ordinary shares and the changes to corporation tax', *Monetary Bulletin*, April (157), London.

'GROUP OF NINE' (1987) 'Report to the representative bodies from the working group on the taxation of exchange rate fluctuations: proposals for legislative change', July.

Hammer, R. M. (1979) 'Comment on Lessard' in *The Economic Effect of Multinational Corporations*, JAI Publications: Greenwich, Connecticut.

Hammond, G. M. S. (1987) 'Recent developments in the swap market', *Bank of England Quarterly Bulletin*, February, pp. 66–79.

Harding, D. (1987) 'A corporate treasurer's approach to foreign exchange risk', *The Treasurer*, March, pp. 17–19.

Harrisson, T. (1988) 'Continuity and change in corporation treasury management', *The Treasurer's Yearbook*, pp. 53–6, Association of Corporate Treasurers: London.

Herring, R. J. (1983) *Managing Foreign Exchange Risk*, Cambridge University Press: Cambridge.

Inland Revenue (UK) (1987) *Statement of Practice (SPI/87) on the Tax Treatment of Foreign Exchange Gains and Losses*, February, Inland Revenue: London.

Inland Revenue (UK) (1989) *Tax Treatment of Foreign Exchange Gains and Losses: A Consultative Document*, March, Inland Revenue: London.

Kambe, M. and Namikawa, K. (1985) 'The future of the city from the Japanese perspective', a project for J. F. Chown & Company Limited, under the supervision of Professor J. R. Franks (London Business School), May.

Kay, J. and King, M. (1985) *Taxing Currency Fluctuations*. Institute for Fiscal Studies: London.

Kenyon, A. (1981) *Currency Risk Management*, John Wiley: London.

Kleinbard, E. D. *et al.* (1987) 'US reduces tax risk for swaps', *International Financial Law Review*, February, pp. 26–7.

KPMG, (1987) *The Tax Treatment of Exchange Gains and Losses*, Peat Marwick: USA.

Lawlor, W. R. (1987) 'Interest deductibility: where to after Bronfman Trust', annual conference report, Chap. 19, pp. 1–41, Canadian Tax Foundation: Toronto.

Lawry, M. (1986) *Australian Income Tax Legislation*, CCH Australia Limited: Australia.

Lawry, M. (1986, rev. 1989) *Australian International Tax Agreements*, CCH Australia Limited: Australia.

Lawry, M. (1988) 'The changing Australian taxation: considerations of inward and outward investment in Australia', *APTIB*, June, p. 259.

Lawry, M. (1989) *Australian Master Tax Guide*, CCH Australia Limited: Australia.

Lessard, D. R. (1979) 'Transfer prices, taxes and financial markets: implications of internal financial transfers within the multinational corporation', in *The Economic Effects of Multinational Corporations*, JAI Publications: Greenwich, Connecticut.

Lessard, D. R. and Lightstone, J. B. (1986) 'Volatile exchange rates can put operations at risk', *Harvard Business Review*, July–August (4), pp. 107–14.

Levey, M. and Ruchelman, S. (1986) 'The US Tax Reform Act of 1986: impact on foreign currency transactions', *Taxes International*, October, pp. 3–16, 79–85.

Levine, H. J. and Berger, H. (1989) 'TAMRA amendments to the foreign currency rules', *Tax Management International*, 10 February, pp. 85–8.

Lodin, S-O. (1979) *International Enterprises and Taxation: Some Preliminary Results of an Empirical Study Concerning International Enterprises*, Nordic Council for Tax Research.

McGarry, S. J. (1988) 'The taxation of exchange gains and losses: a road map', *International Tax Journal*, **14** (1) pp. 25–51.

Muten, L. (1983) 'Some topical issues concerning international double taxation' in S. Cnossen (ed.) *Comparative Tax Studies*, Amsterdam.

Muten, L. (1989) 'Back to plain vanilla?' in B. Fridman and L. Ostman (eds.) *Accounting Development: Some Perspectives*, (forthcoming). Stockholm School of Economics: Stockholm.

OECD (1984) *Transfer Pricing and Multinational Enterprise: The Taxation Issues*, OECD: Paris.

OECD (1988) *Issues on International Taxation No. 3: Tax Consequences of Foreign Exchange Gains and Losses*, OECD: Paris.

O'Reilly, D. (1988) 'Thin capitalisation and offshore banking units', Australia, IBFD 1988/2, p. 84.

Pagan J. C. (1983) *Taxation of Currency Fluctuations*, Butterworth: London.

Piercy, J. (1984) *How to Account for Foreign Currencies,* Macmillan: London.

Pink, G. C. (1985) *Tax Aspects of Commodity and Financial Futures Transactions*, Butterworth: London.

Price, S. (1986) 'Accounting and tax issues of swaps', *The Treasurer*, November, pp. 49–50.

Richardson, S. R. (1988) 'Current developments in debt financing: a Canadian tax perspective', conference paper, Canadian Tax Foundation: Toronto.

Robbins, S. and Stobaugh, R. (1973) *Money in the International Enterprise: A Study in Financial Policy*, Basic: New York.

Rosenbloom, D. (1988) 'International aspects of financial instruments', 3 October, District of Columbia Bar Section of Taxation, Third Annual Federal Tax Institute.

Rosenbloom, D. (1988) 'Application of the new foreign currency rules: Section 988', *Financial Institutions Tax Issues*, 10 November.

Ross, D. (1989) 'Tax planning and the treasurer in international companies', *The Treasurer*, February, pp. 35–7.

Rudnick, R. S. (1989) 'Corporate tax integration and liquidity of investment', *Tax Notes*, 27 February, American Bar Association Task Force.

Stilling, P. (1987) 'Treasury management: accounting for reality', *The Treasurer*, January, pp. 15–17.

Stonehill, A., Ravn, N. and Dullum, K. (1982) *Managing Foreign Exchange Exposure in International Financial Management*, Norstedt & Somers: Stockholm.

Sullivan, D. F. (1988) 'New developments in corporate financing', conference papers, Canadian Tax Foundation: Toronto.

Tiner, J. I. and Connelly, J. M. (1987) *Accounting for Treasury Products*, Woodhead-Faulkner: Cambridge.

'TREASURY 2' (1984) 'Tax reform for fairness, simplicity and economic growth', *The Treasury Department Report to the President.* November, Washington.

Vincent, R. (1988) 'Australia: taxation of foreign-source income', IBFD 1988/11, p. 493.

Wainman, D. (1984) *Currency Fluctuation, Accountancy and Taxation Implications* (2nd edn), Woodhead-Faulkner: Cambridge.

Waldner, S. C. (1986) 'Hedging for strategists', *International Correspondent Banker*, May, pp. 41–3.

Wilkie, J. S. (1987) 'Structured international debt issues: a Canadian perspective', *Canadian Tax Journal*, pp. 1–49, Canadian Tax Foundation: Toronto.

Wiri, Y. (1983) 'Foreign currency accountancy and its translation', (in R. J. Herring (ed.)) *Managing Foreign Exchange Risk*, Cambridge University Press: Cambridge.

Young, A. (1988) 'New Zealand: the imputation system', APTIB, June, p. 280.

Young, A. (1988) *New Zealand Income Tax Legislation*, CCH New Zealand Limited: Auckland.

Abbreviations

APTIB:	Asian Pacific Tax and Investment Bulletin
	2 Nassim Road Singapore 1025
CCH:	Commerce Clearing House
	Tax Business and Law Publishers
	Telford Road
	Bicester
	Oxfordshire OX6 0XD
	England
CTF:	Canadian Tax Foundation
	130 Adelaide Street W
	Toronto
	Canada M5H 3P5
IBFD:	International Bureau of Fiscal Documentation
	Sarphatistraat 124
	P.O. Box 20237
	100 HE Amsterdam
	Netherlands
TMI:	Tax Management International Journal
	1231 25th Street NW
	Washington DC 20037
	USA

Index